Issues in Business Ethics

Volume 44

More information about this series at http://www.springer.com/series/6077

David Rönnegard

The Fallacy of Corporate Moral Agency

Springer

David Rönnegard
Stockholm
Sweden

ISSN 0925-6733 ISSN 2215-1680 (electronic)
Issues in Business Ethics
ISBN 978-94-017-9755-9 ISBN 978-94-017-9756-6 (eBook)
DOI 10.1007/978-94-017-9756-6

Library of Congress Control Number: 2015936147

Springer Dordrecht Heidelberg New York London

Printed on acid-free paper

Springer Science+Business Media B.V. Dordrecht is part of Springer Science+Business Media (www.springer.com)

Abstract

This book is a philosophical analysis of the corporation in society that spans the disciplines of Ethics, Law, Economics, and Political Philosophy. Part I poses a meta-ethical challenge to the position, generally accepted in Business Ethics, that a corporation qualifies as a moral agent. The most prominent theories of corporate moral agency are analysed by evaluating if they can satisfy the three necessary moral agency abilities of intentionality, autonomy, and an ability to act. Part I concludes that, metaphysically speaking, the corporation *itself* does not qualify as a moral agent, in part because the morally relevant sense of the abilities of intentionality and autonomy require *awareness* on behalf of the agent. Therefore, corporations cannot be morally responsible as distinct from their members. Attributions of moral responsibility to corporations are at best an elliptical way of referring to individual corporate members who may be morally responsible.

Part II proceeds from the premise that the corporation is not a moral agent. It seeks to descriptively evaluate what the corporation *is* and to prescriptively evaluate what role the corporation *ought* to have in society. By tracing the historical development of the corporate legal form in English and American law, it is argued that *descriptively* the corporate form is primarily a *legal agent*. It is also maintained that the corporation is a legal fiction granted to associations of individuals, and as such it is descriptively an instrument of the state.

Part II then proceeds to *prescriptively* argue that the corporation also *ought* to be an instrument of the state. As such, the state may legitimately regulate corporate actions to be in accord with national goals of social welfare. It is highlighted that although the corporate *legal form* is an instrument of the state, *actual corporations* are the instruments of their incorporators. Part II then takes issue with the prescriptions of the Corporate Social Responsibility movement which maintain that a wider constituency of stakeholders than merely shareholders ought to be considered in managerial decision-making. It is argued that many of the prescriptions of CSR are very difficult to uphold unless one also mistakenly advocates corporate moral agency. Furthermore, the issues that CSR wishes to tackle are better addressed through public initiatives and legal enactments by the government. The normative force of the argument is that citizens of democratic states ought to *primarily* make calls for *legal enactments* in order to hold the corporate legal instruments accountable to their preferences.

Contents

Part I The Fallacy of Corporate Moral Agency

1 The Importance of Corporate Moral Agency 5
References 8

2 Necessary Conditions for Moral Agency 9
References 15

3 Corporate Intentions 17
3.1 Explication of Peter French's Conception of Corporate Moral Agency 18
3.2 The Metaphysics of Intentions and Its Moral Relevance 22
References 29

4 Corporate Actions 31
4.1 Are Corporate Agents Autonomous? 34
4.2 Free vs. Non-free Agents 38
4.3 Emergent Corporate Moral Agency? 41
References 48

5 Corporate Autonomy 51
References 55

6 Summary of Why Corporate Moral Agency Is a Fallacy 57
6.1 Autonomy 57
6.2 Intention 58
6.3 Action 58
Reference 59

7 The Reference of Corporate Proper Names and Responsibility Attributions 61
References 71

8 Corporate Collective Moral Agency 73
8.1 Joint/Shared Intentions 74
8.2 Group/Corporate Intentions 78
8.3 Corporate Collective Intentions 81
References 90

9 Conclusion: Legitimate and Illegitimate Corporate Moral Responsibility Attributions 91
9.1 Moral Responsibility Attribution to a Collective Whole 91
9.2 Moral Responsibility Attribution to a Corporate Structure 93
9.3 Moral Responsibility Attribution to a Unanimously Intending Collective 94
9.4 Elliptical Moral Responsibility Attribution to a Collective Whole 97
References 99

Part II The Role of the Corporation in Society

10 The Role of the Corporation in Society: The Descriptive View 103
10.1 The First Corporations 104
10.2 The Legal Debate About the Nature of the Corporation 105
10.3 The Shareholder Primacy Norm 108
10.4 The Separation of the Corporation from the Shareholders and the Emergence of the Corporate Share as an Autonomous Form of Property 118
10.5 The Limited Liability of Shareholders 122
10.6 The Reification of the Corporation (and the Legal Influence of the Theories About the Nature of the Corporation) 128
10.7 The Corporation as Socio-economic Instrument 136
References 140

11 The Role of the Corporation in Society: The Prescriptive View 143
11.1 Ought the Corporate Legal Form to Be Used as an Instrument of the State? 144
11.1.1 The Problem with the Descriptive Claims of the Nexus-of-Contracts Theory 145
11.1.2 The Problem with the Libertarian Prescription for Absolute Property Rights 149
11.2 The Wrong with the Corporate Social Responsibility Movement 157
11.2.1 The Philosophical Foundations of the CSR Movement 157
11.2.2 Shareholder Theory vs. CSR 164
11.2.3 The Rationality of the Shareholder Primacy Norm 182

11.3 The Division Between Public and Private Corporate Responsibilities 185
11.3.1 The Public/Private Distinction 186
11.3.2 The Market as a Zone of Moral Exception 192
11.3.3 The Justification for State Regulation 199
11.4 Summary: The Role the Corporation Ought to Play in Society 205
References 206

Conclusion 209
Bibliography 213

Introduction

There has for some time been a heightened interest in the ethical behaviour of business corporations from many areas of society. Consumers in developed countries have displayed a willingness to "vote" with their money by boycotting corporations that use child labour and have increased their demand for products that are environmentally friendly. Investors have increasingly started to put their money into "ethical funds" that vow not to invest in certain industries, for example, the military and tobacco and sex industries. International institutions have set up guidelines for good business practice, for example, the OECD Guidelines for Multinational Enterprises and the UN Global Compact. National governments have also started to make legal reforms, for example, the 2002 Sarbanes-Oxley Act in the USA following the corporate scandals of Enron and WorldCom. Importantly, many corporations and business leaders have begun to declare themselves as champions of Corporate Social Responsibility (CSR) by stating that they regard their corporations as having obligations to serve the communities in which they are active.

The field of business ethics as an academic pursuit has been steadily evolving, although it has received much more attention in recent times due to the enhanced interest from other parts of society. The contemporary academic field of business ethics originated in America during the 1970s and 1980s when several moral philosophers started inquiring whether or not the corporation qualified as a moral agent (e.g., Donaldson 1982; French 1984; Ladd 1970; Werhane 1985), that is, an entity that one may legitimately attribute with moral responsibility. However, since those days the issue of corporate moral agency has not captured the interest of many philosophers. Nowadays, the discourse in the field generally proceeds from the implicit premise that corporations are moral agents and that it is quite acceptable to hold corporations morally responsible.

Many of the ethical prescriptions made by academics and civil society about what corporations ought to do hinge on a conception of corporations as moral agents. Corporate moral agency is generally an underlying assumption for prescribing that corporations should sign up to voluntary ethical guidelines beyond the requirements of the law as well as corporate commitments to CSR. This is because corporations are said to have moral duties that guide their conduct which, if the duties are held by the corporation itself rather than individual members, requires an assumption of corporate moral agency.

The aim of Part I of this book, titled "The Fallacy of Corporate Moral Agency", is to re-evaluate the corporate moral agency debate. The overwhelming consensus in favour of corporate moral agency has led few people to question this fundamental tenet of the field. This debate has lain largely dormant for over a decade, and I aim to re-examine the issue in a more extensive and systematic fashion than previously done. Part I deals exclusively with the issue of corporate moral agency and the attribution of moral responsibility to corporations.

I first put forward three uncontroversial necessary conditions for moral agency. These conditions will serve as the foundation of our evaluation of the corporation's metaphysical status as a moral agent. I then start the analysis by systematically scrutinizing the theories espoused by some of the most influential advocates of corporate moral agency and consider if they satisfy our three conditions. These theories have in common that they allow for the possibility of attributing moral responsibility to a corporation where no moral fault may be found with the corporate members, thus lodging the responsibility with the corporation itself as a moral agent. I show that none of the espoused theories meet the necessary conditions for moral agency in the relevant way. I maintain that if it is *moral* responsibility that we wish to attribute to a corporation for a certain event, then we will not be making a legitimate attribution of moral responsibility if we are lodging that attribution with the corporate entity itself rather than a set of its members.

However, the use of corporate names as the subjects or moral responsibility predicates is clearly part of our use of language, and it is therefore important to make sense of such statements. Therefore, I next move on to inquire what the reference of a corporate name is when used as the subject of a moral responsibility attribution. In other words, does the corporate name refer to an entity that is logically distinct from the corporate members, or is the name used to refer to the set of members that are morally responsible? I suggest that corporate names in moral responsibility attributions implicitly refer to the subset of corporate members that are morally responsible for the event being attributed and that we only use the corporate name because of transparency difficulties in identifying who the responsible individuals are.

Next, I show how one can construct better theories of corporate moral agency with the aid of theories of collective intentionality. The idea is that if we can construct a theory of collective moral agency that is completely dependent on the intentionality of individual members who themselves are moral agents, then we may have a theory that meets our necessary moral agency conditions. Bearing in mind the theories of corporate moral agency that I have criticized and the theories I have constructed with the aid of collective intentionality, I wrap up Part I by presenting a taxonomy of legitimate and illegitimate corporate moral responsibility attributions. The principal conclusion to be drawn from this taxonomy is that moral responsibility may only be legitimately attributed to corporations when that responsibility is meant to lodge with the corporate members and that corporations are never moral agents in and of themselves.

Part II is titled "The Role of the Corporation in Society" and takes as its premise the conclusion from Part I, namely, that the corporation is not a moral agent. Because few have thought to question corporate moral agency, few have also thought of exploring the implications of it not being such an agent. Having argued against corporate moral agency, I need to say something constructive about what the corporation *is* in order to hold it accountable. If corporations are not moral agents, then what are they?

The answer to this question is the first aim of Part II explained in the section titled "The Role of the Corporation in Society: The Descriptive View". I maintain that corporations are primarily legal agents and further that the corporate legal form serves an important role as an instrument of the state. I trace the evolution of the corporate legal form in English and American law from the first chartered craft guilds by the Crown in the fifteenth century up to the establishment of the modern corporate legal form in the second half of the nineteenth century. This historical analysis is also viewed through the perspectives of three competing theories in law over the nature of the firm: the Legal Fiction Theory, the Nexus-of-Contracts Theory, and the Real Entity Theory. Interestingly, these theories overlap with the debate on corporate moral agency. I maintain that the Legal Fiction Theory is a descriptively dominant representation of the nature of corporations.

Clearly, corporations are not *merely* legal agents existing only in contemplation of the law because as organizations they are metaphysically comprised of human members, but from the perspective of holding the entities themselves accountable, corporations are primarily legal agents. As legal agents, corporations differ from moral agents in that they are not ends in themselves. Instead, actual corporations and the corporate legal form are both created for certain instrumental purposes. I suggest that actual corporations are the instruments of the incorporating parties, while the corporate legal form is the instrument of the state to promote economic growth and regulate economic activity for the public good. This provides a useful distinction between the *goal* and the *role* of the corporation: its goal is to be an instrument to further the interests of shareholders, while its social role is to further the interests of the state.

Having answered descriptively what the role of the corporation in society *is*, the second aim of Part II is to answer what role the corporation *ought* to have in our society. This section is titled "The Role of the Corporation in Society: The Prescriptive View". I here make use of the distinction between the goal and the role of the corporation. First, I look at whether the corporate legal form ought to have a *role* as an instrument of the state. This involves scrutinizing the libertarian nexus-of-contracts objection that state use of the corporate legal form is an illegitimate interference with the corporate *goal* because it infringes on the absolute property rights of shareholders. I argue that the foundation for absolute property rights is very weak and instead maintain that the best justification for private property rights is that they are instrumentally beneficial to citizens. If we cannot uphold absolute property rights, this opens the door for the state to use the corporate legal form as an instrument to further the public good.

Next, I consider whether or not actual corporations ought to be primarily the instruments of the incorporating parties. This involves a head-on confrontation between Shareholder Theory and the prescriptions of the Corporate Social Responsibility movement. That is to say, ought the corporation to be an instrument primarily for the shareholders, or should its *goal* be tempered by duties to solve social problems and/or take equal consideration of stakeholder interests? I maintain that the prescriptions of the CSR movement are difficult to uphold without an illegitimate reliance on corporate moral agency and that the corporate goal ought to primarily serve the interests of its shareholders. Furthermore, I suggest that the issues that CSR wishes to tackle are better addressed through public initiatives and legal enactments by the government.

This brings us to my final topic of inquiry which involves the proper division between public and private role responsibilities. It is not possible to answer what role corporations ought to have in society without contrasting it against the role the state ought to have in society, unless the two roles overlap. I come to suggest that given that the corporate legal form is an instrument of the state and that actual corporations are the instruments of the incorporators, we then obtain a public/private distinction where the state regulates the corporate legal form while actual corporations are free to decide on the best means to realize their private goals within the boundaries of the law. I also maintain that the market is a zone of moral exception where it is acceptable to act purely out of self-interest while playing within the rules of the law. In fact, the underlying market justifications of competition and efficiency demand this zone of moral exception.

As we shall see, the position that corporations are moral agents is not tenable, which forces us to rethink how to hold corporations accountable. These issues are of paramount importance today with the expanding popularity of the CSR movement, which largely hinges its prescriptions on corporate moral agency. If corporations are not moral agents, then it is unreasonable to expect corporations themselves to assume *moral* responsibilities. Rather, if we wish to influence and hold corporations accountable, we must see them as the legal agents that they are and hold them legally accountable. The normative force of the argument is that citizens ought to *primarily* make calls for *legal enactments* to hold the corporate legal instruments accountable to their preferences.

We need to keep in mind that this is a work in ideal theory. As such, its conclusions are not immediately applicable to the concrete world. For example, it is not possible to fully endorse the advocacy of shareholder primacy within a democratic system of ideal judicial constraints if parts of that system in the real world are left wanting. Nonetheless, this ideal theory provides a meaningful direction towards which we should strive in order to obtain a just and economically efficient society where corporations are an integral part.

References

Donaldson, T. 1982. *Corporations and morality.* New Jersey: Prentice Hall.

French, P.A. 1984. *Collective and corporate responsibility.* New York: Columbia University Press.

Ladd, J. 1970. Morality and the ideal of rationality in formal organizations. *The Monist* 54: 488–516.

Werhane, P.H. 1985. *Persons, rights, & corporations.* New Jersey: Prentice Hall.

Part I
The Fallacy of Corporate Moral Agency

When events take place within the context of satisfying corporate goals, we may ask, who is morally responsible for the resulting consequences? This question concerns the identification of the proper bearer of *moral* responsibility.

It is uncontroversial that corporations are legal agents that may be attributed with legal responsibilities. However, can corporations also be moral agents that are the proper subjects of *moral* responsibility attributions?[1]

The concept of corporate moral agency (also known as corporate moral personhood) is for many an important implicit assumption within business ethics. This is in part due to the desire to qualify the "business" as a unit of ethical analysis for its actions (see, e.g.: Collier 1998), as well as the desire to identify a placeholder for moral responsibility attributions when no moral responsibility can be found with the corporate members (see, e.g.: Werhane 1989). Corporate moral agency implies that corporations can be the proper bearers of moral responsibilities in a manner that is distinct from their human members. This does not mean that the corporation can perform any actions without its members, but it does mean that the corporation can be morally responsible as a unit that is considered *distinct* from its members. As such, corporate moral agency needs to be kept separate from notions of *collective moral responsibility* that attribute moral responsibility to corporate members.[2]

---

[1] A corporation is formally defined as an association that is given legal status by a state charter to operate as a single unit with limited liability over an indefinite period of time. It is however clear that the type of entities commonly referred to as corporations do not merely have a manifestation in law but are also organizations comprised of individuals. For the current discussion on corporate moral agency I shall not merely consider the corporation in this narrow legal sense, because otherwise it would be a category mistake to speak of the moral agency of a purely legal entity. I shall regard corporations as goal directed organizations comprised of human members.

[2] The distinction between corporate moral responsibility and collective moral responsibility is not always made clearly enough. On the one hand, corporate moral responsibility involves agency that is logically distinct from the corporate members and thus moral responsibility is attributed to the corporation even when no member is morally responsible. On the other hand, collective moral responsibility requires that at least someone within the collective is morally responsible. On some interpretations one or more responsible individuals may represent a group such that the

Over the years most thinkers on the subject have tended to support various conceptions of corporate moral agency (e.g.: De George 1981; Donaldson 1982; Dubbink and Smith 2011; French 1984; Goodpaster 1983; Hess 2013; Manning 1984; Moore 1999; Ozar 1985; Phillips 1992; Seabright and Kurke 1997; Soares 2003; Werhane 1985), while Ladd (1970), and Velasquez (1983, 2003) are exceptions.

As we shall see, it will become important to distinguish between the mere semantics of acknowledging the way we speak about corporations on the one hand and substantial metaphysical arguments for the moral status of the corporation on the other hand. I am assuming (and I believe it is uncontroversial) that moral responsibility attributions are only legitimate to moral agents. Given this assumption, what we need to do is to establish whether a corporation *is* a moral agent without augmenting our basic notions of what a corporation *is* and what a moral agent *is*. The aim is to see if we can move from an understanding of the uncontroversial attributions of moral responsibility to *individuals* (the sense which we are primarily familiar with) to an understanding of attributions of moral responsibility to *corporations* (or collectives of individuals) without a significant shift in meaning. The goal is not to construe the corporation as a moral agent by any means possible, but rather to explore if the corporation possesses certain necessary characteristics for moral agency.

The main tenet of my argument is that the corporation cannot be considered a moral agent primarily because, metaphysically speaking, there is no moral agency that arises or exists that is distinct from the moral agency of the individual members that comprise the organization. The arguments to be made against the various positions of corporate moral agency hinge importantly on what we take to be the necessary characteristics for the metaphysical status of moral agency. There appears to be very little consensus in the field of moral philosophy with regard to necessary and sufficient conditions for moral agency. Therefore I shall proceed by arguing from some fairly uncontroversial necessary conditions with the aim of showing that if these cannot be met then my argument against corporate moral agency will be even more robust than if I rely on a more controversial full blown account of necessary *and* sufficient conditions for moral agency.

I shall assume that the ability to intend an action, the ability to carry out an intentional action, and the ability to choose an intentional action autonomously are necessary conditions for moral agency. I shall start by first explicating these three necessary conditions for moral agency. Given these necessary conditions for moral agency I shall consider the positions of several philosophers with regard to the moral status of corporate entities themselves conceived as logically distinct from their members.

---

entire group is considered morally responsible. Keeping the distinction between corporate moral responsibility and collective moral responsibility in mind is important because with the latter the agency is entirely dependent on the abilities of the members while with the former it is not.

I then go on to discuss what it is we are referring to when we us corporate names as the subjects of corporate moral responsibility attributions. In other words I discuss what the reference of a corporate proper name is in the context of attributing moral responsibility. This inquiry is the flipside of analysing whether or not corporations are moral agents because only moral agents can legitimately be attributed with moral responsibility.

Next, I suggest that one may construct better theories of corporate moral agency by making corporate moral agency contingent on the moral agency of corporate members rather than being logically distinct from the members. I show, with the aid of theories of collective intentionality, that one can have certain collectives of individuals towards whom corporate moral responsibility attributions are legitimate. Finally, I conclude with a classification of legitimate and illegitimate corporate moral responsibility attributions.

The structure of Part I is[3]:

- Chapter 1: The Importance of Corporate Moral Agency
- Chapter 2: Necessary Conditions for Moral Agency
- Chapter 3: Corporate Intentions
- Chapter 4: Corporate Actions
- Chapter 5: Corporate Autonomy
- Chapter 6: Summary of Why Corporate Moral Agency Is a Fallacy
- Chapter 7: The Reference of Corporate Proper Names and Responsibility Attributions
- Chapter 8: Corporate Collective Moral Agency
- Chapter 9: Conclusion: Legitimate and Illegitimate Corporate Moral Responsibility Attributions

References

Collier, Jane. 1998. Theorising the ethical organization. *Business Ethics Quarterly* 8: 621–654.

De George, R.T. 1981. Can corporations have moral responsibilities? *University of Dayton Review* 5: 3–15.

Donaldson, T. 1982. *Corporations and morality*. Englewood Cliffs: Prentice Hall.

Dubbink, W., and J. Smith. 2011. A political account of corporate moral responsibility. *Ethical Theory and Moral Practice* 14: 223–246.

French, P.A. 1984. *Collective and corporate responsibility*. New York: Columbia University Press.

Goodpaster, K.E. 1983. The concept of corporate responsibility. *Journal of Business Ethics* 2: 1–22.

Hess, K.M. 2013. "If you tickle us . . . ": How corporations can be moral agents without being persons. *Journal of Value Inquiry* 47: 319–335.

Ladd, J. 1970. Morality and the ideal of rationality in formal organizations. *The Monist* 54: 488–516.

[3]Chapters 1, 2, 3, 4, and 5 in part draw on Rönnegard (2013).

Manning, R.C. 1984. Corporate responsibility and corporate personhood. *Journal of Business Ethics* 3: 77–84.
Moore, G. 1999. Corporate moral agency: Review and implications. *Journal of Business Ethics* 21: 329–334.
Ozar, D.T. 1985. Do corporations have moral rights? *Journal of Business Ethics* 4: 277–281.
Phillips, M.J. 1992. Corporate moral personhood and three conceptions of the corporation. *Business Ethics Quarterly* 2: 435–459.
Rönnegard, D. 2013. How autonomy alone debunks corporate moral agency. *Business and Professional Ethics Journal* 32(1–2): 77–106.
Seabright, M.A., and L.B. Kurke. 1997. Organizational ontology and the moral status of the corporation. *Business Ethics Quarterly* 7(4): 91–108.
Soares, C. 2003. Corporate versus individual moral responsibility. *Journal of Business Ethics* 46: 143–150.
Velasquez, Manuel G. 1983. Why corporations are not morally responsible for anything they do. *Business and Professional Ethics Journal* 2: 1–18.
Velasquez, Manuel G. 2003. Debunking corporate moral responsibility. *Business Ethics Quarterly* 13: 531–562.
Werhane, P.H. 1985. *Persons, rights, & corporations*. Englewood Cliffs: Prentice Hall.
Werhane, Patricia H. 1989. Corporate and individual moral responsibility: A reply to Jan Garrett. *Journal of Business Ethics* 8: 821–822.

Chapter 1
The Importance of Corporate Moral Agency

The metaphysical issue of corporate moral agency is highly abstract, however, the conclusion one reaches has important wider ramifications. These ramifications are both legal as well as morally prescriptive. Anyone who is concerned with identifying the correct bearer of moral responsibility for events that take place in the context of satisfying corporate goals will be concerned with the metaphysical issue of whether or not the corporate entity qualifies as such a bearer of responsibility. This is not just of interest to a narrow group of philosophers. Many laws that are enacted are in part dependent on moral reasoning, not least who or what we take to be the subjects of moral responsibility.[1] For example, we don't extend full legal rights and duties to children because we do not deem them to be fully morally responsible for their actions, but as soon as they mature to an age when they are considered to be fully fledged moral agents then the attending legal rights and duties also follow. If we were to regard the corporation as a moral agent then this could form a moral basis for extending to them similar legal rights and duties as human moral agents.[2]

The metaphysical conclusion we reach on corporate moral agency has potentially huge ramifications. Regarding the corporation as a moral agent may for example

[1]This does not mean that only moral agents can or should be legal agents. There are good instrumental reasons for creating purely fictive legal agents (such as corporations) with attendant legal responsibilities that have no relation to moral agency. For example, it is useful that the estate of a deceased person is a legal agent until all pecuniary matters have been settled. However, if someone or something does qualify as a moral agent then this provides moral (and not only instrumental) reasons for extending certain legal rights and duties to such agents.

[2]McMahon (1995) has made a strong argument suggesting that even if social science were to prove that organizations are real and distinct entities from their members that qualify as moral agents, that should not accord them any moral consideration over and above their individual members who have primary consideration in their own right (although this does not preclude organizational consideration or responsibility attributions that does not conflict with individual rights).

D. Rönnegard, *The Fallacy of Corporate Moral Agency*,
Issues in Business Ethics 44, DOI 10.1007/978-94-017-9756-6_1

justify extending to them the full Bill of Rights,[3] while on the other hand denying them moral agency may justify revoking some rights (such as the 14th Amendment to the US constitution which first established the corporation as a "person" before the law).[4] Interestingly, the recent US Supreme Court case *Citizens United v. Federal Election Commission* (2010) held that First Amendment rights to free speech apply to corporations for the purposes of independent political expenditures. The majority opinion (5–4) did not make reference to the 14th Amendment nor to corporate personhood,[5] although Justice Stevens' forceful dissent (joined by Justices Ginsburg, Breyer, and Sotomayor) suggests that the majority opinion implicitly assumes it. Stevens writes:

> "The fact that corporations are different from human beings might seem to need no elaboration, except that the majority opinion almost completely elides it . . . [C]orporations have no consciences, no beliefs, no feelings, no thoughts, no desires. Corporations help structure and facilitate the activities of human beings, to be sure, and their "personhood" often serves as a useful legal fiction. But they are not themselves members of "We the People" by whom and for whom our Constitution was established."

Justice Stevens is expressing the fear that we forget at our peril that corporations are "persons" only as *fictions* before the law. To confer to corporations the rights of natural persons is an erroneous move and may hinder citizens from exercising those very rights.

Furthermore, the truth of corporate moral agency is a necessary condition for corporate *criminal* liability. Criminal sanctions are only applicable to morally responsible agents that are deemed to *deserve* retribution. Therefore corporate moral agency is a prerequisite for criminal punishment (Hasnas 2012). Civil law primarily serves the purposes of deterrence and compensation for harm, while

---

[3]Hess (2013) argues that the corporation's status as a moral agent does not imply extending rights to corporations that are normally associated with persons. This is maintained on the basis that the concept of a "person" is much richer than the concept of "moral agency", for example that persons have the ability to be "vulnerable" which is needed to make rights meaningful. On my view the labeling of "moral agent" and "person" is a nominal concern. An account of moral agency with *sufficient* conditions (beyond the necessary abilities of intentionality, action, and autonomy), will be indistinguishable from an account of persons, and thus anyone that meets such sufficient conditions should be afforded the rights associated with personhood.

[4]Qualifying corporations as "persons" before the law has been used on several occasions to confer rights normally held by natural persons, starting with Santa Clara v. Southern Pacific Railroad (1886) which held that corporations are persons for the purposes of the 14th Amendment. The granting of such rights have often relied on arguments of derivative corporate rights from shareholders as citizen, although such a move might also be argued on the basis that corporations themselves are real moral agents/persons deserving of such rights. For example Peter French advocates such a view. He says that corporations are "full-fledged moral persons and have whatever privileges, rights and duties as are, in the normal course of affairs, accorded to moral persons" (1991: 290).

[5]The majority opinion relied on the free speech rights of corporate members (shareholders) as associations of individuals in granting such rights to corporations. This is a surprising move given that corporations are legally considered to be entirely separate entities from their members (see Sect. 10.4).

criminal law alone serves the purpose of punishment. Although there are several jurisdictions in the world that allow for corporate criminal liability the US system is the most developed (Diskant 2008).[6] It is however highly questionable if corporate criminal liability is fair as sanctions fall on corporate members collectively, many of whom are entirely innocent. Hasnas (2012: 191) correctly affirms that "[c]orporate punishment is inherently vicarious collective punishment" because the imposition of criminal fines inevitably affect corporate stakeholders. And collective punishment that falls on the innocent is not only unjust but also a breach of article 33 of the Geneva Convention (Ronnegard 2008).[7]

But the ramifications of corporate moral agency are not only *legal* in character; the ramifications are also *morally* prescriptive. Corporate moral agency is important for the behaviour that we prescribe for corporations. To argue that a corporate entity ought to do something (a negative or positive duty), such as care for its employees, reduce its environmental footprint, or solve problems in its local community, requires a different form of argumentation from one that prescribes that a corporate member or a group of members do the same thing. If a corporation were regarded as a distinct moral agent from its members, this would require moral justifications of the corporate entity's treatment of stakeholders in a manner that does not appeal to the duties of its members. An example of this type of justification is Donaldson's (1982) Social Contract Theory whereby the corporation's moral duties are maintained on the basis that the corporation *itself* must strike a fair contract with the rest of society in order to legitimize its existence.

By implication we cannot simply regard corporate moral responsibility as a metaphor that is actually meant to refer to the moral responsibilities of corporate members. To argue that a corporate member or group of members ought to act on *corporate moral duties* is by no means a straight forward exercise. One would need to show how and why corporate members would have *individual* or *collective* moral responsibilities that are equivalent to the prescribed *corporate* moral responsibilities. Corporate members can have moral duties but they cannot have *corporate* moral duties; that would be a category mistake.

Note that in arguing against corporate moral agency I am not saying that no one is morally responsible for events that happen in business; rather I argue that if anyone is responsible then it is one or more members who are the proper moral agents. Fully realizing this should help form justifications for greater individual responsibility before the law. For example, if BP had a moral responsibility to clean up the oil spill in the Gulf of Mexico, then presumably BP *ought* to do it because BP realizes it is the right thing to do. If BP is not a moral agent that is capable of having such a

---

[6]These examples all apply to an American context because of the relevance of recent developments there. However, in other jurisdictions there is in principle nothing that hinders granting corporations legal rights normally associated with natural persons based on a conception of corporate moral agency.

[7]A further danger with statutes of corporate criminal liability is that it may lead to mistaken views that a moral agent is being punished and may thus appease demands to pierce the corporate veil in order to punish those members who are actually morally responsible.

moral duty, then there is all the more reason for legislation that targets the corporate legal agent (to compensate affected stakeholders) as well as legislation that targets the corporate members that are actually morally responsible (for deterrence and punishment). [8]

References

Diskant, E. 2008. Comparative corporate criminal liability: Exploring the uniquely American doctrine through comparative criminal procedure. *Yale Law Journal* 118: 126–176.

Donaldson, T. 1982. *Corporations and morality*. Englewood Cliffs: Prentice Hall.

French, P.A. 1991. The corporation as a moral person. In *The spectrum of responsibility*, ed. P.A. French. New York: St. Martin's Press.

Hasnas, J. 2012. Reflections on corporate moral responsibility and the problem solving technique of Alexander the Great. *Journal of Business Ethics* 107: 183–195.

Hess, K.M. 2013. "If you tickle us . . . ": How corporations can be moral agents without being persons. *Journal of Value Inquiry* 47: 319–335.

McMahon, C. 1995. The moral status of organisations. *Business Ethics Quarterly* 5(3): 541–554.

Ronnegard, D. 2008. Collective responsibility: Collective punishment. In *Encyclopaedia of business ethics and society*, ed. Robert W. Kolb. Thousand Oaks: SAGE Publications.

[8] If the corporation is not a moral agent but merely a legal agent then business activity should primarily be regulated by the rule of law. The justification for what corporations ought to do then shifts from the moral domain of reasoning towards political justifications that regulate corporate activity.

Chapter 2
Necessary Conditions for Moral Agency

Goodpaster asks: "[I]s the concept of moral responsibility, as we are pursuing it, a normative concept or a descriptive concept or a mixture of the two?" (1983: 5). The way I see it the *attribution* of moral responsibility is a *description* about what a moral agent has done (or should have done).[1] However, what is required to *be* a moral agent is *normatively* decided by us given an understanding of the central abilities that we think the metaphysics of moral agency requires. In other words the attribution of moral responsibility to an agent is an event-description founded on a normative conception of what it should mean to *be* morally responsible. And what it should mean to be morally responsible involves a thorough understanding of the abilities for moral agency and their moral relevance.[2]

If corporations are to be ascribed the metaphysical status of moral agency then they will have to satisfy the conditions for moral agency as they arise in individual humans from which the notion of moral agency originates. It might be argued that the conditions that satisfy corporate moral agency differ from those that satisfy individual moral agency, and thus corporations need not have abilities that are equivalent to their human counterparts. For example, that corporate intentionality

[1]Moral agents may be attributed with moral responsibility for specific events. An event attributed to a moral agent will be characterised by a certain description of that event. For example, if chemical waste has been dumped into the river, then this event might be described as "the polluting of the river". Let us assume that "the polluting of the river" is a breach of a negative moral duty if intentionally brought about by a moral agent. A moral agent X who has intentionally brought about "the polluting of the river" may then be correctly attributed with the following moral responsibility: "moral agent X is responsible for polluting the river".

[2]Velasquez (2003) argues that attributions of intentionality to corporations are prescriptive; i.e. we should treat them *as if* they did possess intentionality. I do not disagree with this interpretation, but it is more precise to say that the conditions for moral agency are *prescribed*, but when we then attributed moral responsibility to an agent this is a *description* of what the moral agent has done.

D. Rönnegard, *The Fallacy of Corporate Moral Agency*,
Issues in Business Ethics 44, DOI 10.1007/978-94-017-9756-6_2

and human intentionality[3] are different and need not display the same qualities. But if the conditions for moral agency are not metaphysically equivalent then the senses of individual moral agency and corporate moral agency will be different.

It is the possession of the characteristics of individual moral agency that makes the attribution of moral responsibility meaningful to us. What would this new corporate sense of moral agency mean if it is not analogous to the human moral agency in which the notion originates? Does this new sense of corporate moral agency have any morally relevant properties in common with individual moral agency? Several philosophers (e.g. De George 1981; Donaldson 1982; Dubbink and Smith 2011; French 1995; Held 1991; Phillips 1992; and Werhane 1985) adhere to the view that corporate moral agency is a *special kind* of moral agency, but none of them say in what sense it has morally relevant characteristics.[4] For example De George (1999: 196) says, "[b]ecause the moral status of corporations is different from the moral status of human beings, the moral obligations of corporations are different from the moral obligations of human beings". It is unhelpful to use the term 'moral agency' in the corporate sense meant by these philosophers when it implies a very different concept from the human concept we are familiar with. Thus as we now look closer at the conditions of moral agency they will be developed with reference to how those abilities are understood in us.

Velasquez has done important work on debunking the concept of corporate moral agency. His first piece on the subject, *Why Corporations are not Morally Responsible for Anything they do*, appeared in 1983, and his follow-up, *Debunking Corporate Moral Responsibility*, appeared in 2003. In his articles Velasquez responds to the most prominent theories advocating corporate moral agency. In so doing he debunks their contention that corporations can satisfy the necessary moral agency abilities of intending and acting. One of his primary lines of argumentation is that "the concept of intentional action is rooted in the concept of an agent with certain mental and bodily unity which corporations do not have" (1983: 72). He emphasises that "[p]rocedures and policies, however simple or complex, cannot create a group mental-state nor group minds in any literal sense" (2003: 546). At best attributions of corporate moral responsibility are metaphorical as corporations can never literally intend an action. This seems quite right.

[3]"Intentionality" is the property of being about something; for something to have content. For example, intentionality is a pervasive feature of propositional content of many different mental states. Beliefs, desires and intentions are examples of intentional mental states. The attribution of intentionality to an agent does not specifically entail the state of intending, but merely that it has at least one of the several states which contain propositional content.

[4]All ethical theories hinge on the existence of moral agents towards whom the prescriptions of behaviour apply. If entities that do not meet the conditions of individual moral agency are to be considered special kinds of moral agents, then it is not clear that our ethical theories are applicable to them. If not, then what types of prescriptions are applicable to them? How are we to treat them and how are they to treat us? Are we to develop an entirely new realm of moral philosophy dealing with the behaviour between them and us (not to speak of their behaviour to each other)?

In responding to extant theories of corporate moral agency Velasquez has replied to them on their own terms, thus narrowly focusing on debunking the concepts of corporate intentions and corporate actions. However, besides the ability to intend and the ability to act, it is generally recognized that autonomy is a necessary condition for moral agency (Clarke 1992). Hardly any of the theories of corporate moral agency even touch upon the issue of autonomy. They do not because they cannot. I will show that the concept of autonomy alone debunks corporate moral agency and it further informs why corporations cannot intend nor act. Quite simply, if corporations cannot satisfy the autonomy condition they also cannot intend autonomously nor act autonomously, and thus cannot be moral agents. But we are getting ahead of ourselves. I shall consider each condition separately, as has been the tradition in the past, but autonomy will prove to be the central hurdle that corporations cannot pass.

I shall assume that there are three uncontroversial conditions for the metaphysical status of moral agency which we regard as necessary for ascribing such a status as it arises in individual humans. If corporations are to be ascribed the metaphysical status of moral agency then they will at least have to satisfy these three conditions. These three conditions are an ability to intend an action, an ability to perform an action and finally, an ability to autonomously choose an intentional action.

- Three Necessary Conditions for Moral Agency:
  - An ability to *intend* an action.
  - An ability to *perform* an action.
  - An ability to *autonomously choose* an intentional action.

Firstly, the ability to intend an action is a necessary condition for moral agency because it is by virtue of the intention that the event which takes place is considered an action attributable to the agent as a subject, rather than merely an accident or causal sequence of events. Actually intending an action (which requires the ability to intend an action) is only necessary for the ascription of moral responsibility for performed actions. For example a moral agent can only breach a negative duty[5] not to harm someone by intentionally performing the harmful action. Omissions on the other hand, involve the non-performance of an action and in such circumstances moral responsibility attributions do not require an actual intention to act, but merely the *ability* to intend an action. For example if a moral agent has a positive duty[6] to prevent harm, it[7] may breach that duty by *not* intending the preventive measures. However, the subject of the moral responsibility attribution must have the ability to intend an action to be blamed for not having intended as prescribed. The agent

[5] A negative duty is a duty to abstain from a certain action.

[6] A positive duty is a duty to perform a certain action.

[7] I will generally be referring to a moral agent as "it". This is because referring to a moral agent as a he or a she tends to imply that the agent is a person which is often associated with the attributes for moral agency. A corporation's status as a moral agent is precisely the topic of contention so it seems to be misguiding to refer to a moral agent as a he or a she.

is held morally responsible because it ought to have acted when it did not, and this at least requires that it had the ability to intend an action. (As we shall see it will become important to distinguish instrumental attributions of intentions from intrinsic attributions of intentions based on mental states.)

Secondly, the ability to perform an action is a necessary condition because we blame moral agents for the actions they perform (or abstain from performing), which requires that they have the ability to perform an action in the first place.

Finally, autonomy to choose an intentional action is a necessary condition for moral agency, and its central importance has been recognized since the first days of theorizing on the subject. The earliest philosopher to construct a theory of moral agency was Aristotle who in the *Nicomachean Ethics* set forth the view that only those who possess the *ability* to make choices following deliberation can be morally responsible (Eshleman 2009). The importance of the ability to make choices is still central to our more modern conceptions of autonomy. Nowadays it is important to keep "personal autonomy" and "moral autonomy" separate (Taylor 2005). Waldron says that personal autonomy involves "a person in charge of his life, not just following desires but choosing which desires to follow... Moral autonomy, by contrast, is associated specifically with the relation between one person's pursuit of his own ends and others' pursuit of theirs" (2005: 307). In other words personal autonomy is devoid of moral content about how an agent ought to treat others and is exclusively concerned with the capacity for independent choice. On the other hand, moral autonomy involves a comprehensive view of moral agency, which includes the ability to choose right from wrong.[8] I will be employing the condition of personal autonomy (rather than moral autonomy) because it is merely a necessary and not a sufficient condition for moral agency. If corporations cannot meet this necessary condition for moral agency then they certainly will not meet the richer sufficient condition.

There are a number of instructive phrases used to describe the concept of personal autonomy (from now on "autonomy"), such as: "free will", "self-determination", "self-rule", and "self-government". These phrases all draw on the intuition that autonomy involves an agent's ability to hold a vantage point that is distinct from the agent's desires and allows the agent to choose which desire to act upon. Autonomy is thus not merely about the ability to make choices, importantly it is about *how* choices are made. Harry Frankfurt (1971) points out that a central difference between humans and animals is our ability to reflect on our desires and beliefs when we choose to act. For example, an ass can choose between a pile of hay and a sugar cube based on their relative desirability, but it cannot reflect on higher-order desires

[8]Moral autonomy does contain moral prescriptions. For example for Kant moral autonomy involves practical reason (i.e. our ability to use reasons to choose our own actions) which itself presupposes that we see ourselves as free. In order to be free an agent must follows his own authority (not an external authority) which involves the self-imposition of universal moral law (e.g. Categorical Imperative).

for choosing either one or the other. A human on the other hand might desire to eat meat, but on reflection may not desire to kill animals, and on that basis may choose not to eat meat.

According to Frankfurt (1971) an autonomous agent must have desires regarding his desires (in order to be able to independently *choose* intentional actions)[9] which Frankfurt has called "second-order intentionality". In terms of the previous example, the desire to eat meat is an instance of "first-order intentionality", while the desire not to desire meat due to animal welfare is an instance of "second-order intentionality". This ability to have second-order intentionality forms the basis of our autonomy because we are able to *independently* choose our intentional actions rather than merely reacting to our desires.[10] As such, autonomy refers to an agent's ability to be directed by desires that belong to the agent.[11] This is why autonomy is necessary for lodging *ownership* with an agent for an intentional action. This ownership of actions is the foundation for attributing moral responsibility to an agent.[12]

The ability to independently choose an intentional action is a necessary moral agency condition because we attribute an action to an agent by virtue of it being its choice, which would not be the case if the agent lacked the *ability* to choose otherwise. It is common to articulate the autonomy condition by saying that the agent must be *free* to choose otherwise than it did. Although an agent's lack of freedom to choose otherwise will often exculpate an agent from its action (because the agent desired to choose a different course of action), a plurality of options is not strictly a necessary condition for moral responsibility attribution.[13] Frankfurt (1969) has pointed out that although an agent may lack *options* to choose otherwise, the choice that the agent in fact makes may nevertheless be the choice the agent would have chosen regardless of the availability of a plurality of options. In such cases the agent is clearly morally responsible despite not being free to choose

---

[9]Frankfurt assumes that intentions consist of a desire-belief complex.

[10]An autonomous agent does not merely react to external influences; rather it chooses how to act. Animals that merely react to external influences are not autonomous and are not morally responsible for their actions.

[11]There is a distinction between internalist and externalist accounts of autonomy (Buss 2008). Internalist accounts focus only on the coherence between an agent's lower and higher-order desires for autonomous action. Externalist accounts also evaluate whether an agent is responsive to an adequately broad range of higher-order desires (reasons) for and against actions. Frankfurt's (1971) account is internalist and such a weaker account is sufficient for our present purposes.

[12]There are several overlapping accounts of autonomy (see e.g. Bratman 1979; Watson 1975). All "hierarchical" accounts are augmentations of Frankfurt's view of autonomy (Buss 2008). Central to my argument, and common to all hierarchical accounts, is that autonomy involves the agent's ability to reflect on its own first-order desires for action. It is not my aim to develop or argue for a particular account of autonomy. Given Frankfurt's prominence in the autonomy debate I will be relying on his account.

[13]An ass may be *free* to choose between a pile of hay and a sugar cube, but it does not have the *autonomy* ability to reflect on its choice, and thus cannot choose otherwise than it does.

otherwise. Frankfurt says (1971: 19) "it is quite irrelevant to the evaluation of his moral responsibility to inquire whether the alternatives that he opted against were actually available to him". Therefore the necessary condition for moral agency that we are working with is the *ability to independently choose an intentional action* (rather than having a plurality of options).[14]

In Chap. 3 "Corporate Intentions" I will make further specifications to the criteria of "intention" and "autonomy" for moral agency. We will come to see that an important point of contention in the debate over corporate moral agency rests on two interpretations over the nature of intentions. Most advocates of corporate moral agency adhere to an instrumental attribution of intentions. However, I shall maintain that we must make a metaphysical claim about what intentions are in order to meet the metaphysical status of moral agency, and I shall argue that the morally relevant sense of an intention is as a mental state. I will make the following further specification to the criteria of "intention" and "autonomy":

- **An ability to intend an action.** The morally relevant sense of an intention is one that a moral agent is *aware* of which suggests that it is metaphysically a mental state.
- **An ability to autonomously choose an intentional action.** In order for a moral agent to be able to choose its intentional actions it must be *aware* of the process of choosing an intentional action which suggest that metaphysically the ability is mental.

In Chap. 4 "Corporate Actions?" I will make a further specification of the "action" criterion for moral agency. I will argue that a moral agent must be able to perform an action on its own or through the help of non-free agents who do not act independently when representing their principal. This is because moral responsibility is not transferable from the actions of individuals who act *independently*. I will make the following further specification to the "action" criterion:

- **An ability to perform an action.** In order to be attributed with moral responsibility for an event a principal must have some way that it can realize its intention either through its own corporal movements or by instructing a non-free agent to realize its intention.

I will not argue here for these further specifications of the three necessary criteria for moral agency, but will defend these views in the indicated chapters.

[14]The significance of regarding autonomy as an *ability* may be further underscore. Under circumstances of coercion a moral agent may be exculpated for intentional actions if the agent desired to choose otherwise but could not. Circumstances of coercion may vary from one situation to another, but it is necessary that a subject has the *ability* to independently choose an intentional action in order to be the subject of a moral responsibility attribution irrespective of the circumstances. The ability of autonomous choice enables the agent to choose a different course of action from the one that is actually chosen.

Although I believe that most philosophers would regard the stated conditions as necessary for moral agency, I believe that few would accept that these three conditions would jointly qualify as sufficient conditions for moral agency. For example Kant required moral agents to possess capacities for practical reason, while Hume required moral agents to have the ability to sympathise. Nevertheless, a moral agent at the very least possesses these three *necessary* abilities, plus whatever other conditions you believe are *sufficient* for moral agency. The metaphysical notion of moral agency is here left open-ended to accommodate the conditions you regard as *sufficient* for moral agency. However, I am assuming that most adult humans qualify as moral agents.

References

Bratman, M.E. 1979. Practical reasoning and weakness of the will. *Noûs* 13: 131–151.

Buss, S. 2008. Personal autonomy. In *The Stanford encyclopedia of philosophy,* ed. Edward N. Zalta. http://plato.stanford.edu/archives/fall2008/entries/personal-autonomy/.

Clarke, R. 1992. Free will and the conditions of moral responsibility. *Philosophical Studies* 66: 53–72.

De George, R.T. 1981. Can corporations have moral responsibilities? *University of Dayton Review* 5: 3–15.

De George, R.T. 1999. *Business ethics*. Upper Saddle River: Prentice Hall.

Donaldson, T. 1982. *Corporations and morality*. Englewood Cliffs: Prentice Hall.

Dubbink, W., and J. Smith. 2011. A political account of corporate moral responsibility. *Ethical Theory and Moral Practice* 14: 223–246.

Eshleman, A. 2009. Moral responsibility. In *The Stanford encyclopedia of philosophy,* ed. Edward N. Zalta. http://plato.stanford.edu/archives/win2009/entries/moral-responsibility/.

Frankfurt, H.G. 1969. Alternate possibilities and moral responsibility. *Journal of Philosophy* 66: 828–839.

Frankfurt, H.G. 1971. Freedom of the will and the concept of a person. *Journal of Philosophy* 68: 5–20.

French, P.A. 1995. *Corporate ethics*. Brace: Harcourt.

Goodpaster, K.E. 1983. The concept of corporate responsibility. *Journal of Business Ethics* 2: 1–22.

Held, V. 1991. Can a random collection of individuals be morally responsible? In *The spectrum of responsibility*, ed. P.A. French. New York: St. Martin's Press.

Phillips, M.J. 1992. Corporate moral personhood and three conceptions of the corporation. *Business Ethics Quarterly* 2: 435–459.

Taylor, R.S. 2005. Kantian personal autonomy. *Political Theory* 33: 602–628.

Velasquez, Manuel G. 1983. Why corporations are not morally responsible for anything they do. *Business and Professional Ethics Journal* 2: 1–18.

Velasquez, Manuel G. 2003. Debunking corporate moral responsibility. *Business Ethics Quarterly* 13: 531–562.

Waldron, J. 2005. Moral autonomy and personal autonomy. In *Autonomy and the challenges to liberalism*, ed. J. Christman and J. Anderson. Cambridge, MA: Cambridge University Press.

Watson, G. 1975. Free agency. *Journal of Philosophy* 72: 205–220.

Werhane, P.H. 1985. *Persons, rights, & corporations*. Englewood Cliffs: Prentice Hall.

Chapter 3
Corporate Intentions

Peter French is one of the most discussed advocates for the position that corporations are moral agents. He regards the corporate entity itself as a moral agent that is logically distinct from its members. This position may be contrasted with other views that attribute moral agency and responsibility to the corporation as a collective whole of structured individual members.[1] This difference becomes an important one because it distinguishes if corporate moral responsibility attributions refer to the corporate entity or its members (either individually or collectively). As we shall see later on I do believe that certain corporate moral responsibility attributions are legitimate when they implicitly refer to its members, but that it is imperative that we reject any such attributions to corporate entities themselves as logically distinct from their members. French's position is widely discussed due to its extreme nature but not widely held for the same reason. However, French is a good starting point because his controversial view helps to highlight some of the main issues at stake in this debate.[2] I shall explicate French's position of corporate moral agency which will involve presenting his views on the conditions for moral agency. I will then criticise French's position in the light of the necessary conditions for moral agency which will help to further specify the morally relevant sense of the intention and autonomy conditions for moral agency.

[1]As noted earlier it is crucial to distinguish corporate moral agency from notions of collective moral agency. Corporate moral agency involves agency that is logically distinct from the abilities of corporate members, while collective moral agency is entirely dependent of the abilities of members.

[2]I will start by considering French's view of corporate moral agency because it is the most discussed view, but more importantly because debunking his view will allow us to further specify the morally relevant sense of the intention condition.

D. Rönnegard, *The Fallacy of Corporate Moral Agency*,
Issues in Business Ethics 44, DOI 10.1007/978-94-017-9756-6_3

The structure for this chapter will be:

- Section 3.1: Explication of Peter French's Conception of Corporate Moral Agency
- Section 3.2: The Metaphysics of Intentions and Its Moral Relevance

3.1 Explication of Peter French's Conception of Corporate Moral Agency

French has as a premise that anything that is an intentional agent is also a moral agent. Therefore he views his task as showing us that a corporation is an intentional agent and thus by reference to his premise he has shown that a corporation is a moral agent. He regards the two crucial abilities for agency to be an ability to intend and an ability to act (which is not controversial), and his aim is to show us that the corporation has these abilities in a manner that is logically distinct from its members (which is controversial).[3]

His starting point (1984) is that there is an all-important difference between what he calls an "aggregate collectivity" and a "conglomerate collectivity". An aggregate collectivity is merely a collection of people who bring about a certain event through the aggregation of their individual efforts. The conglomerate differs from the aggregate collectivity in that it has an internal organization with decision procedures for concerted actions. It also has enforced standards of conduct and members have defined roles. It is this structure of the conglomerate collectivity that French argues stands as the basis for the corporation's ability to act intentionally and thus to be an independent moral agent.

- Aggregate Collectivity: An aggregate collective consists of a group of individuals who together bring about a certain event through the aggregation of their individual efforts. For example, the members of the group "motorists" in a city individually contribute to the aggregate level of air pollution.
- Conglomerate Collectivity: A conglomerate collective is an organized group of people with an established decision procedure to make collective decisions. The members of a conglomerate collective work concertedly in the pursuit of a common goal. For example, a corporation, an orchestra, or government agency.

French (1984: 10) says: "Moral responsibility predicates cannot be legitimately ascribed to aggregate collectivities. Aggregates simply fail the test for membership

[3] I have assumed that there are three necessary conditions for moral agency, but French only addresses two of these and leaves out the condition of autonomy. French is not alone in doing so. Most corporate moral agency advocates merely focus on the intention and action conditions. One could reject corporate moral agency purely on the basis that such theories use insufficient conditions for moral agency. However, to fully debunk corporate moral agency I shall show that such theories cannot meet *any* of the necessary moral agency conditions.

into the moral community. It is crucial that they are not intentional agents in and of themselves." His reason for saying that moral responsibility predicates cannot be legitimately ascribed to aggregate collectivities is that the aggregate is not an entity, and so is not responsible as such. Rather when we talk about aggregates these terms act as general terms. For example, in the phrase "a mob of people" the word "mob" acts as a general term, and what a mob is responsible for, each member of the mob is responsible for. Therefore each individual member of an aggregate is morally responsible.

On the other hand when we talk about conglomerates these terms act as singular terms. For example on his conception the phrase "the Example Corporation" would act as a singular term and name an entity, given that it has an established decision and action procedure that concerts the intentions and actions of members. The Example Corporation has an identity that is not merely the aggregation of its members. If we say "the Example Corporation was responsible for polluting the river", we are then not trying to attribute moral responsibility to a specific subset of corporate members who acted so as to pollute the river, but rather to the entity itself which is the Example Corporation. French maintains that we must be referring to an entity that is distinct from its members because otherwise the referent of the Example Corporation could vary depending on a speaker's intention of referring to different specific members,[4] which he finds inconsistent with the meaning of statements that contain corporate names. For conglomerates responsibility is predicated to the conglomerate entity itself rather than to some individual member. Some member must have done something, but the responsibility we predicate to the conglomerate entity need not fall upon any individual member. For the Example Corporation to be responsible for polluting the river, some individual corporate member must have acted, but not necessarily so that this member can be attributed with the responsibility for polluting the river. Thus the entity may be morally responsible although no member is. That is to say, individual corporate members A, B, and C, may perform actions X, Y, and Z, which causally leads to corporate act Q, although no individual member is morally responsible for Q.

Aggregates according to French are identical to the sum of their members. On the other hand conglomerates, such as corporations, are indifferent to the changing of individual memberships. Individuals hold positions within the organization, but who those individuals are that hold those positions is a contingent property of the corporation.[5]

French (1991a: 290) says that corporations can be "full-fledged moral persons and have whatever privileges, rights and duties as are, in the normal course of affairs, accorded to moral persons." We should note in order to understand what is being expressed that French does not distinguish between moral agents and moral

[4]In other words, on different occasions for different events the speaker might refer to different corporate members when using the corporate name.

[5]French (1984: 29) maintains that the name of a corporation is in Saul Kripke's terms a "rigid designator" which picks out the same object in every possible world.

persons, nor does he distinguish between intentional agents and moral agents; the three notions seem to be used interchangeably.[6] He writes: "I shall define a moral person as a referent of any proper name or description that can be a non-eliminable subject of what I shall call a responsibility ascription of the second type" (French 1991a: 296). French explains that a responsibility ascription of the second type amounts to a conjunctive proposition, where the first conjunct identifies the subject's action as causally efficacious for an event and the second conjunct maintains that the subject intended to bring about the event through its action. Thus a moral agent must legitimately have such a conjunctive proposition attributed to it. This clearly identifies French's two crucial conditions for moral agency as having the ability to *act* and the ability to *intend* its actions.

Now we come to the most crucial part of French's position. What is it that counts as an intentional agent? What characteristics must an intentional agent have? He writes: "To say that something acts intentionally is to say that it has purposes, plans, goals, and interests that motivate some of its behaviour . . . Obviously, corporations cannot, in any normal sense, desire and believe. If intentional actions must reduce to desires and beliefs, then corporations fail to make it as intentional actors" (French 1991b: 10). Of course he does not believe that they fail to be intentional actors. Instead French employs theories of intentional action that do not hinge on agents necessarily having any real desires or beliefs when these are construed as mental states. He thus quite explicitly admits that the metaphysical similarity with individual moral agents cannot be met. French (1991a: 298) says: "If corporations are moral persons, they will be non-eliminable Davidsonian agents." For something to be a Davidsonian agent some events must be describable so as to make sentences about the entity intending the events true. There must be a description which says that the corporation itself intended the event in question.

I must here briefly explicate the Davidsonian notion of agency so that we understand this very central aspect of French's theory. Davidson's account of agency is a semantic rather than a metaphysical account of intentional agency. It is a very weak notion of agency and it says that if there is at least one true description under which an actor brought about an event intentionally, then that actor is the agent of the event. Davidsonian agency is a weak account of agency because it is not necessary for an actor to intend an event under a certain description in order to be the agent of the event under that description. Ouyan and Shiner (1995) give the following example: The description "Don intentionally spilled the contents of the cup" will make true that Don did what he did intentionally, but under another description "Don intentionally spilled the coffee" it will be false that Don did what he did intentionally, because Don thought it was tea in the cup and not coffee. According to Davidson, Don is the agent of spilling the coffee because we find at least one description under which "Don did it intentionally" is true. The weakness of the account is that Don is not only the agent of the event of spilling the cup which he

[6] It is not clear if French believes that these terms are synonymous, but he never explains their different senses nor explains why the terms are used interchangeably.

intended, but he is also the agent of the event of spilling the coffee which he did not intend. Therefore actually intending a specific act description is not necessary to be the agent of that event as long as there is another act description under which the act was intentional.

- Davidsonian Agency: Davidson's account of agency says that if there is at least one true description under which an actor brought about an event intentionally, then the actor is the agent of that event. This is a weak account of agency because the actor is also the agent of the same event under a different event-description that the actor did not intend.[7]

However, for there to be any true description at all which says that a corporation itself performed an act intentionally, one must have a theory which says that corporations possess the *ability* to intend actions. Due to the obvious lack of a "corporate mind" French needs a theory of intending that in no way relies on mental states. So what notion of intending does French have in mind? He employs two different notions. The first is the notion of an "intentional system" borrowed from Daniel Dennett which French employs in his earlier work. Dennett's notion of an "intentional system" is a system whose behaviour can be explained by ascribing beliefs and desires to the system. But these beliefs and desires need not be "real" in any sense akin to mental states. For example, a spring can qualify as an intentional system because describing the spring as intending what it does is useful in predicting its movement. In other words, we can find it instrumentally useful to talk about the spring *as if* it intended what it did. The second notion of intending French has borrowed from Michael Bratman's planning theory of intention. Bratman's theory presents itself as an alternative to the traditional view of intentions that regards intentions as reducible to a desire-belief complex. Rather for Bratman intending is an entirely separate state from desiring and believing and the operative element of intending is to plan. Bratman says that when we form an intention we make future directed plans that set out a course of action and the plan is conduct-controlling because we commit to it.

Real desires and beliefs are part of Davidson's account of intentions which presumably he would require for there to be a true description under which an agent brings about an event intentionally. However, French divorces real desires and beliefs from Davidson's account of agency and replaces it with Dennett's instrumental account of intentions (or Bratman's account) in order to obtain a description of an agent intending that does not rely on the mental states of belief and desire.[8]

---

[7]Nevertheless, one should note that Davidson is presenting an account of agency and is not aiming to present an account of moral agency as such. As we shall see the weakness of the account is not a problem for Davidson but for French who uses Davidson's account of agency for the purpose of moral agency.

[8]French is borrowing a part of Davidson's theory of agency, but Davidson himself would not qualify corporations as agents as they have no real desires and beliefs.

French's claim is that the corporate structure, which he calls Corporate Internal Decision Structure (CIDS), is the intentional element that is consistent with Dennett's notion of an intentional system and Bratman's planning theory of intention. French says that the CIDS functions as a redescription device that allows us to predicate intentionality upon a corporation.

Corporations' CIDS have two main characteristics. The first is an organizational responsibility flow chart which delineates positions and levels of authority. The second is the corporate decision rules that are usually manifested in corporate policy. "The CID structure accomplishes a subordination and synthesis of intentions and acts of various persons into a corporate decision" (French 1991a: 300). French likens the CIDS to the rules of a game, where the organizational chart defines the players with their corresponding lines of responsibility. The corporate policy dictates the goal of the corporation (the aim of the game) and corporate "recognition rules" define what count as corporate decisions (the moves with in the game). "When the corporate act is consistent with, an instantiation of... established corporate policy, then it is proper to describe it as having been done for corporate reasons, as having been caused by a corporate desire coupled with a corporate belief and so, in other words, a corporate intention" (French 1991a: 302). On French's conception this intentional agency of the corporation is not reducible to the intentions and actions of its members. It is central that the intentional agency is of the corporate entity itself.

According to French, the CIDS is intentional because it can be regarded as a conduct-controlling plan (Bratman) or a system with directedness (Dennett). The CIDS allows for a description of a corporate act as being intentional and thus the corporation qualifies as a Davidsonian agent. The CID structure "accounts for the personality of the corporation.... A corporation is that particular one because it has a particular CID Structure" (French 1992: 139). The CIDS is all important. It distinguishes corporations from aggregate collectivities. It also licences the redescription of events as corporate intentional actions and thus, as intentional agents, corporations are moral agents according to French.

- Corporate Internal Decision Structure (CIDS) & Corporate Moral Agency: The CIDS together with Dennett's theory of intentions (or Bratman's) gives a non-mental account of the corporation's *ability* to intend and thus according to French enables the corporation to be attributed with Davidsonian agency. Because French equates intentional agency with moral agency, French concludes that corporations are moral agents.

3.2 The Metaphysics of Intentions and Its Moral Relevance

In this section I will argue that the morally relevant sense of an intention is as a mental state and that the ability to choose an intention autonomously is a mental ability.

If we take French's two moral agency conditions and regard the entities that exist in the world, what would qualify as a moral agent? Keeping in mind that French's conception of intentionality is borrowed from Dennett and does not require any mental states to qualify as an intentional system, we could enumerate mature people, infants, cats, dogs, colonies of ants and even corporations as moral agents. Do we really mean for all of these to qualify as moral agents?

Let us first look at the inadequacy of French's view of intentionality for the purposes of moral agency. He subscribes to both Dennett's and Bratman's views of what it is to intend. Let us start with Bratman. I do not find Bratman's planning theory of intention per se to be inadequate as a description of the intending criterion for moral agency. Bratman's aim is to illuminate the notion of intention as it appears in humans who are planning creatures. He rejects that intentions are reducible to a desire-belief complex and rather maintains that intending is a different mental state altogether. However, it is important for our purposes to note that although Bratman regards intentions as plans they are nevertheless mental plans which we have as believing and desiring humans. French seems to have used a piece of Bratman's theory without acknowledging the greater context of which it is a part. So although it may (or may not) be appropriate to regard a CIDS as a conduct-controlling plan, it cannot on Bratman's theory be regarded as an intention separate from the corporate members because the CIDS is not a mental state.

The corporation is clearly not an agent in the sense of having mental states. If I write down a plan of mine on a piece of paper, we do not say that the paper has an intention. The paper perhaps contains a representation of my intention, but it is only I, with my mental state that has an intention. One might say that the CIDS is conduct controlling because it is a plan consisting of rules, guidelines and a mission statement, which the individual members may make a commitment to adhere to. However, with this representation we have a state of affairs consisting of intentions and commitments of the individual members and not something that qualifies in any metaphysical sense as a separate corporate intention.

- French's Use of Bratman's Planning Theory of Intentions: French uses Bratman's planning theory of intentions in order to attribute intentions to a corporation's CIDS. This is an illegitimate use of Bratman's theory because Bratman conceives of intentions as mental plans and because a CIDS clearly does not possess any mental states it cannot have any intentions in the sense of Bratman's theory.

Next, Dennett's view of an intentional system is not appropriate as a condition for moral agency. His conception of what it is for something to intend requires no real mental states of desiring and believing, it requires only that we can predict the behaviour of the system by relying on ascriptions of intentional states. However, for the purposes of moral agency it is not sufficient that we can merely predict a system's behaviour through such ascriptions; rather the intending agent must actually possess the relevant mental states. Fisse and Braithwaite (1993: 24) write:

> "If responsibility is conceived as a metaphysical concept, then the intrinsic features of responsible entities assume special importance. But if responsibility is taken to be a functional concept of social action, then nothing necessarily hinges on the intrinsic characteristics of different social entities".

The concept of moral responsibility that we are working with is a metaphysical one. We are discussing what moral agency *is* and whether or not corporations possess the necessary characteristics for moral agency. We are not here discussing the *function* that attributions of moral responsibility play in our society. Therefore the intrinsic features of the corporation are of fundamental importance for attributing moral agency and responsibility to the corporation. The problem for French in employing Dennett's intentional system is that it is an instrumental account of intentionality and has nothing per se to say about the metaphysical nature of intentions.[9] You cannot simply jump from an instrumental attribution of intentions which says that the corporation behaves *as if* it intends, to a metaphysical attribution of intentions which says that the corporation does have intentions.[10]

The concept of what intentions are comes from our introspective awareness of our own planned actions suggesting that they are primitively mental states. If intentions are mental states then they are only attributable (in a literal sense) to entities that actually possess such mental states. Our attribution of intentions to other humans or animals is based on the belief that they have the mental states that we can identify in ourselves. It is an epistemological leap of faith that beings other than ourselves possess what we experience as intentionality. We infer that other beings behave intentionally not only from their apparently purposive behaviour, but also from our belief that their brains experience the mental states found in us. Dennett's intentional systems seem better described as "systems that tend towards a certain state" rather than "systems that intend certain behaviour". It is only by virtue of a similarity with the intentions we are capable of having that we, in a literal sense, attribute intentions to others.

Dennett maintains (1987) that there is nothing special about minds and brains with regard to intentionality. He argues that all intentionality is merely attributed intentionality, even the attribution of intentionality to ourselves. He maintains that we merely attribute intentionality to other people, to ourselves, and to external objects for certain instrumental purposes. However, John Searle (1980) distinguishes between the instrumental attribution of intentionality to objects on the one hand, and what he calls intrinsic intentionality (also called original intentionality) on the other hand. He says that although we may instrumentally attribute intentionality

[9] This is a problem for French, not Dennett. Dennett has no ambition to establish a metaphysical account of intentions because he believes that there is nothing more to intentions than the instrumental attribution of intentions. However, it is part of French's project to establish a metaphysical account of moral agency, and for such a project an instrumental account of intentions will not do.

[10] One can argue that moral responsibility attributions in society would not serve the functions they do unless there exists an underlying belief that the entities attributed with moral responsibility are aware of their conduct and choices, and can appreciate the responsibility being attributed to them.

for certain practical purposes to external objects, minds are special in that they possess intrinsic intentionality. Searle points out that there must be some intrinsic intentionality in the world because the very act of attributing intentionality is itself an intentional act. Therefore not all intentionality can be merely attributed intentionality. There must be something like minds that possess intrinsic intentionality that originally attribute intentionality to the external world.

Searle (1980) has put forward an argument called the Chinese Room argument. It is based on a thought experiment where we are to imagine that an individual who only knows English sits in a room and follows instructions in English for manipulating Chinese characters in such a way that for someone outside the room it seems as if the person inside speaks Chinese. The aim of the argument is to show that if a computer is programmed to functionally perform the speaking of Chinese, and thus be instrumentally attributed with the ability to speak Chinese, the computer is still incapable of *understanding* the language. Similarly this would go to show that instrumentally attributing intentionality (along the lines of Dennett) to intentional systems that have no mental states ignores the appreciation of propositional content of an intention. Dennett however believes that Searle is conflating intentionality with awareness of intentionality. Nevertheless, it might be argued that awareness of an intention is inseparable from the intention itself. If that is so then there is an aspect of an intention which involves awareness, which for our purposes is a characteristic that minds may have and corporations may not. Even if awareness of an intention is conceptually separable from the intention itself I would like to maintain that the morally relevant sense of an intention is one that a moral agent is consciously aware of.[11]

Peter Cane (2002: 65) writes: "Philosophically it is generally agreed that a minimum level of *mental* and physical capacities is a precondition for culpability. A person should not be blamed if they lacked basic *understanding* of the nature and significance of their conduct, or basic control over it" (emphasis added).

Cane points out that a moral agent must be able to understand the significance of its conduct which would at least seem to suggest that awareness of the content of one's intention is a necessary part of a moral agent's ability to intend. If anything different from systems with brains possess the ability to intend it must at least display the mental qualities for intentions found in us. Now, clearly a corporation's CIDS does not possess intentionality in any way that requires mental states- French himself admits as much. Rather, as we have noted, French likens the CIDS to the rules of a game, but rules define a frame of legitimate action and do not in themselves intend. Donaldson (1982: 22) has picked up on this and writes: "[T]he rules of a game fail to tell us what the game *itself* intends- in fact, it makes little sense to say that the game intends anything- and one can argue that the same is true for corporations".

[11]Being able to intend an action is one of the three necessary conditions for moral agency. I am now saying that the morally relevant sense of an intention is such that the moral agent must be aware of its intention. One might object that I am now introducing a fourth necessary condition for moral agency, but I am here only explicating the morally relevant sense of an intention rather than adding new conditions for moral agency.

The task that needs to be achieved in order to show that the corporation is a moral agent is an exercise in metaphysics. French needs to show that corporations have the same or similar characteristics that are necessary for moral agency. The problem for French is that his account of corporate moral agency is a *semantic* account and not a metaphysical account because it is based on a Davidsonian conception of agency and on Dennett's instrumental conception of intentionality. Ouyang and Shiner (1995: 287) say that Davidsonian agency's "character as a *semantic* account of agency apparently leaves the account-giver free to predicate genuine agency of some entity without reference to that entity's metaphysical status as possessor of a mind or soul or will".

A semantic account of agency tells us when it is a meaningful and useful use of language to attribute actions to beings or things. However, a semantic account does not tell us what metaphysical characteristics agents have. To say that a corporation is the agent of an event may be a useful use of language in a non-literal sense (just as it is useful to speak of the sun rising and setting in a non-literal sense), but it does not tell us what the characteristics of a corporate agent are.

- French's use of Davidsonian Agency: French employs Davidson's account of agency in order to justify that a corporation is an agent (and by extension also a moral agent on French's account). However, Davidsonian agency is a semantic account of agency which is meant to explain when it is a meaningful and useful to say that someone is the agent of an event. But as a semantic account of agency it does not say anything about the metaphysical properties of agents. It is precisely the metaphysical properties of being an agent that French needs to substantiate in order for the corporation to be a moral agent.

Moreover, Dennett's instrumental conception of intentionality has nothing to say about the metaphysical status of intentions. However, *it is* part of French's project to make the metaphysical claim that corporations are moral agents. Therefore French is basing his theory of corporate moral agency on an instrumental account of intentionality and a semantic account of agency. This in effect leaves him with an account of corporate moral agency that does not say anything about the corporation's metaphysical characteristics as a moral agent.

Giving a semantic account of moral agency does not amount to much more than an explanation of proper linguistic usage. People may find it useful, for whatever reason to speak of corporations as moral agents, but if such usage is all that is required for corporate moral agency then we could have saved ourselves a lot of trouble and just listened to how people speak in order to identify the proper subjects of moral responsibility attributions. There would be no need for French to go through the entire process of invoking Dennett's intentional system to legitimize his descriptive CIDS account as an intentional system in order to then qualify the corporation as a Davidsonian agent. Ouyang and Shiner (1995: 298) say: "If the goal is to prove that organizations have a certain robust kind of agency that normally presupposes mentalistic intentions, then the goal will not be achieved by showing that they have some weaker form of agency".

Whether ascriptions of intentionality to non-mental actors serves as good explanations or good predictive tools is not my concern here, but rather my concern is whether the sense of intention attributed is morally relevant. The fact is that the concept of "intention" in its primary sense is as a mental state. One might argue that I need to show that it is *only* as a mental state that an intention qualifies in the morally relevant sense. But I believe (due to an intention's primacy as a mental state) that it is those who give a non-mental account of intention who bear the onus of showing that their account and sense of intention is morally relevant. I recognize that corporations do have a CIDS with its mission statement and policies, but the issue is not whether it is *useful* to attribute intentionality to such a structure, but rather whether or not it is *morally relevant* to do so. Jan Edward Garrett (1989: 540) hits the nail on the head when he writes: "French's view that corporations are persons in the same sense as human beings would seem to require that we sometimes rightfully attribute moral responsibility to a person's *code of conduct*, rather than (as we actually do) holding the *person* responsible for action on the basis of his or her code of conduct." In other words, we hold the person responsible for their autonomous choice and action which may be motivated by (but not controlled by) their code of conduct.

- Dennett's Theory of Intending is not Morally Relevant: Dennett's account of intending is merely an instrumental account of intending and does not make any metaphysical commitments or demands. I believe that being *aware* of one's intention is a necessary aspect of the morally relevant sense of an intention which seems to suggest that the morally relevant metaphysical status of an intention is as a mental state. This is clearly not a property of a CIDS.

I think there is a tendency to believe that when untoward events occur someone or something must be morally responsible. This is the intuitive force of French's argument. Nonetheless, it is misguided because it fails to realise that some events occur where only causal responsibility attributions are possible. It may always be possible to attribute causal responsibility for an untoward event (assuming all events have causes), but not always moral responsibility. That is to say, no one may have intended for the event in question to occur. French needs the CIDS to qualify as an "intentional system", so that responsibility can be attributed to the corporation as an agent. However, we must recognize that events that no one intended occur all the time. To the extent that a system is intentionally created to bring about certain events, the creators of that system are morally responsible for the intended results. And to the extent that an event is caused by an unintentional system we can only identify a chain of causal responsibility attributions, but no one is morally responsible. Either way the corporation as a system is not morally responsible in itself. Either its creators are morally responsible or no one is, but we must resist any inclination we may have to think that someone or something must be *morally* responsible for untoward events.

- No one Needs to Be **Morally** Responsible for Untoward Events: When untoward events occur we are often inclined to find out whom or what is responsible. Sometimes the events are intentionally caused by a moral agent and then it may be appropriate to attribute *moral* responsibility to the responsible party. Moral agents may also be merely *causally* responsible for an event without being morally responsible. Unless someone intended an event or had the ability and duty to prevent an event, then no one is morally responsible. In such situations only causal attributions of responsibility are legitimate.

To sum up, French's account of intentionality is inadequate for the purpose of moral agency because of his reliance on Dennett's notion of an intentional system yields merely an instrumental, and not a metaphysical account of intentionality. When this is further conjoined with the Davidsonian account of agency (which is a semantic account of agency) it implies that French's theory only stands as a semantic account of moral agency having contributed no substantial justification on a metaphysical level. Through an analysis and critique of French's view of corporate moral agency we have managed to further specify the "intention" condition for moral agency:

- **An ability to intend an action**. The morally relevant sense of an intention is one that a moral agent is *aware* of which suggests that it is metaphysically a mental state.

An intention that an agent is consciously aware of is the morally relevant sense of an intention because it has an important relation to autonomy. In order for an agent to be autonomous it must be able to choose its intentional actions rather than merely perform intentional actions by reacting to its desires and environment.[12] It seems reasonable to say that for an agent to be able to autonomously choose an intentional action it must be aware of what it chooses. It is difficult to conceive of the ability to autonomously choose an intentional action without the property of the agent being aware of the choice that is made. Therefore the agent is aware of the chosen intention itself because the agent will inevitably be aware of the intention it forms.[13] Furthermore, not only is a moral agent aware of its intention but also aware of the process of choosing an intentional action. It is this awareness that makes

[12]In the language of Harry Frankfurt, the condition of autonomy requires second order intentionality, which in this context requires that one has desires regarding one's desires. The ability to have second order intentionality enables an agent to choose its actions rather than merely react to its desires and environment. An agent can only have (second order) desires regarding its (first order) desires if it is aware of its first order desires. First order desires combine with beliefs to from the agent's intention.

[13]One might object that the ability to be aware of one's intention is not a property of the intention condition but is an ability already contained in the autonomy condition (second order intentionality). Fair enough, but this merely reiterates the necessity of the condition of autonomy which is absent in French's theory. Furthermore, if a moral agent's second order intentionality is mental (its desires concerning its desires), then certainly its first order intentionality will be so too. It makes no sense to speak of an instrumental (and non-mental) account of first order intentions for an agent that also possesses second order intentionality. For example the following makes no sense: "the spring intends (instrumental) to stretch five inches, but it only second order desires (mental) to stretch three inches". Desires are mental states and that applies to both first and second order desires.

the choice attributable to the moral agent and that is why we lodge blame with the moral agent as a locus of responsibility. This awareness of the intention itself and the awareness of the choosing of the intentional action suggest that metaphysically both the abilities of intending and choosing autonomously are mental states. We can now therefore further specify the autonomy condition for moral agency as:

- **An ability to autonomously choose an intentional action**. In order for a moral agent to be able to choose its intentional actions it must be *aware* of the process of choosing an intentional action which suggest that metaphysically the ability is mental.

This concludes my analysis of the intentionality condition for moral agency, specifically with regard French's position. We shall now consider in greater detail the condition of being able to *perform* an action for moral agency with regard to French and other proponents of corporate moral agency. To this we turn next.

References

Cane, P. 2002. *Responsibility in law and morality*. Oxford: Hart.

Dennett, D. 1987. Fast thinking. In *The intentional stance*, 324–337. Cambridge, MA: MIT Press.

Donaldson, T. 1982. *Corporations and morality*. Englewood Cliffs: Prentice Hall.

French, P.A. 1984. *Collective and corporate responsibility*. New York: Columbia University Press.

French, P.A. 1991a. The corporation as a moral person. In *The spectrum of responsibility*, ed. P.A. French. New York: St. Martin's Press.

French, P.A. 1991b. *Corporate ethics*. Brace: Harcourt.

French, P.A. 1992. *Responsibility matters*. Kansas: University Press of Kansas.

Garrett, J.E. 1989. Unredistributable corporate moral responsibility. *Journal of Business Ethics* 8: 535–545.

Ouyang, G., and R.A. Shiner. 1995. Organisations and agency. *Legal Theory* 1: 283–310.

Searle, J. 1980. Minds, brains and programs. *Behavioral and Brain Sciences* 3: 417–457.

Chapter 4
Corporate Actions

French's position that the corporation directs its members to act in accord with its intentions can be represented as a vicarious relationship, by which the corporate members only act as the representatives of the organization and therefore their intentions and actions are attributed to the corporation. Larry May (1991: 320) defines vicarious action as "action 'a' done by 'y' but attributable to 'x' due to the fact that 'y' has been delegated to do 'a' as a substitute for 'x'". Vicarious action as stated is represented by a vicarious relationship or as it is often called a principal-agent relationship; in this case 'x' is the principal and 'y' is the agent of the relationship. The notion of vicarious agency is important for many advocates of corporate moral agency because the corporation's lack of corporal existence requires human agents to causally affect the physical world. By representing the corporation as the principal in a vicarious relationship the corporation is able to satisfy the necessary moral agency condition of being able to perform an action by virtue of the acts performed by its constituents that are then attributed to the entity itself. French's position can be represented in such a way that the corporation itself is the principal and the corporate members are the agents. The Corporate Internal Decision Structure (CIDS) (being the personality of the corporation) directs its employees into action in accord with its intentions and the actions of the employees are then attributed to the corporate entity. The diagram below (Fig. 4.1) represents this relationship.

Representing French's position in this way does not add anything to his argument. The corporation's supposed ability to intend and direct the actions of its members still needs to be established by independent metaphysical argumentation. This representation does not establish the corporation as a moral agent. An analogy by John Ladd is illuminating on this issue. If in a stage production of Hamlet the actor says "to be or not to be" we ascribe those words to Hamlet, not the actor. But this is a fictitious interpretation; what is actually being done is done by the actor

D. Rönnegard, *The Fallacy of Corporate Moral Agency*,
Issues in Business Ethics 44, DOI 10.1007/978-94-017-9756-6_4

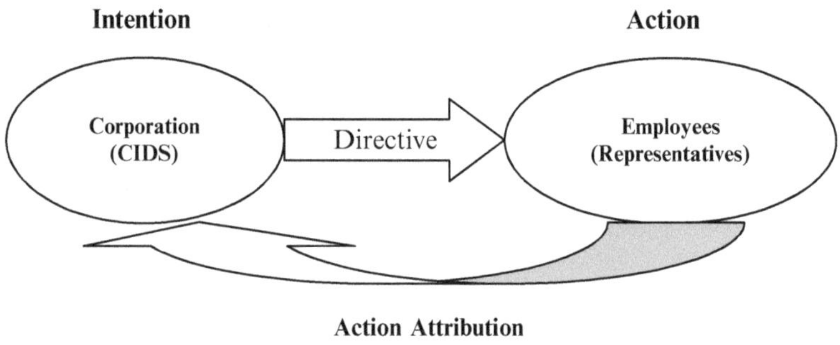

Fig. 4.1 Peter French's theory of corporate moral agency represented as a vicarious relationship

before us. "Insofar as responsibility and morality are concerned in the real world, it is a categorical mistake to apply them to the play world of the corporation" (Ladd 1991: 308).

May takes the slightly different view that the shareholders are the principals and that the corporation is a placeholder of the shareholders' intentions. The shareholders are then able to act through the corporate employees. The following diagram represents his position (Fig. 4.2).

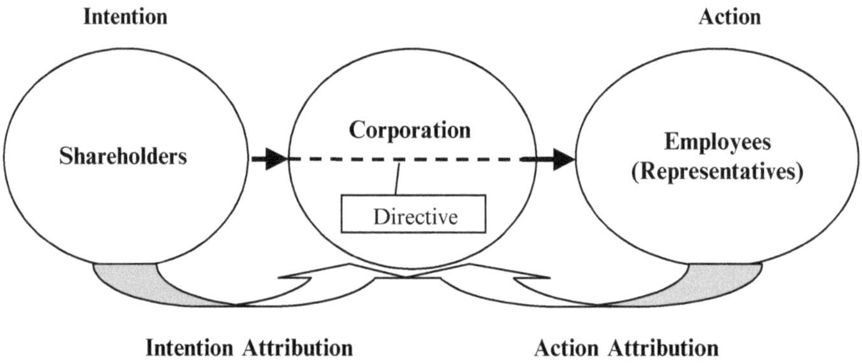

Fig. 4.2 Larry May's theory of corporate vicarious agency

May's position differs from French's in that he does not believe that the corporation can have intentions of its own as distinct from its members. He maintains that such intentions originate from the corporation's shareholders. However, on my interpretation this is the main difference between their two views which otherwise are very similar. May believes as French does that the corporate structure is the defining characteristic of the corporate entity and that it incorporates the acts of its members. The shareholder's intentions are attributed to the corporate entity and so are the actions of the representing employees. According to May the vicarious relationship between shareholders and employees licenses a descriptive transformation through which agency is attributed to the corporation. Furthermore, he believes that the corporate entity itself can be imbued with moral responsibility. For example if the corporation has a duty to perform a certain action that none of its members perform, moral blame may be attributed to the corporation because there exists a "causal nexus" among the corporate members (due to the corporate structure) that ought to have activated personnel to perform the corporate duty. The idea is that the corporation ought to have had a system in place for activating its personnel to avoid certain outcomes, for example a system of safety checks. Due to a failure in this system the appropriate actions were not taken and thus May attributes moral responsibility to the corporate entity itself.

Although May dispenses with notions of the corporation itself having an intention his position is susceptible to similar criticism as French. May has as a premise that the corporation has a duty, but in order for the corporation to have a duty we must first establish that it is a moral agent capable of having duties. This is exactly what we are trying to establish but it seems that May is implicitly assuming it. Furthermore, if the shareholders are the principals and the employees are the agents, why does May insist that the actions of employees be attributed to the corporation rather than the shareholders? Rather than one vicarious relationship between shareholders and employees, May claims there are two: one vicarious relationship between the shareholders and the corporation, and the other between the corporation and the employees. The corporation is the agent of the former relationship and the principal of the latter. Why invoke the corporate entity as an intermediary placeholder for action and intention attributions? I do not know why May has opted for this representation, but a possible answer is that it closely resembles the way that corporate liability is represented in law.[1]

If we for the sake of argument accept that corporate employees can be thought of as the agents of the corporation, and thus their actions are attributable to the corporate entity rather than straight to the shareholders, then the employees are still the only *moral* agents in the principal-agent relationship. As long as the intention for a corporate act is seen as emanating from the corporation itself as with French, or that intentions are attributed to the corporation in place of the shareholders as with May, then the employees are the only moral agents involved in corporate events.[2] The corporation itself is not a morally responsible agent. For example we can imagine a principal-agent relationship consisting of me and my cat. My cat meows at me until I eventually get up. It runs toward its food bowl and continues meowing. I believe my cat desires food and I believe that my cat's intention for doing what it just did was to get me to give it food. So I go out and kill a dog, chop it up and feed it to my cat. The principal in this relationship is my cat and I am

[1]The attribution of corporate liability will be discussed in greater detail in Part II.

[2]May does say that the corporation cannot be described as having any intentions without the intentions of its shareholders, but never mentions any moral blame attributable to the shareholders. It seems like the corporate intention, which emanates from the shareholders, gets disconnected from the shareholders because May's focus on the attribution of moral responsibility is the vicarious relationship between the corporate entity and the employees.

the agent. However, the only moral agent, and the only one morally responsible for the act of killing the dog, is me. Similarly, if the corporate charter says "we shall profit maximize within the fast food industry" and I as the marketing manager go out and kill our competitors, I am the only moral agent in the purported principal-agent relationship.

The shareholders of a corporation agree to assume the financial risk of their investment in the corporation. They agree that the employees of the corporation manage their assets and the shareholders agree to assume liability for the financial consequences of the actions of the employees to the extent of the value of their investment. This is the extent of the legal liability of shareholders who have shares in a company with limited liability. May's view of corporate vicarious agency is very similar to how corporations as legal entities are attributed legal liability.

Feinberg identifies vicarious liability as a type of strict liability. Vicarious liability can be characterised as a situation where one party is morally responsible and another incurs the liability. He says: "There is *vicarious liability* when contributory fault, or some element of it, is properly ascribed to one party, but liability is ascribed to a different party" (Feinberg 1968: 675). Such is the case for corporations as legal agents. As long as an employee acts within the confines of his job description on behalf of the corporation, then his acts are legally attributable to the corporate legal entity that must bear legal liability for untoward consequences of the employee's acts. This characterization of responsibility is appropriate for the position I am advocating, because the corporation itself is not at fault because it is not a moral agent. It is merely due to a legal convention that the corporation gets attributed with the liability for the act of the morally responsible employee.

4.1 Are Corporate Agents Autonomous?

Whether a corporation can be an autonomous *principal* in a vicarious relationship will be discussed in the following chapter (Chap. 5 "Corporate Autonomy"). Our present concern is whether corporate *agents* in a vicarious relationship are autonomous and the implication that has for the potential transferability of moral responsibility to the principal.

According to French the CIDS licences a redescription of acts performed by its members as corporate acts done for corporate reasons when they are performed consistently with corporate policy. As we have seen he says that the CIDS subordinates and synthesises the intentions and acts of its members into acts attributable to the corporate entity. Furthermore he says: "The corporation's only method of achieving its desires or goals is the activation of the personnel who occupy its various positions" (French 1984: 303). That French views the intentions of corporate members as "subordinated" and that the members are "activated" into action seems to suggest that he regards them as the implementation devices of a corporate intention.[3] French does admit that corporate members may be attributed with morally responsibility without also attributing moral responsibility to the corporation, but this appears to be limited to situations where members break with corporate policy. Are corporate members really ignorant automatons directed by a corporate "intention"? Corporate members who are directed to act by their superiors may at times do so with little insight about the ultimate intentions of the actions they are asked to perform, but at least someone in the organization who is directing the actions is aware.

The corporation is often represented as a machine where the individual members are the replaceable cogs within the machine. Jerry Mander (1992: 56) writes, "Seeing corporate behaviour as rooted in the people who work within corporations is like believing that the problems caused by armies are attributed to soldiers. With corporations, as with the military, the basic problems are inherent in the forms and rules by which these entities are compelled to operate ... Form determines content. Corporations are machines".

The argument that corporations are machines has been used to argue both for and against corporate moral agency. For example, French suggests that individual corporate members are often not morally responsible because of their lack of autonomy within the corporate structure and thus suggests that the corporation itself is morally responsible. On the other hand John Ladd (1970) argues that because the corporation is like a machine incapable of choosing its own intentions it does not itself possess the requisite autonomy for moral agency.

Are corporations machines? It must be pointed out that even a very rigidly structured organization such as the military has commanders (and heads of state) who make decisions that direct the soldiers. Thus even if we are unwilling to attribute the intentions for the resulting military actions to the soldiers themselves, they are at least attributable to the superiors and not the structure of the organization. One might argue that individual members in organizations to some degree give up part of their autonomy and follow orders without much reflection. In other words, they abstain from exercising their ability to choose their intentional actions. Ladd speaks of subordinates' acceptance of authority as giving up their personal autonomy. Herbert Simon writes:

> "A subordinate is said to accept the authority whenever he permits his behaviour to be guided by the decisions of a superior without independently examining the merits of the

[3]Albert Flores and Deborah G. Johnson (1983) explicate a position (which they argue against) that depicts the members of a corporation as lacking the autonomy to choose actions. This depiction helps us understand what French has in mind. They say: "[A]n individual is considered responsible for his actions only if the action is free and the individual is himself at the time of the action ... When one acts in a professional role, one acts within a certain fixed framework which is defined by the constrictive rules of the organization ... To this extent individuals in these roles are not free .... The individual as a private person seems to disappear in the organization as he takes a public role. The actions or decisions of any particular person apparently could or would be made by any individual in the same role or position" (Flores and Johnson 1983: 541).

decision." Hence, the subordinate "holds in abeyance his own critical faculties for choosing between alternatives and uses the formal criterion of the receipt of a command or signal as his basis for choice" (source Ladd 1970: 494).

To what extent members of corporations blindly follow the orders that direct them is an empirical issue. However, prescriptively speaking subordinate employees ought not to give up their autonomy by simply reacting to the directives of their superiors. It is part of our moral intuition that those who possess the abilities for moral agency ought to use those abilities to act as moral agents. Certain organizations may be structured so as to reduce individual members' autonomy of choice to get them to blindly act as directed. By getting individual members to believe that their personal goal is to follow whatever orders are given, they then give up their own autonomy. By reducing the element of choice for individual members the risk of non-performance of individual tasks for the organization decreases. The instrumental desirability of this is understandable from the perspective of military generals because they do not want soldiers to freely ponder the difficult moral dimensions of the actions they are directed to perform. Nevertheless, I believe that we as moral agents have an underlying moral duty to use our ability to reflect on the moral implications of our actions. We ought not to accept a superior's desire for us to give up our autonomy and stop choosing our own intentional actions. We cannot obtain moral immunity by simply claiming "I was just following orders".

It is worth recognizing that members that relinquish their autonomy may often not do so as a matter of conscious choice, but subconsciously because "the broader ethical climate and culture of an organization influence employees' thoughts and behaviours" (Treviño and Weaver 2003: 160). Members that are new to an organization where unethical behaviour is customary may be "subjected to specific socialization processes that lead them to accept the prevalent activities as normal" (Anand et al. 2004: 40). When a moral agent enters a new normative environment that differs from that of the rest of society he may gradually and subconsciously come to accept these norms as normal. When an agent then performs voluntary actions based on a normative framework that is not his own this may be construed as a subconscious relinquishment of autonomy. Through socialization and rationalizations for "unethical" behaviour the agent believes that he is acting autonomously, but he has in fact surrendered his autonomy because his decisions are no longer based on his own normative framework.

When an individual *subconsciously* relinquishes his autonomy do we not absolve him of moral responsibility for his actions? An individual that enters an unethical work climate[4] requires strong conviction and character in order to retain his autonomy and this might be too much to expect from most individuals. According to Treviño and Weaver (2003: 167) "the large majority of employees in work organizations reason at the conventional level, and thus they rely on rules and leaders

[4] According Schneider (1975: 474) a work climate is defined as prescriptions that are "psychologically meaningful molar descriptions that people can agree characterize a system's practices and procedures".

to guide them in their thinking about what is right. They are, by definition, looking to others and to the situation to help define what is right and wrong".[5]

Given that many employees reason at the conventional level many will be susceptible to a subconscious surrendering of their autonomy if they enter an unethical work climate. However, I do not believe that this absolves employees of moral responsibility for their actions. This might mitigate responsibility but it does not eliminate responsibility. We cannot have distinctly different standards of morality dependent on peoples' level of moral development. Moral prescriptions are an ideal to live up to and not an average of what everyone in fact does.[6] People have a duty to develop morally and further they ought not to relinquish their autonomy.[7] This may be difficult, but not all moral prescriptions are easy.

If an unethical work climate is intentionally created and perpetuated by the managers of a corporation then they also bear moral responsibility for the unethical behaviour of their subordinates. Treviño and Weaver (2003) say that those in positions of authority in organizations bear the responsibility for the ethical frameworks and guidance they create for subordinates; these signal to subordinates what is, and is not acceptable. This means that if someone is morally responsible for untoward events it is the employees and their managers that are responsible, not a CIDS that is logically distinct from the corporate members.

A CIDS may just be a corporate mission statement together with an organizational chart, which together set the aim of the business and delineates areas of responsibility to certain positions of authority. The corporate mission may be to become a market leader within a specified industry, where the organizational chart shows which positions are responsible for achieving such goals for certain product categories. Such a structure sets a general aim for the organization, which is

---

[5]According to Lawrence Kohlberg (1981) people can progress through three levels of moral development, called the (1) pre-conventional level, (2) conventional level, and (3) post-conventional level. Very briefly, behaviour at the first level is motivated by egocentric concerns; at the second level behaviour is motivated by social approval; and at the third level behaviour is motivated by abstract reasoning and universal principals of justice.

[6]Moral prescriptions set an ideal behaviour and thus also require an ideal moral development. Moral agents cannot simply excuse their relinquishment of autonomy within organizations because they have not developed their moral reasoning sufficiently. Anyone who has the *ability* to develop their moral reasoning has a moral duty to do so. However, children and the mentally handicapped are exempt. "Ought" implies "can". Children are exempt because they need time to develop morally, and the mentally handicapped are exempt because they are unable to develop morally.

[7]I have specified the autonomy condition for moral agency to be in accordance with Frankfurt's notion of second order intentionality (see Chap. 2 "Necessary Conditions for Moral Agency"). This means that a moral agent is *able* to have desires about his desires, and thus does not merely have to react to his first order desires and external environment, but is able to choose his own intentional actions. An agent that does not develop morally (in accordance with Kohlberg's (1981) theory of moral development), but is *able* to have second order intentionality, should still be considered a moral agent. A moral agent's lack of moral development might lead to a subconscious relinquishment of autonomy within organizations (i.e. the moral agent stops choosing for himself and merely reacts to the new normative environment), but as a moral agent he still has a moral duty not to relinquish his autonomy.

ethically neutral as long as it does not specify how certain parties ought to be treated. Although certain organizational structures may be more specific than others, it is impossible and redundant for such a structure to specify what employees should do in each specific situation that may arise. Members need to make decisions in the face of changing circumstance. The CIDS only shows the general goal of the organization, but it does not need to specify the means employees ought to take to realise such goals. This is the decision of the individual employees. The directive to become a market leader does not tell the individual marketing manager to go out and physically murder the competition, although this might be an effective means to realise this goal. And a firm called "Murder Inc.", may direct its employees to the act of murder, but this does not confer moral immunity to the employees that commit the acts.[8] No matter how intricate a CIDS becomes, in the end it is always individuals as moral agents that create such structures, and therefore it will always be individuals that are morally responsible for the resulting events that take place, as long as the events are intended or ought to have been prevented. Individuals create structures, individuals have intentions, and individuals choose to perform actions; corporations do not have these abilities.

Irrespective of the empirical constraints on moral agents in their corporate roles, Flores and Johnson (1983: 542) are right when they say: "One must distinguish between the requirements imposed on the individual by the role and the individual's willingness to fulfil these requirements. Though the role contains the content and structure of one's actions to a considerable degree, it does not force or initiate action". In the end it is the individual members as moral agents that choose to accept the roles they play.

- Corporations are Not Machines: At the very least there is a director at the top of every structure who is a moral agent and may be morally responsible for events caused by "activating" corporate members. To the extent that it is descriptively true that corporate members relinquish their autonomy to directors, it is nevertheless the case prescriptively that they ought to hold on to their autonomy. In the end it is individual persons who choose to assume roles within a structure.

4.2 Free vs. Non-free Agents

There is an important distinction to be made among two different types of vicarious relationships having to do with the degree of discretion that is granted to the agent. In the first type of relationship (type one) the agent merely acts as a delegate who follows the instructions of its principal to the letter. In the second type (type two)

[8]French would object by saying that murder is not a legitimate corporate end, but I believe that moral agents must possess the autonomy to choose whatever ends they desire in order to be considered moral agents, in which case murder can be a moral agent's intention.

the agent has a wider degree of discretion to act as he sees fit within some defined boundaries. Feinberg (1968) calls such agents "Free agents", and they are hired to exercise their professional judgment on behalf of the principal.

I believe that there is a point to be made that principals of a type one relationship are morally responsible for the actions of their agents in a manner that type two principals are not. The agents of a type one vicarious relationship are not employing their own judgment with regard to choosing the actions they perform; they are choosing to act as an extension of the principal. For example, if someone has been given a letter of appointment in order to vote in a certain manner on behalf of someone else then they would be acting as a type one agent. As such the resulting moral consequences of the agent's actions ought to be attributable to the principal, because there is an important sense of the principal acting through the agent.[9] This type of vicarious attribution of moral responsibility to the principal is consistent with French's position because he regards the corporation as morally responsible (vicariously) for the actions of its employees that lack autonomy in their corporate roles.

However, in a type two relationship the agent is hired specifically to employ his professional judgment, and therefore is acting in a manner that is significantly independent from the principal. A point needs to be highlighted here: we can never strictly speaking be morally responsible for the *independent* action of another person, it is merely the liability of the action that can be transferred. Even if we consent to "assume responsibility" for the independent action of another person, this only means that we will assume the liability for his actions and thus take care of any compensation that is required.[10] Feinberg (1968: 676) writes: "There is an important point about all vicarious punishment: even when it is reasonable to separate liability from fault, it is only the liability that can be passed from one party to another." The force of the argument is that when an agent in a vicarious relationship acts independently there is a significant sense in which his actions are disconnected from the principal, i.e. not a direct consequence of the intention of the principal, and thus the moral responsibility from the agent's action is not transferable to the principal. Thompson makes a related point with regard to politicians incurring blame for the failures of others. He says, "[attributions of] strict liability in politics may sometimes be morally justifiable; they do not establish that such liability is equivalent to moral responsibility. When we hold officials strictly accountable in this way, we usually do not condemn them morally" (Thompson 1987: 43).

The important point about a *type one* vicarious relationship is that the principal asks the agent to bring about a specific event. For example, person X might hire person Y to steal classified information from competitor Z. As the principal of the relationship person X may be attributed with moral responsibility for the event of

[9]Note that the agent will usually also be morally responsible in this situation because he has accepted to carry out the directives of the principal.

[10]At most one might be morally responsible for negligence, i.e. not preventing the action of another, but never morally responsible for the action itself.

"stealing classified information from Z" which is carried out by person Y. Person Y may have discretion as how to illicitly obtain the competitor's information, but the event of "stealing classified information from Z" is still the same. However, a manager who is the agent in a *type two* vicarious relationship is not generally asked to bring about a specific *event*. A manager is usually asked to employ his expertise to further the ends of the shareholders by whatever means deemed appropriate by the manager (within certain boundaries of discretion). The goal a manager is asked to pursue will usually be general (e.g. profit maximization) and not the realization of a specific *event*. The manager then employs his own judgment forming his own intentions regarding the best means to realize the goal of shareholders. The means employed by managers may generate certain event descriptions for attributing *moral* responsibility, but these will not be attributable to the principal because the agent has formed the intentions independently.

Note that both free and non-free agents are *autonomous*, in that they both possess the ability of forming autonomous intentions. Both choose their actions and as such both are responsible for their own actions. But non-free agents choose to act on the intentions of a principal to realize a specific event. It is thus the principal's intention that is being realized and therefore the responsibility for the event is transferred to the principal too. Free-agents, on the other hand, form their intentions for specific events *independently* from the principal, and thus responsibilities for actions of such free-agents are not transferred to the principal.

To the extent that we wish to talk about the relationship between the corporation itself and its members as a vicarious relationship, I certainly think it is fair to depict corporate members as having a role as free agents. The CIDS of a corporation clearly does not have specific instructions for its members. Now, even if we grant that the corporation itself is a principal of a type two vicarious relationship, we can still not attribute moral responsibility to the corporation for the actions of its employees. The independence of the free agents means that they perform actions on their own initiative that are not directed by a specific intention from the principal. There is not a sense of the principal acting directly through the agent, because the principal is not directing the actions of the agent. The free agents are morally responsible for the actions they perform and it is merely the liability of their actions that is legally transferable to the corporate principal. The employees need to act in the interest of their corporate principal, but it is they who choose the means of realizing that end given certain loosely defined boundaries of their job description.

- Moral Responsibility is not Vicariously Transferable: Even if we were to accept that a CIDS counts as a principal with an intention that directs corporate members (who are free agents), it is still not possible to claim that the corporation is *morally* responsible because the members independently form their intentions regarding how to achieve corporate goals, which disconnects the transfer of moral responsibility to the principal. It is only the members that are *morally responsible* although the *liability* for the repercussions of their actions may be transferred to the corporate legal entity.[11]

This non-transferability of moral responsibility for independent intentions counts as a further specification of the moral agency ability to perform an action. As previously mentioned the criterion for "action" when further specified is:

- **An ability to perform an action.** In order to be attributed with moral responsibility for an event an agent must be able to realize its intention through its own corporal movements or by being a principal instructing a non-free agent to realize its intention.

4.3 Emergent Corporate Moral Agency?

Patricia Werhane (1985) has put forward a theory of corporate moral agency that can also be represented as a vicarious relationship with the corporation as the principal and the employees as the agents. However, her notion of corporate moral agency seems to suggest that it is an emergent property from the individual employees that might circumvent the problem of the non-transferability of moral responsibility because the corporate moral agency emerges from the members and is not per se transferred to the corporation. Nevertheless the emergent moral agency of the corporation is to be regarded as a form of moral agency that is distinct from the agency of the constituent members.

Werhane believes that corporate action is a "secondary action". She says that a corporation performs a secondary action if and only if it is correctly attributable to the corporation on the basis of an action of some other agent. This is just a different formulation of what we have called a vicarious relationship between a principal and an agent. Werhane (1985: 50) writes:

> "[A]ll corporate actions are secondary actions that result from a series of primary actions by persons. Corporations *function*, then, as if they were real, autonomous, individual entities... corporations are what I shall call *secondary collectives* whose actions are ontologically reducible to, but not identical with, actions of individuals performing on behalf of the corporation... A corporation functions as a unit, dependent upon, but distinct from its constituents".

Werhane states that the actions that are attributed to corporations are not to be literally taken as actions of some physical entity, but are rather actions that are carried out through the corporate members. However, she also maintains that not

[11]The difference between Responsibility and Liability: Responsibility is a metaphysical concept that attributes ownership for actions to an agent. Liability on the other hand is primarily a legal concept that when attributed to an agent makes that agent the subject of certain legal responses/sanctions.

all actions of corporations are redescribable in terms of individual actions. It would seem that Werhane holds that corporate moral agency in some sense supervenes on the individual members of the organization. I understand her to be saying that anything that is describable as an action of a corporation is metaphysically dependent on individuals, but ascriptions of actions that are made to corporations need not translate into descriptions of individual actions. She (1985: 53) says: "It makes sense to talk about corporate "action" only if whatever activity is attributed to a corporation is a result of primary actions of individuals."

For Werhane it is the structure of the corporation that authorizes the primary actions of individual members and it is thus through that very structure that we attribute collective secondary action to the corporation. This is an important distinction between French and Werhane. For Werhane the performance of corporate actions are made by primary agents who intend and perform their actions on behalf of the corporation and the corporate structure serves to authorize the attribution of those actions as corporate actions. Her position is different from French who maintains that the CIDS dictates an intention that is separate from the intentions of the corporate members.

For Werhane the corporate charter sets the corporate goals and together with the by-laws specifies the authorization process through which constituents operate. Werhane (1985: 54) writes: "Corporate constituents function in terms of these goals, acting in accordance with their interpretation of the directives of the charter". We can see here that it is the constituent members that are the source of the corporate intentions as it is up to them to interpret the corporate charter; the members are not simply directed into action like cogs in a machine. Of course the members are constrained in what they may pursue because the organization is created for certain purposes, but they are not directed by something to be regarded as the non-human intention of a corporate charter. Below is my representation of Werhane's theory in terms of a vicarious relationship between the corporation and its members (Fig 4.3).

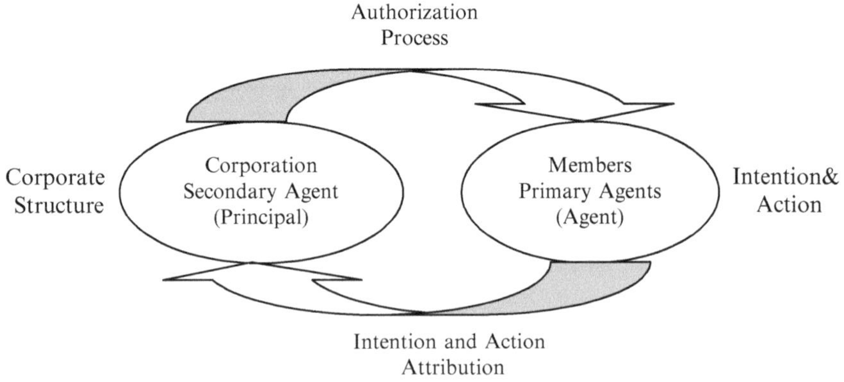

Fig. 4.3 Werhane's theory of corporate moral agency represented as a vicarious relationship

The diagram shows how the corporate members as primary agents perform intentional actions that are authorized by their interpretation of the corporate charter and by-laws. The intentions and actions of the members are then attributed to the corporation who is a secondary agent and the principal of the vicarious relationship.

Werhane holds that action attributions to corporations may be non-distributive, and hence the responsibility for the actions need not be distributed to the constituent members. For instance, the corporate action attribution "the Example Corporation polluted the river" will in all corporations (except for the very smallest) be a series of actions performed by constituents none of whom may have intended the event in question.[12] She (1985: 56) writes: "Thus, at least in principle, it is possible that there could be corporate immoral "action", that is the result of a series of blameless primary actions." My interpretation that corporate moral agency is an emergent property of the constituent members comes from statements like: "Because secondary actions are, in a derivative way, actions of persons, they can be moral or immoral actions, and one may evaluate them accordingly" (Werhane 1985: 57).

My difference with Werhane rests primarily with the attribution of moral responsibility in a manner that may be distinct from the constituents of the corporation. This is clearly her position, but it seems to be driven by a desire to make sense of our use of corporate names as the subjects of our moral responsibility attributions. But how does one at the same time reconcile the notion that a corporation can be morally responsible for an action for which no moral fault lies with its members, if at the same time the corporation is ascribed moral agency because the primary actions are performed by the members who are moral agents?

I agree that the result of a collective performing a series of individual actions may be a result that no one intended. This result may have been brought about by an unintended process of individual actions working within a corporate structure. However, this analysis would give a causal explanation resulting in a causal responsibility attribution for the result of the individual actions. Given that a necessary condition for a moral responsibility attribution (with respect to the breach of a negative duty) is that the action was intended, then the absence of an intention consequently implies that there is no legitimate moral attribution to be made with regard to the result. We might wish to blame the corporate structure if it was causally efficacious with regard to the result, but such an attribution of blame is merely a causal responsibility ascription rather than a moral one. If the creators of the structure intended the result in question (or breached a duty of care) then they are morally responsible, but the structure itself is at most only causally responsible.

---

[12]Cooper (1968) has said that predicates used to describe collectives can be divisible or indivisible. A divisible attribution applies to each and every member of a collective, in contrast with an indivisible attribution where the predicate applies only to the collective whole. An example of the latter is the taste of a stew. Someone may dislike each individual ingredient of the stew but nevertheless like the stew as a whole. This bears relevance to Werhane's theory because, for her, predicating responsibility to the corporation may be an indivisible predicate that applies only to the corporation and is not divisible among the corporate members.

An objection might be raised that an actual intention is not necessary for the attribution of moral responsibility. Some advocates of corporate moral agency point out that many corporate moral responsibility attributions involve negligent behaviour on behalf of the corporation and thus an omission has occurred rather than a specific action. This is meant to serve as an argument for corporations qualifying as moral agents without necessarily being *able* to intend actions. However, negligence is a form of omission and a moral agent may only be responsible for an omission X because it did not perform an action Y, which it had a duty to perform. To be held morally responsible for an omission presupposes that a moral agent has a positive moral duty (i.e. it ought to acts so as to prevent X, by doing Y). For an agent to have a positive duty to perform Y it must have the ability to intend Y, otherwise it would not have the ability to act in the pursuit of Y. The morally blameworthy aspect of an omission is that an intentional action which ought to have been performed was not performed, and thus for an agent to be negligent it must have had the *ability* to intend the action.[13]

- Corporations are Not Morally Responsible for Omissions: Negligence is a form of omission that involves a lack of an intention to perform an action. However, it is only possible to blame someone for negligence who has the *ability* to intend an action, because it is by virtue of an absence of an intention that ought to have materialised that blame is attributed. Clearly it is only possible to expect someone to intend an action if they have the *ability* to intend an action. And obviously any omission that involves intentionally abstaining from action also requires the *ability* to intend.

It is widely accepted in moral philosophy that "ought implies can". That is to say, one can only have a duty to perform an action if one is capable of doing it. This is why the necessary moral agency condition we are working with is an *ability* to intend an action and not a condition that requires the existence of an actual intention.

Werhane (1985: 57) says that although corporations have "some of the characteristics of persons, they lack the autonomy necessary to perform primary actions". I have assumed as uncontroversial that a necessary condition for moral agency is that an agent possesses the autonomy to choose its own intentional course of action. Werhane seems to claim that the corporation *itself* has no such autonomy, which I agree with, but then it is difficult to understand in what sense the corporation is a moral agent. But she also says "corporations, like persons, are and should be held morally responsible for actions within their control when, all things considered, they could have done otherwise" (Werhane 1985: 59). It seems inconsistent

[13]Moral responsibility is legitimately attributed to moral agents with certain abilities. It would be senseless to morally blame something for not having the requisite abilities; it is not something that is chosen. Some moral agents, in certain situations, for example soldiers in the army, might suppress or disregard their moral abilities and choose to simply follow orders. But in such situations the agents possess the abilities but choose not to engage them. They may thus be blamed for not using the abilities they possess. However, we cannot blame something for a lack of moral abilities, for example a lion. The actions of non-moral agents are amoral actions.

with the corporation's lack of autonomy that it could have chosen an alternate intentional action and done otherwise than it did. Without the requisite autonomy the corporation *itself* cannot have done otherwise than it did. (The possibility of the corporation qualifying as an autonomous principal will be discussed in greater detail in the next chapter.)

If the moral agency of the corporation were fully dependent on the actions of the primary agents, who are autonomous moral agents themselves, then it is possible to understand that the corporation could have done otherwise than it did, as the autonomy of the corporation could in some sense be regarded as a reflection of the autonomy of its members. But Werhane insists that the corporation is dependent upon but distinct from its constituents. Why this insistence that the corporation is distinct from its members? I believe that at the heart of it lies a desire to make sense of corporate moral responsibility attributions where no fault can be found with the members of the organization. This responsibility, as with French, falls on the corporate structure. The idea being that through no fault of their own, merely the way in which the members are structured with regard to one another, untoward events occur and that there is a relevant moral responsibility attribution to be made towards the corporate structure. But this (as we noted earlier with French) is to misconstrue the nature of our moral responsibility attributions. We do not hold people responsible for their codes of conduct; we hold them responsible for their actual chosen conduct. The code of conduct like a corporate structure might explain the resulting event or action that takes place, but this is at best a causal and not a moral responsibility attribution.[14]

The reason for this confusion is that one is taking the corporate action ascription as literally being *one* action, i.e. the corporation's action. But, the corporate "action" is only a consequence of individual actions and not literally an action of the corporation. We are attributing a result, event, or state of affairs to a series of actions performed by individuals, which when we speak we commonly attribute to the organization as *one* action. But this manner in which people speak cannot be merely taken at face value. The corporation's actual ability to perform an action requires independent metaphysical argumentation. It is misguiding to construe the consequence of the concerted efforts of corporate members as *one* action, because it adds to the belief that there is some sort of super-agent that has intentions and reasons for acting that are separate from the individuals that comprise the organization.

Richard De George tries to get around some of these problems by rejecting corporate moral agency and instead maintains that corporations are *moral actors*. The important thing about moral actors is that their intentions are not the proper object of moral evaluation but their actions. Corporations are to be regarded as moral actors rather than moral agents because "corporations lack the interiority characteristics of human individuals" (De George 1999: 101). But this does not so

[14]Moral agents possess the ability to autonomously choose intentional actions. Structures and codes of conduct may influence (provide reasons for) action, but it is the moral agents that autonomously choose whether to act on those influences.

much circumvent the problem of moral agency as much as it only ignores it. In what relevant sense is such an action "moral"? It seems that De George is employing the notion of a moral actor primarily to make sense of the way we use corporate names as the subjects of moral responsibility predicates. He does say: "A corporation has no conscience, no feelings, no consciousness of its own ... Because a corporation acts only through those who act for it, it is the latter who must assume moral responsibility for the corporation, although due to a lack of transparency who may not always be clear" (De George 1999: 100). I agree with this statement, but De George still wishes to say that "a corporation can be held responsible for its actions", because clearly people do hold corporations responsible. He says: "Because the moral status of corporations is different from the moral status of human beings, the moral obligations are different from the moral obligations of human beings" (De George 1999: 196). But once again we have a void between the metaphysical status of moral agency and the mere semantic attribution of moral responsibility. If those who attribute moral responsibility intend the ascription to lodge with the corporation itself, then it is a misattribution because it does not lodge with a moral agent. Moral responsibility is only legitimately attributable to moral agents and to say that such attributions lodge with moral actors instead (with none of the requisite metaphysical characteristics) at most suggests that semantically the attribution is a meaningful use of language. As I have said before, we can meaningfully speak of the sun rising and setting, but that does not mean that the sun actually does rise and set.

If we are simply going to morally evaluate events that affect people without consideration to intentions, are we then also going to morally evaluate natural events that affect people that also are not intentional? For both De George and Werhane there is something morally important in the fact that corporations are run by corporate members who are moral agents which makes the corporations susceptible to moral evaluation. To get at the heart of the issue let us ask the following: How is an unintended event resulting from the actions of the members of a collective morally different from a natural event? For example, what is the difference between a tree falling naturally and killing a man or as a result of several people concertedly trying to fell the tree? Is the fact that the latter is dependent on the actions of people morally relevant? It is only relevant if it can be argued that at least one individual (or set of members) had a duty to avoid or prevent the untoward event in question. If no one intended the untoward event, and no one had a duty to prevent it from happening, then there is no moral responsibility to be attributed. There is only a causal responsibility attribution to be made and thus there is no moral difference between the result caused by the falling tree and the collective. If someone does have a duty then it is that individual(s) that is responsible and not the separate corporate entity itself. The feeling that there is a moral difference between the tree and the collective seems to arise from the potential for moral responsibility that an individual or collective of individuals might have within an organization, while the tree can never be attributed with moral responsibility. The fact that the corporation consist of individuals that are moral agents makes it possible that those individuals may be morally responsible for certain events, but it does not in itself add credence to the view that the corporation as distinct from its members can be attributed with moral responsibility.

- Corporate Members have the Potential of Being Morally Responsible: The moral difference between a natural event and one caused by a collective of humans is that there is a potential for attributing moral responsibility to the human members of a collective. However, if no human member intended the event in question nor had a duty to prevent it, then no one is morally responsible and it is not *morally* different from if it was a natural event.

Some might feel that there is nothing puzzling about the idea that the corporation is fully dependent on its constituents and yet the corporation may be regarded as a distinct moral agent because they might argue that corporate moral agency supervenes upon its individual members. But whether or not we agree with organizational descriptions supervening on their constituents or not, this cannot be the only justification for similarly saying that corporations are moral agents. If corporate moral agency is to be regarded as a different level of description of social events (i.e. different from a description in terms of individuals), then one still needs to argue in what sense that level of description is *morally* relevant, because as long as we believe that certain characteristics are necessary for moral agency we still need to show through independent argumentation that the social entity possesses the relevant characteristics. And one cannot simply obtain such an argument by saying that the social entity has those moral properties by virtue of the characteristics of its members, because there is no reason that the social entity should have the same characteristics as its members. That the social properties supervene on individuals is merely to say that the higher level descriptions are metaphysically dependent on lower level descriptions; it does not say that the two description levels have the same properties. In fact the very point of having two levels of description is that they are useful by virtue of displaying different properties.

Werhane (1985: 50) writes: "corporations can be said in a particular sense to 'act'" and that corporations "*function* as if they were real autonomous individual entities". She also says that her theory of collective secondary action "will ascribe sufficient secondary or institutional moral agency to justify the *ascription of a form* of moral responsibility" (1985: 50). It seems that the sense of moral agency that she has in mind for corporations is meant to differ from the sense we normally understand when we speak of individual human moral agents. As I have previously maintained it is far from clear what a different sense of moral agency would mean. I think that for Werhane "corporate moral agency" means that we morally evaluate corporate structures or codes of conduct for the behaviour they motivate.[15] But this

[15]Corporate policies and procedures that are meant to guide corporate members to act ethically is the domain of "organizational ethics". Organizational ethicists may evaluate the ethicality of organizational policies and procedures based on how various stakeholders are meant to be taken into account for corporate decisions, while the notion of moral agency concerns the identification of the proper bearer(s) of moral responsibility for the actual treatment of the stakeholders. A policy may be unethical, but it cannot be morally responsible. Policies and procedures are important tools in order to steer an organization in an ethically desirable direction, but these tools are not themselves the bearers of moral responsibility.

severs as a source of confusion because it is moral agents that we normally attribute with moral responsibility and not their codes of conduct. A code of conduct is only relevant as the motive of behaviour if it is adopted by a moral agent for his actions. It is difficult to understand how a code *itself* can possess an independent status of moral agency.

Werhane, French, and De George assign a form of moral agency to the corporation by virtue of the way we speak without reference to metaphysical foundations to support such a claim.[16] But we cannot move from speaking about corporations *as if* they are moral agents and then proceed to hold them responsible as if they *actually* are. It would seem that French, De George, and Werhane, in their different ways, are reifying the corporation.

We have seen how the status of corporate members as independent free-agents precludes their actions from being attributable to a corporate principal. But can a corporate principal be autonomous from its members? So far we have noted that French does not consider the autonomy condition while Werhane (although she advocates corporate moral agency) holds that corporations do not have the ability to autonomously choose intentional actions. Given that autonomy is a necessary condition for moral agency we need to consider whether corporations can autonomously choose intentional actions. Philip Pettit (2002) has put forward a theory that tries to maintain just that. To this we turn next.

References

Anand, U., B.E. Ashforth, and M. Joshi. 2004. Business as usual: The acceptance and perpetuation of corruption in organizations. *Academy of Management Executive* 19: 9–23.
Cooper, D.E. 1968. Collective responsibility. *Philosophy* 43: 258–268.
De George, R.T. 1999. *Business ethics*. Upper Saddle River: Prentice Hall.
Feinberg, J. 1968. Collective responsibility. *Journal of Philosophy* 65: 674–688.
Flores, A., and D.G. Johnson. 1983. Collective responsibility and professional roles. *Ethics* 93: 537–545.

[16]In the nineteenth century legal developments (in the UK and US) led the corporation to be regarded as a completely distinct legal entity from the shareholders. The corporation nowadays is usually referred to in the singular, "it", but in the early nineteenth century when shareholders were still regarded as forming the corporation it was referred to in the plural "they". Many advocates of corporate moral agency cite the need to make sense of our linguistic use of corporate names as the references of moral responsibility attributions. Perhaps a plausible explanation is that the legal linguistic development of referring to corporations as "it" instead of "they" lead to the public also employing the singular to refer to a corporation. If this is the case then the public have adopted a legal use of language to make their moral responsibility attributions. This use of language would therefore not imply that people are referring to a distinct moral agent called the "corporation". When people blame corporations it may on the one hand mean that they are making a *legal* responsibility attribution, or on the other hand they are making a *moral* responsibility attribution to a fictional legal entity (which is a category mistake). We cannot infer corporate moral agency from responsibility attributions to an abstract legal entity.

French, P.A. 1984. *Collective and corporate responsibility*. New York: Columbia University Press.
Kohlberg, L. 1981. *The philosophy of moral development: Moral stages and the idea of justice*. San Francisco: Harper & Row.
Ladd, J. 1970. Morality and the ideal of rationality in formal organizations. *The Monist* 54: 488–516.
Ladd, J. 1991. Corporativism. In *The spectrum of responsibility*, ed. P.A. French. New York: St. Martin's Press.
Mander, J. 1992. The myth of the corporate conscience. *Business and Society Review* 81: 56–63.
May, L. 1991. Vicarious agency and corporate responsibility. In *The spectrum of responsibility*, ed. P.A. French. New York: St. Martin's Press.
Pettit, P. 2002. Groups with minds of their own. In *Socializing metaphysics*, ed. F. Schmitt. Lanham: Rowman & Littlefield.
Schneider, B. 1975. Organizational climate: An essay. *Personnel Psychology* 28(4): 447–479.
Thompson, D.F. 1987. *Political ethics and public office*. Cambridge, MA: Harvard University Press.
Treviño, L.K., and G.R. Weaver. 2003. *Managing ethics in business organizations*. Stanford: Stanford Business Books.
Werhane, P.H. 1985. *Persons, rights, & corporations*. Englewood Cliffs: Prentice Hall.

Chapter 5
Corporate Autonomy

I have so far shown that the founding theories of corporate moral agency (that focus on the corporate structure as the locus of independent abilities) do not meet the morally relevant moral agency conditions of an ability to intend and an ability act. As regards the autonomy condition I have so far primarily considered the autonomy of members in their role as corporate agents performing actions on behalf of the corporate principal. I now turn to considering whether the corporation itself can qualify as a principal with autonomous intentions (that direct corporate agents into action).

The theories considered so far do not present corporate intention and action abilities that meet the autonomy condition. But to be fair these theories do not even try to address the autonomy condition. However, in *Groups with Minds of Their Own*, Philip Pettit (2002) has specifically tried to address the issue of corporate and organizational autonomy.[1]

Pettit says that a certain type of decision procedure within a purposive organization can result in a decision being made that no one in the organization desired. Pettit explains how the above scenario is possible (and he claims commonly occurring) and maintains that we must regard purposive organizations, such as a corporation, as being intentional and personal subjects in their own right. This is a different approach from what we have seen so far. For Pettit the members are actively involved in the decision of what the collective should do, while with French the corporate intention is *teleologically imposed* by the corporate charter. Also, for

[1]In *Responsibility Incorporated* (2007) Pettit draws on his earlier account (2002) of group autonomy to explicitly address the moral agency of groups. I shall however maintain focus on his 2002 account in *Groups with Minds of Their Own* because it provides a more extensive view of corporate autonomy which is my concern in this section. (Furthermore, Pettit's (2007) conditions for moral agency are drawn from Christian catechisms for what constitutes responsibility for a serious sin. Besides autonomy these conditions do not correspond to the necessary conditions that I am employing, and it is unclear why Pettit regards Christian catechisms as a relevant foundation for moral agency conditions.)

D. Rönnegard, *The Fallacy of Corporate Moral Agency*,
Issues in Business Ethics 44, DOI 10.1007/978-94-017-9756-6_5

Pettit, the collective decision is attributed to the organization because of a particular voting procedure, while with Werhane the decision is *authorized* by the corporate charter which the members interpret. Let us take a closer look at Pettit's theory and see what he has in mind.

Pettit (2002: 167) starts by saying: "There is a type of organization found in certain collectivities that makes them into subjects in their own right, giving them a way of being minded that is starkly discontinuous with the mentality of their members. This claim in social ontology is strong enough to ground talk of such collectivities as entities that are psychologically autonomous and that constitute institutional persons." Pettit also wishes to maintain that the properties that these organizations have are such that they are the type of entity that we can hold responsible. It would seem that Pettit's aim is to give an account of organizational agency that at least meets the moral agency condition of autonomy and may thus potentially be regarded as an autonomous principal that directs corporate members into action.

Pettit asks us to consider a situation where a collective of employees in a factory need to decide if they agree to a pay-sacrifice in order to obtain safety improvements in their workplace. There are three premises to consider with regard to this issue. Firstly, is there a serious danger under the current work conditions? Secondly, will the suggested measures for improvement be effective? Thirdly, is the loss in pay bearable? Consider the following matrix of the decision situation assuming that the collective consists of three individuals, A, B and C:

	Serious danger?	Effective measure?	Bearable loss?	Pay-sacrifice?
A	Yes	No	Yes	No
B	No	Yes	Yes	No
C	Yes	Yes	No	No
	Yes	Yes	Yes	?

Initially let us consider two primary decision procedures to settle the matter of if the collective should agree to a pay sacrifice. The first is called the conclusion-centred approach and involves each individual making up his or her own mind with regard to each premise and concluding that the pay-sacrifice is worth it only if each premise is considered in the affirmative. Each individual having reached a conclusion on their own then casts a vote, yes or no, and the pay-sacrifice is decided upon if a majority votes for it (vertical column to the right). The second decision procedure is called the premise-centred approach and involves each member casting a vote on each premise. The collective view on each premise is decided by a majority of votes cast. A collective decision in favour of the pay sacrifice is then reached if and only if the collective view on each premise is affirmative (horizontal column at the bottom). The particular situation represented in the matrix shows that the collective decision under the conclusion-centred approach would reject the pay sacrifice (unanimously), while under the premise-centred procedure the collective decision would be to accept the pay sacrifice. Therefore, applying the premise-centred approach, in this instance, leads to a situation where every single member is against a pay-sacrifice but the collective decision is to accept such a sacrifice. This result is called the “Doctrinal Paradox”.

When a collective needs to make decisions on separate issues over time they will need an established procedure by which to make collective decisions. Pettit points out that the premise and conclusion-centred procedures do not exhaust the possibilities when considering this inter-temporal aspect of group decision making. If the collective consistently uses either of the two procedures the collective runs the risk of making decisions that are inconsistent with decisions made in the past. For example, one can imagine that due to the votes cast by party members at one point in time the party decides to be for abortion, but against abortion at a different point in time.[2] An inconsistent decision might have detrimental consequences because the collective is perceived as irrational and thus not a credible promoter of its agenda. In order to accommodate for collective consistency Pettit says that one can have a decision procedure that is first premise-centred, but secondly also allows for the possibility to ignore the majority vote on *one* of the premises, letting the majority votes on the remaining premises together with the majority vote on the individual members’ conclusions determine the collective decision. The idea here is for the decision procedure to allow for a wider discretion to be consistent with past decisions.

Collectives are faced with a choice of whether to opt for a conclusion-centred procedure which displays individual responsiveness with regard to the views of its members (at the potential expense of collective inconsistency), or to opt for a premise-centred approach which allows for collective consistency (at the expense of potentially reaching a decisions that few if any members endorse). Collectives that opt for the premise-centred approach “collectivise reason”. Such groups are called “social integrates” and according to Pettit they deserve metaphysical recognition as intentional and personal subjects.

A social integrate represents an integration of individuals (not merely an aggregate) because it has a shared purpose and forms judgments and intentions in relation to that purpose, and importantly because it collectivizes reason in forming judgements and intentions. A social integrate must be regarded as an intentional subject because “it is going to display all the functional marks of an intentional subject and that there is no reason to discount those marks as mere appearances” (Pettit 2002: 182).

Important for our purpose is that Pettit regards the social integrate as distinct from its members. He does not mean for it to be metaphysically distinct from its members, but rather that it is distinct “in the sense of being a centre for the formation of attitudes that are capable of being quite discontinuous from the attitudes of the members” (Pettit 2002: 183). On Pettit’s characterization it would be wrong to think that the individuals form their intentions which then become the intentions of the

---

[2]The issues need not be identical as in my abortion example but merely be “rationally connected” so that a decision on the new issue can be judged as consistent or inconsistent with regard to some past decision.

collective. Rather, the group makes its decision on a specific issue in a manner capable of being discontinuous from the attitudes of the members due to the decision procedure. At this procedural level an organizational intention can be announced. It is only after the organizational intention is announced that the members form their own intentions to concertedly perform the intended action.

So far we can see that Pettit has put forward a theory that aims to show the distinct manner in which a purposive organization possesses the ability to act through its members, and importantly the collective has an ability to elect its intentions in a manner that is discontinuous from the attitudes of the members. Is this a theory that satisfies the necessary conditions for moral agency?

Let us start by considering the autonomy of the corporate agent. The autonomous nature of the corporation for Pettit is displayed in part by the doctrinal paradox, which may result when employing a premise-centred procedure. The autonomy is also displayed when employing the other (inter-temporal) premise-centred procedure, because the corporation may make a decision which is not responsive to the attitudes of current members, but rather responsive to decisions made in the past. Does this corporate "choice" that is discontinuous with the attitudes of the individual members actually count as autonomy in any morally relevant sense?

Pettit's voting procedure is based on mental states (or rather votes of members), and one could also construe a temporal premise-centred voting procedure as a procedural (non-mental) second-order intentionality that enables the members to stay consistent over time. However, because the resulting corporate intention is merely the result of a procedure there is no sense in which the corporation is *aware* of its choice. Such a voting procedure is similar to an algorithm. It is like programming a computer to run an algorithm (with votes as inputs) and then saying that the output is the autonomous choice of the computer. The fact that the procedural choice is discontinuous with member attitudes does not shift any agency ability or moral responsibility onto the procedure. All the morally relevant choices are done by *devising the procedure itself* and by the *members accepting* to abide by the result of the voting procedure.

The distinctness that the corporation presents through the adoption of a premise-centred procedure is only apparent. The members choose the premise-centred procedure due to their desire to be collectively rational over any desire they may have to let their decision procedure be individually responsive (conclusion-centred). This choice of procedure by the members cannot be represented as a decision made autonomously by the organization because the choice is prior to the potential establishment of a premise-centred procedure. Therefore this foundational decision made by the corporate constituents makes at least those members morally responsible for creating a voting system that may lead to decisions that are unresponsive to the attitudes of current members.

A related but separate issue regards the purported autonomy of the actual corporate decisions made. Pettit (2002: 177) says that a purposive group "must avoid automatic recourse to revision of past commitments; it must show that those commitments are sufficiently robust for us to be able to expect that the group will frequently be guided by them for future judgments." It is thus not strictly necessary for such a social integrate to act consistently with past decisions, but Pettit never addresses how the members are meant to choose their decision procedure; i.e. if they are going to accept or revise past decisions. If such a decision is to be regarded as autonomous by the corporation, it would require a meta-decision-procedure that is also discontinuous from the attitudes of the members. Such a procedure, however, would be pointless because one wants to accommodate the desire of current members to be consistent (or not) with past decisions which requires a decision procedure that is responsive to the attitudes of current members. Inevitably it will be the attitudes of the current members that in some way decide if the collective should be responsive to current attitudes or let a past decision dictate the current decision for the sake of inter-temporal consistency.

For the purpose of attributing moral responsibility the precise form of the collective decision procedure is not important. For example, a collective using a premise-centred procedure may lead to a decision that no one endorses, but it is the members at the end of the day that have to accept to follow it or not. The notion of "collectivizing reason" serves as an explanation for why the collective of individuals decided to pursue a course of action that they individually did not desire. It does not serve as a legitimate justification for attributing their actions to the organizational entity itself.

- Collective Decision Procedures are not per se of Moral Importance: It is quite simply not possible to obtain autonomy (or moral agency) from any decision procedure because after a procedural decision is made it is still up to the individual members (who are moral agents) to realize the decision through autonomous intentional action. Just like a code of conduct cannot be morally responsible, neither can a decision procedure be morally responsible. We attribute responsibility to an agent's intentional action and not its decision procedure. A decision procedure can at most *explain* the actions of individual members, but a procedure is not per se *morally responsible* for the intentional actions of members.

References

Pettit, P. 2002. Groups with minds of their own. In *Socializing metaphysics*, ed. F. Schmitt. Lanham: Rowman & Littlefield.

Pettit, P. 2007. Responsibility incorporated. *Ethics* 117: 171–201.

Chapter 6
Summary of Why Corporate Moral Agency Is a Fallacy

6.1 Autonomy

Among the three necessary conditions for moral agency autonomy has emerged as the most crucial condition that any theory or corporate moral agency must overcome. Autonomy is of special importance because it is only by having intentions that are independent from the corporate members that the organizational structure could potentially be the locus of moral responsibility instead of the members. It is only then that it could qualify as a principal and potentially direct corporate (non-free) agents into action.

The autonomy condition was specified by appealing to Frankfurt's notion of second-order intentionality. This ability to have desires regarding one's desires is the foundation of independent choice and places *ownership* of an intention with an agent because it is *aware* of the choice that is made. Autonomy was thus specified as the *ability to independently choose* an intentional action.

I have explored if Pettit's (2002) corporate voting procedure that could lead to the Doctrinal Paradox could be construed as having the ability to independently choose an intentional action. It was argued that this could not be the case because the procedure is not aware of the choice being made. Furthermore, the choice of voting procedure itself cannot be discontinuous with the attitude of members, and any 'choice' of intention made by a voting procedure still requires the acceptance of autonomous members to enact the intention.

The autonomy of organizational structures seems implausible because they are created by humans for humans. Either the consequences of the organizational structure are intended by their creators (or ought to have been avoided), in which case the creators are morally responsible for those events, or the consequences are not intended by the structural creators (or could not reasonably been have avoided), in which case no one is morally responsible for the consequences. No one needs

D. Rönnegard, *The Fallacy of Corporate Moral Agency*,
Issues in Business Ethics 44, DOI 10.1007/978-94-017-9756-6_6

to be *morally* responsible for events. There may only be *causal* responsibility where the corporate structure might play an important role. If anyone is morally responsible for an event then it must at least be one member.

6.2 Intention

The ability to intend an action has been slightly left behind in the preceding discussion of corporate moral agency theories. This is primarily because of the importance of the criterion of *autonomy* which must be met by a corporate structure if there is to be any separation between the intention of the corporation and its members. If the corporation lacks the autonomy ability to deliberate and choose its own intention, but must be given the intention by its members, then there is an important sense in which the intention continues to belong to the corporate members.

Furthermore, an agent can only have second-order desires regarding first-order desires that it is aware of, which suggests that the ability to have intentions is also a mental ability. Clearly corporate structures or voting procedures are not consciously aware.

6.3 Action

Discussing French I inquired if a corporate structure could be construed as a principal and the corporate members as the agents in order to justify the corporation's ability to perform an action. Because the corporation has no corporal existence it is important for advocates of corporate moral agency to manifest the corporate structure as a principal because it has no way of performing an action on its own. However, the construal of the corporation as a principal is heavily contingent on the corporation's ability to have an intention (which is itself contingent on autonomy).

Nevertheless, even if we were to hypothetically assume that a corporate structure qualifies as a principal, Feinberg has shown that moral responsibility is not transferable from the actions of *independent* "free agents" to the principal (merely the liability for the action is transferable). This implies that irrespective of the corporation's status as a principal it can still never be morally responsible for the actions of its free-agents. I have argued that corporations are not principals as they have no autonomous intentions, and furthermore that the corporate members are free-agents whose responsibility is not transferable.

French, De George, Donaldson, and Werhane's support for corporate moral agency is in part driven by a desire to make semantic sense of attributions of moral responsibility to corporations. The corporate structure, however, is not up to the task of being the locus of moral responsibility- at most it can be the locus of causal responsibility. It would seem that in their different ways these philosophers are reifying the corporation.

Corporations do not possess second-order intentionality (autonomy ability), and they do not possess first-order intentionality (intention ability); nor do they possess the ability to act (directing non-free agents). Therefore corporations cannot perform autonomous intentional actions. Corporate moral agency is a fallacy.

Some might argue that nothing great hinges on the fallacy of corporate moral agency because if corporate moral agency is not true then we simply stop regarding corporate names as part of moral responsibility attributions literally, and instead start viewing them as placeholders for corporate members without anything significant changing. If such use of corporate moral responsibility attributions is fully appreciated as merely a metaphor then it is a convenient use of language for elliptically assigning blame to corporate members. But if it is not fully appreciated as a metaphor then we run the risk of reifying the corporation with attendant legal consequences, such as extending the full Bill of Rights to corporations based on an erroneous assumption of corporate moral agency.

Furthermore, for the purposes of corporate prescriptions, the metaphorical attribution of moral responsibility to corporations will not do. It is simply a category mistake to argue from corporate duties to member duties. If the concept of corporate moral agency is untenable, then different justifications must be used to prescribe corporate conduct, which in turn influences the nature of those prescriptions and ultimately the role of the corporation in society. In short, the fallacy of corporate moral agency implies that our moral prescriptions and responsibility attributions should focus on corporate members.

In the next section I shall consider what corporate moral responsibility attributions refer to. It is uncontroversial that statements attributing moral responsibility to an individual refer to the individual moral agent, but what does a moral responsibility attribution to a corporation refer to? If corporate structures are not the locus of moral responsibility then how do we make sense of the use of corporate names as the subjects of moral responsibility attributions? To this I turn next.

Reference

Pettit, P. 2002. Groups with minds of their own. In *Socializing metaphysics*, ed. F. Schmitt. Lanham: Rowman & Littlefield.

Chapter 7
The Reference of Corporate Proper Names and Responsibility Attributions

It is clear that corporations are capable of being the subjects of moral responsibility predicates. We ascribe moral responsibility to corporations all the time. "Ford is responsible for deaths caused by safety deficiencies in its Ford Pinto model". "BP is responsible for the oil leak in the Gulf of Mexico". "Union Carbide is responsible for thousands of deaths following an explosion at its Bhopal plant". The list can go on and on.

So far I have inquired whether corporations satisfy our necessary conditions for moral agency, while now I shall inquire what it is we are referring to when we use corporate names as the subjects of moral responsibility attributions. The following question needs an answer: what is the reference of corporate proper names when used in ascriptions of moral responsibility? Are we literally referring to something that may be called the corporate entity itself such as the structure, or are we referring to its members or perhaps both? As only moral agents can be attributed with moral responsibility this question is the flipside of asking if corporations have the necessary and sufficient characteristics for moral agency. The answer to this question will tell us what we are referring to when we make corporate moral responsibility attributions.

French suggests that we should interpret corporate moral responsibility attributions quite literally. "The Example Corporation is responsible for polluting the river", should be interpreted as the corporate entity itself is morally responsible for the event. Conglomerate collectivities are distinguished from aggregates in that they have a structure with policy and decision procedures. It is this Corporate Internal Decision Structure (CIDS) which supplies the corporation's intentionality and moral agency, and this structure is the reference of corporate proper names (i.e. the subject of a responsibility ascription of the second type). Therefore when we attribute moral responsibility to corporations French maintains that we are referring to the corporate structure and the responsibility ascription is not distributed to its members.

D. Rönnegard, *The Fallacy of Corporate Moral Agency*,
Issues in Business Ethics 44, DOI 10.1007/978-94-017-9756-6_7

Virginia Held (1991) distinguishes between two notions of group action: action as a "Random Collection" of individuals and action as a "Collectivity".[1] For her the main difference is that the latter group of people have a common decision procedure which the former lacks. French and Held express their views on this in slightly different ways but are on the whole in agreement on this specific issue. Although their conceptions of the distinguishing feature of conglomerates are similar French's CIDS is a far more extensive concept than Held's mere commitment to a "decision procedure". The CIDS contains a common goal in which members conspire as well as corporate policy and by-laws. What this amounts to is that corporations are purpose-built organizations. On the other hand, Held's "decision procedure" would qualify a commune of hippies (who decide how they are going to live their lives together through a voting procedure) as an organised group. That is to say there is no need to have a common goal which everyone is working towards achieving in concert, but only a decision procedure for solving disputes.

While French and Held are in agreement that the decision procedure distinguishes the two types of groups, Held does not attribute moral responsibility to the collective's structure as distinct from its members, but rather to the collective considered as a whole group of individuals. I interpret her as saying that it is legitimate to make responsibility attributions to collectives without knowing any of the actions taken by its individual members.[2] She believes as French does that "judgments about the moral responsibility of its [the collectivity's] members are not logically derivable from judgments about the moral responsibility of a collectivity" (Held 1991: 269). It may not be possible to derive that "member z is morally responsible for b" from the statement "collective x is morally responsible for b". However, I think the important point is that we can derive that there exists a person or subgroup of persons such that he/they are morally responsible for b.[3]

Downie (1969: 50) writes that "non-moral responsibilities of some collectives are *not* analysable in terms of those of its members; but... if a collective is *morally* responsible for something then it does [mean that it is analysable in terms of its members]". The idea here is that the ascription of moral responsibility

[1]In order to avoid confusion I shall stick with French's labelling of aggregate and conglomerate collectivities. Although French and Held's notions are not identical I believe they are close enough for our current purposes to use interchangeably.

[2]In what follows I am careful to point out that the position I am attributing to Held is my interpretation. Her writing has a holist flavour to it as if she does not wish to succumb to individualist demands of reduction. Nonetheless, I believe her position suggests that it is individuals that are the responsible moral agents and that we can legitimately attribute moral responsibility to conglomerates, not because they are the legitimate holders of moral responsibility, but because we are unable in practice to identify the responsible agents.

[3]If the collective action is taken as primitive or distinct from the members then this derivation is not possible. But as long as we assume that collective action is in some sense the action of members then this derivation is possible. However, this derivation does not add anything substantial to the argument for or against corporate moral agency, because the heart of the issue is indeed if corporate action is in a morally relevant sense distinct from its members or not.

must lodge with those who are the moral agents, which it is assumed are the corporate constituents rather than the organizational structure. Such a view differs substantially from French's position because for him actions predicated upon a conglomerate are not necessarily predicated upon any individual member because they refer to the entity as distinct from its members. But for Held, although the responsibility predicated upon the collective may not be attributable to any individual member it is still attributable to the collective as a group of individuals rather than the separate organizational structure. A conglomerate collectivity for Held is an organized group that may have officials who can act so as to represent the group or have a voting procedure to arrive at decisions. In her view, due to this decision structure it may be impossible to say that any member is morally responsible.

- Moral Responsibility Attribution to a Collective Entity that is Logically Distinct from its Members vs. Moral Responsibility Attribution to a Collective that is Dependent on the Members: French's attributes moral responsibility to the organizational structure of a conglomerate collective as logically distinct from its members while Held attributes moral responsibility to the whole membership of the conglomerate collective (in a non-distributive sense).

Held maintains that an aggregate collective can be represented as the conjunction of its members and that if the aggregate is responsible so is each and every member. French and Held are in agreement here and further this view of regarding the group as a conjunction of its members seems to be the basis for French using the term "aggregate". However, if the same members formed an organized group we could not simply represent the group as a conjunction of its members because we would be lacking the group decision procedure. Due to this difference of a conglomerate collectivity "the distribution of moral responsibility over such a combination would not seem plausible" (Held 1991: 273). It seems that Held is saying that the decision method hinders the distributive attribution of moral responsibility to the members of the group in practice because it obscures the identification of responsible members.

- Distinction between Distributive and Non-Distributive Attributions of Collective Responsibility: A distributive attribution of collective responsibility is one that aims to distribute responsibility to the individual members of a collective. A non-distributive attribution of collective responsibility is one that lodges with the whole membership of the collective rather than any individual members. It is generally accepted that attributions of responsibility to aggregate collectives are distributive, while it is contentious whether or not attributions of responsibility to conglomerate collectives are distributive or non-distributive. I shall argue that they should always aim to be distributive although the distribution may not always be apparent due to transparency difficulties.

Held is correct both with regard to the ability to represent an aggregate as a conjunction of its members and the necessity to include the decision procedure for the representation of the conglomerate. Furthermore, I can see why the added structure of a conglomerate causes difficulties for distributing moral responsibility to its members, but is this not just a more complex problem of evaluation? From the outside there may be transparency difficulties into an organization, but surely they can be overcome. The decision procedure is a defining aspect of a conglomerate, but it is just an extra factor to take into consideration when evaluating the responsibilities of the individual members. This does not in itself sanction solely non-distributive attributions of moral responsibility to conglomerates. If a member votes against an act that nevertheless is enacted and performed by some other member, surely this is a morally relevant factor to consider despite the existence of a collective decision procedure.[4] Held would probably agree, but believes that because we do make collective responsibility attributions without knowledge of the responsibility of any individual members so "we have no intentions of accepting reductionist demands in practice, it is dishonest to concede them in 'principle'" (Held 1991: 268).

I concede that conglomerates present difficulties for distributive moral responsibility attribution, but they are not so great that they cannot be overcome and exist only in "principle". Furthermore, we should not let our potential epistemological inabilities of identifying responsible members blind us from recognising that our moral responsibility attributions reside with the members responsible who are moral agents. That is to say, we should not believe that it is legitimate to blame the entire corporate collective of individuals simply because we do not have access to information about the parties who are actually responsible.

- We must distinguish between the metaphysics of discerning who is morally responsible when we make moral responsibility attributions from the epistemology of being able to identify who is morally responsible.

What does a non-distributive attribution of responsibility to a group amount to? Who are we attributing responsibility to? I interpret Held as saying that it is legitimate for us to attribute responsibility to a conglomerate collectivity in a non-distributive sense when we believe someone is morally responsible but lack the knowledge of who is responsible due to transparency difficulties. Furthermore, Held never states that conglomerates are moral agents, but only that we can attribute moral responsibility predicates to them. Therefore I do not interpret her as saying that the conglomerate as a collective whole is literally responsible, but only as a way of attributing responsibility with uncertainty regarding with whom within the group responsibility resides. One might argue that if we hold a conglomerate responsible as a collective whole we are then implicitly holding each individual member responsible to some extent, because the members are attributed responsibility by virtue of being a member of the collective. Unless we attribute moral agency and responsibility to the structure as French does, which Held does not wish to do, we must then be attributing responsibility to the members of the group as part of the collective moral responsibility attribution. The attribution is to the

[4] I shall later consider the problems associated with attributing moral responsibility to a collective when an individual is acting as the elected representative for the collective.

members collectively, not individually (thus not distributively), but each member is nevertheless encompassed by the attribution. It seems then that Held implicitly attributes responsibility to some unknown subset of the group's members through the corporate name, but does not believe it is possible to *distribute* responsibility to those who are morally responsible because of the impeding group structure.

Manuel Velasquez (1983: 74) says with regard to corporate moral responsibility attributions that "[w]e are often forced to adopt this elliptical way of speaking because, as outsiders, we are usually ignorant of the inner workings of a corporation". This problem of transparency is precisely why we often use the corporate name in our moral responsibility attributions. We believe that at least some member of the corporation is morally responsible for an event, but we do not know whom. For example, the managing director of the Example Corporation would not attribute moral responsibility for polluting the river to the corporation as a separate entity or a collective whole, simply because his position within the organization allows him to see with which members moral responsibility actually resides. When have you ever heard a managing director or CEO of a corporation say "it was not our fault, it was the corporation's fault"? It often happens that a representative of a company says that no member within the organization is responsible for a certain event because they attribute the event to a systemic fault. However, the natural interpretation of this excuse is not that the system is morally responsible, but rather that the systemic fault serves to causally explain an event which no member intended.

Using a corporate name as the subject of a moral responsibility attribution in order to elliptically refer to a member or subset of corporate members requires that one assumes that someone within the organization is morally responsible for the event and acted in his or her role on behalf of the corporation. This is to distinguish the actions done by individuals in their own personal capacity from the actions done in pursuit of realizing a collective corporate goal. For example, Bad Bob is a member of the Example Corporation and Bad Bob is also a bad friend. The statement, "Bad Bob is morally responsible for hitting his friend Ian", does not due to transparency difficulties legitimize the elliptical responsibility attribution, "the Example Corporation is responsible for hitting Ian", because the person who is performing the immoral action of hitting Ian (who is Bad Bob) is not acting in his role as a member of the Example Corporation. Therefore the untoward event that we are elliptically attributing to the corporation must in some way be consistent with an overriding collective goal of the corporation; otherwise the untoward event will be performed by members in their private capacity and the corporate name may not be used to elliptically attribute them with responsibility.

Clearly I believe that our corporate moral responsibility attributions refer to corporate members and as I shall argue that they are distributive. Contrary to Held, corporate moral responsibility attributions are distributive because we *can* distribute the responsibility, but we may at the present time abstain from specifying the distribution due to transparency difficulties. I am not saying that there is no difference between the distributive attributions we make to aggregates and the ones we make to conglomerates. I agree that the distinguishing feature of conglomerates is that members have a decision procedure and that members may have a common goal to pursue. A corporation that exists over a period of several generations may not have any members left from when the organization was started but the current members may still consistently achieve the same goal as their predecessors. This is why it is inadequate to simply represent a corporation as a conjunction of its members, because it misses their interrelations and common goal. It is right to regard a CIDS as that aspect of an organization that persists through time. But we should not thereby attribute responsibility to the group structure as opposed to the group members.

The corporate structure allows us to consistently refer to those individuals who are engaged as current members in the pursuit of a common end as given by the formal or informal structure of the group. The structure encircles those who are members and acts as a divider between members and non-members. Anyone who enters the structure becomes a corporate member.[5] On the other hand no one can ever become a member of a pre-existing aggregate; either you are or you are not. You cannot come and say to an aggregate "can I join you?" because there is no representative to ask and they do not have a decision procedure by which to decide. A conglomerate requires both its structure and its current members in order to be adequately represented. The corporate name however does not directly refer to the current members. Rather it refers to the corporate structure which in turn specifies the set of current members. The structure acts like a pointer that says "at this moment in time the individuals who occupy the following positions are members of the corporation". Therefore corporate moral responsibility attributions refer to the set of corporate members that are delineated by virtue of the corporate structure, although such an attribution need only aim to *distribute* responsibility to a subset of its members.[6]

[5]On this view members are those who hold role defined positions as given by the corporate structure. Are shareholders members? I am inclined to say that this depends on if a shareholder has voting stock or not. The ownership of non-voting stock does not bring with it a role that affects the corporation's activities; it is merely an ownership of capital and thus such shareholders are not members of the corporation as far as moral responsibility is concerned. On the other hand owners of voting stock do obtain a role that can influence the activities of the corporation, but only if the right to vote is exercised. So I am inclined to say that shareholders who exercise their right to vote may be considered members of the organization. Christopher McMahon (1995) explains that the associationist view of organizations distinguishes members from non-members by whether or not they are party to the authority relations within the organization. Therefore he explains that if shareholders are considered as "forming a collective principal that has created a hierarchical structure of agents to carry out its purposes, they will be party to the authority relations associated with the corporation and thus members of it. By contrast, if they are appropriately regarded as a group of investors [i.e. merely supplying capital] they are not party to the corporations authority relations and thus not members of it" (McMahon 1995: 546). Therefore if we combine McMahon's view with my initial suggestion, we can say that those individuals who have voting stock (and exercise their right to vote) may be regarded as a collective principal encompassed by the corporations authority relations and thus may be regarded as members of the corporation.

[6]On the other hand a responsibility attribution to an aggregate distributes responsibility to all its members, because it is only by virtue of one's responsibility in the event in question that one becomes a member of an aggregate.

The reference of the name of an aggregate collective is simply its extension, which is the individuals who are said to be its members at the moment of producing the event in question. The reference of a conglomerate name is also its members, but it has the added feature of a structure that specifies the extension through fixed positions that demarcate members from non-members. Although the corporate structure persists through time corporate members change and therefore the members referred to by the corporate name change too. The reference of the corporate name is the corporate structure, but it in turn specifies the positions that are filled by corporate members where the moral responsibility attribution lodges. One can say that the identity of conglomerates consists of both its structure and its current members, and because members change the reference of our responsibility attributions are indexed in time. For example consider the moral responsibility attribution: "The Nestlé Corporation is morally responsible for the deaths of infants in underdeveloped countries through its irresponsible marketing of breast milk substitutes". If a new responsibility attribution of this type were to be made once again today as it was in the 1970s it would refer to different corporate members. We may not know who the responsible corporate members are, but we can be pretty sure that they are not part of the same set of members as in the 1970s.

The importance of varying membership for the identity of a conglomerate is clear when we refer to the government. For example we refer to the US government 1997–2001 as the Clinton administration. The presidential post and the ministerial posts remain fairly constant over time but the individuals who hold the different positions change. If government policy under the Clinton administration causes a severe injustice we do not then proceed to hold the current administration morally responsible for those events. We may hold the government legally responsible, but that is a different responsibility attribution and should not be conflated with the *moral* issue at hand.

As mentioned previously, I take it that moral responsibility attributions are distributive. I interpreted Held's (1991) position as saying that it is legitimate to attribute moral responsibility to conglomerates in a non-distributive sense, but that moral responsibility nevertheless resides with the group's members. She maintains the non-distributive sense of the responsibility attribution because she does not believe it is possible to distribute responsibility to the group's members due to the epistemic difficulties created by the decision procedure. What I maintain is that the moral responsibility attribution is distributive, but we abstain from distributing the responsibility until it becomes transparent which members are responsible. This is only a small difference, but the important point is that our positions abstain from attributing moral responsibility to the group as a whole in a *distributive* sense.

Our denoting terms such as corporate names are referentially opaque and therefore we must ultimately rely on speakers' intentions to understand the desired reference. When we make corporate moral responsibility attributions I believe that speakers intend, or ought to intend, to attribute moral responsibility to the responsible members who are moral agents that can bear the moral responsibility. One important reason is that it goes against our moral intuition to attribute moral responsibility to a group as a whole because many of the members may never have intended or contributed to the act in question and are thus not morally responsible. To the extent that a group responsibility attribution is connected with any form of punishment, a collective punishment is an unfair[7] sanction for those in whom no moral responsibility resides.[8]

All agents that are denoted by being members of a corporation may not intend nor act in the process of corporate activity. Some members, such as janitors and other auxiliary employees may be totally oblivious to the actions and intentions of employees acting within the context of the core business. Perhaps more importantly, shareholders (although it may be debatable if they are members of the organization) are often ignorant of the intentions and actions of management (as free agents). Furthermore, some employees may be acting upon the directives of their superiors without full insight into the intended overall result of the actions that they perform. To this extent it is unfair to hold all corporate members morally responsible for actions taken within the operational context of the organization. It is unfair to punish all corporate members because many, having neither intended nor acted, are not morally responsible. Our corporate moral responsibility attributions are distributive, but the distribution is not necessarily an equal distribution of responsibility to all corporate members. We must, despite the transparency difficulties created by the corporate structure and in part through the aid of that very structure distribute moral responsibility to those in whom responsibility resides.

- Corporate moral responsibility attributions are distributive and the reference of the corporate name in responsibility attributions is the organizational structure which in turn specifies the positions which the corporate members fill.

Recall that French maintains that the corporate name must refer to an entity that is distinct from the corporate members because otherwise the referent of the corporate name could vary depending on a speaker's intention to refer to different specific

[7]I am assuming that punishment is only fair when administered to those subjects with whom moral responsibility resides. Some utilitarian conceptions of justice may not regard moral responsibility as a central criterion for punishment but simply punish people in such a manner that it maximises utility. I choose to disregard such utilitarian conceptions of punishment as I regard moral responsibility as a condition for punishment, while the act of punishment itself may be justified on instrumental grounds (Ronnegard 2008).

[8]The sentencing of the auditing firm Arthur Andersen is an example of an unfair collective punishment. Arthur Andersen was the auditor for both Enron and World Com (which have come to be associated with the biggest corporate governance scandals in history). Arthur Andersen as a corporation was convicted of complicit involvement in accounting fraud for its clients Enron and World Com, and was consequently heavily fined and lost virtually all of its clients worldwide. This was the result of the fraudulent behaviour of a number of individuals at Arthur Andersen in the United States, however the sentencing of the corporate entity ruined the livelihoods of all the other Arthur Andersen partners in the world whom had no involvement whatsoever with the scandals. It would have been fair to pursue the fraudulent individuals within the organization with criminal charges rather than sanctioning the corporate entity. Technically the sanctioning of a corporate entity is not legally considered a "collective punishment"; it is merely the sanctioning of a legal person. However, in practice the corporation consists of individual members who all may be affected by the corporate legal sanction.

corporate members. How does my view compare to French's position? Because I believe that it is only the corporate members that can be morally responsible I maintain that if we know who the responsible members are we would never have any use for using corporate names in our moral responsibility attributions.[9] My position is that corporate names refer to the corporate structure which in turn specifies the positions held by the members. Corporate *moral* responsibility attributions must lodge with at least one moral agent and because the corporate structure does not qualify as a moral agent the attribution must refer to one or more members of the corporation.[10] At first glance, employing the corporate name in a moral responsibility attribution implies that one casts one's net too wide because it encompasses members who may not be responsible. However, the attribution is only intended to elliptically refer to those members who are responsible and therefore the attribution of responsibility does not specify a distribution of responsibility. The corporate name is only used until the corporate veil is pierced and moral responsibility can be attributed and distributed to the responsible members.

- Corporate Moral Responsibility Attributions are Distributive, because the aim is to distribute responsibility to individuals who are moral agents and are morally responsible, but we may currently abstain from distributing responsibility to those individuals until we know who they are.

Moreover (as a separate argument), one can argue that it is of little use to blame a corporation as a moral agent. For French the intention and moral agency of a corporation resides in the CIDS. If we for a moment accept that this structure counts as a corporate intentionality and moral agency, in what sense is it *useful* for us to blame a structure for its "intentions" and for the resulting consequences? We usually attribute blame to an agent in order to induce guilt or shame, or to justify some other kind of formal or informal sanction in the hope that the agent

---

[9]The only exception is the case of a "unanimously intending collective". In this case we can find it useful to use the corporate name because we know that *all* the members are morally responsible. This will be discussed in greater detail in the next section.

[10]However, note that the reference of *descriptive* statements that contain corporate names need not change with varying membership because the reference of the name refers in the first instance to the corporate structure which causally explains the event being attributed to the corporate collective. A mere description of the form "the Example Corporation produced a car" does not hinge in any important sense on the identity of the individual members nor on if they intended to produce a car. Descriptions using a corporate name serve to attribute an event to the causal process within the organization that led to the event. The structure is the essential component of an organization which causally explains the coordinated result of the actions of the members. For example, individuals A, B and C perform actions X, Y and Z which due to the structure causally produce the result Q. The result Q is not an intentional result of the corporate entity nor is it relevant if the members intended the result. It is a mere itemization of the events that causally led to Q. Members must necessarily perform actions, but the actions could equally have been performed by different members because it is merely their causal contribution that is important. The members could equally be robots as human beings. This type of use of a corporate name in a descriptive statement would resemble the manner in which French mistakenly attributes *moral* responsibility to the corporation where constituents lack their own autonomy and are merely directed by the structure.

will augment its behaviour. The corporate structure cannot feel shame, it cannot be incarcerated, and it cannot learn from its mistakes. If we utter statements blaming structures then those statements do not serve the purpose of communicating the moral responsibility attribution to the subject of the attribution. That is to say, there is no sense in which a structure understands it is being blamed or that it is *morally* blameworthy for an untoward event. It simply has no mental states with which to appreciate the nature of the consequences it has brought about. The corporation is instrumentally attributed an intention, but the corporation (or CIDS) is not aware of its intention. If corporate moral responsibility attributions referred to the CIDS people simply would not bother making them. It is like assigning moral blame to a tree that falls and kills a man. Although the man's wife may curse at the tree in her despair I cannot imagine her morally blaming the tree for her husband's death. As I have previously maintained attributions of responsibility to structures are only legitimate in a causal sense. Therefore in order to make the concept of attributing moral blame to a corporation consistent with our moral intuitions, we must assume that we are implicitly referring to the individuals who comprise the corporation and can feel and respond to the blame being attributed.

The concept of moral agency is not just important for identifying the referent of the attribution of moral responsibility, i.e. identifying a holder of moral duties that may break those duties and thus be attributed with moral responsibility. Moral agents are also capable of having *rights* as well as duties. Ought we to take corporate moral rights seriously? Analysing corporate moral rights quickly leads to absurd consequences. If a corporation is a distinct moral agent from the corporate members then presumably corporate moral rights are not derivative from the moral rights of the individual members (because then it would not be a distinct moral agent). Does it not seem wrong that the rights of the corporation could conflict with the rights of the members? For example, the corporation's hypothetical moral right to life (or rather its right to exist) could conflict with the shareholders right to dispose of their resources. These rights may conflict if it is more profitable to liquidate the corporation than it is to keep the business running. Are we committing murder when we shut down the corporation and creating life when we start a new one? No, of course not. Corporations are not moral agents and they have no *moral* rights to be taken seriously.

Summary French regards the reference of corporate names to be the corporate structure which is also the reference of our moral responsibility attributions. I have argued that the structure is the important distinguishing feature of conglomerates but it is not the reference of corporate moral responsibility attributions. Rather, the structure delineates who qualifies as a corporate member (indexed in time), and it is the members who are the reference of our moral responsibility attributions. Moral responsibility resides with those members who intentionally acted in pursuit of an event or ought to have intentionally prevented an event. However, we may attribute moral responsibility to a corporation while abstaining from distributing responsibility if it is not transparent who is responsible. This is in line with our moral intuition of only attributing moral responsibility to those who are morally responsible. Furthermore, it only useful to blame those who are aware of the moral nature of their acts.

In the next section I shall consider the legitimacy of corporate moral responsibility attributions when such attributions specifically refer to the corporate members.

References

Downie, R.S. 1969. Collective responsibility. *Philosophy* 44: 66–69.

Held, V. 1991. Can a random collection of individuals be morally responsible? In *The spectrum of responsibility*, ed. P.A. French. New York: St. Martin's Press.

McMahon, C. 1995. The moral status of organisations. *Business Ethics Quarterly* 5(3): 541–554.

Ronnegard, D. 2008. Collective responsibility; Collective punishment. In *Encyclopedia of business ethics and society*, ed. Robert W. Kolb. Thousand Oaks: SAGE Publications.

Velasquez, Manuel G. 1983. Why corporations are not morally responsible for anything they do. *Business and Professional Ethics Journal* 2: 1–18.

Chapter 8
Corporate Collective Moral Agency

The argument so far has focused on the short-comings of the view that corporate entities themselves can be regarded as moral agents. Although Werhane and Pettit develop theories that are metaphysically individualistic the moral agency of the corporation is nevertheless said to exists at a social level of description that functionally acts as an autonomously intending entity, while for French the moral agency of the corporation is metaphysically distinct from its members.

As I have tried to maintain, corporate entities themselves do not exhibit the necessary characteristics for moral agency. However, a stronger argument can be made for corporate intentions and actions if we dispense with the notion that the corporation can possess the necessary characteristics for moral agency in a manner that is descriptively discontinuous with the characteristics of its members. Instead, it may be possible to develop a view of the intentions and actions of individuals together with the structure of their interrelations that may constitute a legitimate foundation for collective intention and action attributions. This constitutes a shift away from French's teleological conception of a corporation's intention (given as a directive by the corporate structure), to a conception whereby the collective intention originates from the corporate members themselves. I am also aiming to shift away from a conception of moral agency that rests on social level descriptions of the characteristics for moral agency that are in some way distinct from the constituent members.

If one can develop an account of corporate intentionality that is not distinct from its members, then the step to corporate responsibility attributions is not too far away. If the collective intention originates from the members who are moral agents and can intend, then we can arguably attribute collective intentions that do not constitute a social level description that is discontinuous with the attitudes of members. In other words, one may be able to build morally relevant collective characteristics from the

D. Rönnegard, *The Fallacy of Corporate Moral Agency*,
Issues in Business Ethics 44, DOI 10.1007/978-94-017-9756-6_8

individual members who themselves possess those characteristics.[1] This analysis of corporate moral responsibility attributions that are *dependent* on corporate members together with our previous analysis of corporate moral responsibility attributions that are *distinct* from corporate members will help us construct a taxonomy of legitimate and illegitimate corporate moral responsibility attributions.

If Corporate Moral Agency denotes moral agency that is logically *distinct* from the corporate members, then let us call moral agency that is *dependent* on members "Corporate Collective Moral Agency".[2] The two should be kept separate.[3]

I shall consider Michael Bratman and Raimo Tuomela's views of collective intentions. Bratman does not specifically expand his account to encompass moral agency or responsibility attributions to collectives, and while Tuomela (2007) does touch upon collective responsibility. Nevertheless both their views are significant in constructing a framework for collective intention and action attributions.[4] When considering their views it will be important to identify if their positions imply that collective intentions must necessarily be attributed to the collective whole or if such attributions are reducible to the individuals that comprise them, because this has implications for the *distribution* of moral responsibility. If the collective intention is not reducible to the members then arguably any attribution of moral responsibility to the collective for its intentional action will also not be reducible to its members. I shall focus more heavily on Tuomela's (1993) account because he develops his view to specifically deal with *corporate* intentions and actions.

8.1 Joint/Shared Intentions

Bratman's (1987, 1993) view on collective intentions (what he calls "shared intentions") is based on his planning theory of intentions for individuals. His account of collective intentions aims at explaining how for a pair of individuals "shared intentions support the goal-directed coordination of shared activity, in part by way of coordinated planning and relevant bargaining" (Bratman 1993: 103). What Bratman

---

[1] An account of corporate moral agency that in some sense is an account of the collective properties of the individuals who are moral agents could potentially satisfy not just our stated necessary conditions for moral agency but also whatever sufficient conditions we deem appropriate.

[2] "Corporate" in "Corporate Collective Moral Agency" signifies that the collective is structured and purpose driven. (Also the phrase "Corporate Collective Moral Agency" does not result in the same acronym as "Corporate Moral Agency" which is useful in keeping the notions separate.)

[3] All too often these two notions are not kept separate which creates confusion in the debate. For example, Arnold (2006) makes a defence of Corporate Moral Agency in terms of the *collective* intentions of members.

[4] Margaret Gilbert (2000) gives an account of collective intentions that she expands to encompass moral responsibility attributions. However, I shall not consider her account because it starts from a holistic standpoint. She simply assumes the irreducibility of collective intentions, which is a central aspect of the present discussion.

has in mind for a shared intention is a situation consisting of appropriate attitudes of each individual participant and their interrelations. Individuals are considered to have a shared intention when they have a common goal that they wish to achieve through joint coordinated activity with certain proper interrelations among the participants.[5] By having a shared intention to achieve a goal J, individuals can coordinate their individual intentional actions by planning the steps needed to achieve the goal. The shared intention functions as the foundation for bargaining about how the goal is to be achieved.

The conditions for a shared intention are as follows:

We intend to J if and only if:

1. (a) I intend that we J and (b) you intend that we J.
2. I intend that we J in accordance with and because of 1a, 1b, and meshing sub-plans of 1a and 1b, you intend that we J in accordance with and because of 1a, 1b and meshing sub-plans of 1a and 1b.
3. 1 and 2 are common knowledge between us.

(1) Simply states that we individually have the goal J in common. (2) States that the individual's intention to achieve the common goal is in part due to the other person's intention to contribute to that goal. It also states that the individual intends to J by meshing sub-plans, which means to coordinate and bargain for the means by which J is to be achieved. The meshing of sub-plans need not yet be realized for a shared intention to be established; all that is required is that we intend that we will J by way of meshing sub-plans. This second condition should also be understood to be specifying the *content* of the cited intending. (3) States that our individual intentions to participate in a joint activity are public, in the sense of being mutually believed. This guarantees that a shared intention is not simply a coincidence of intentions, whereby we happen to have a common goal but neither is aware of the other's intention to achieve it.

Is Bratman's view of collective intentions reducible to individual intentions? According to his own account it is. He points out that "a shared intention is not an attitude in the mind of some super-agent consisting literally of some fusion of the two agents" (Bratman 1993: 98). For Bratman a shared intention is not a state of mind in the participants, but rather a state of affairs about the attitudes of the participants and the interrelations of those attitudes. As such the state of affairs of a shared intention can be explained in individualistic terms by appealing to the intentions of the individuals and their interrelations. This would be consistent with my view that the identity of conglomerates consists of both the group's structure and its members. The structure represents the interrelations of the members while the members themselves possess the intending mental states. Of course the case for most corporations is that many corporate members may not be engaged in all the goals that a corporation may have nor need they necessarily be engaged in an overarching goal, say to profit maximise. However, if we make a very strong assumption and

[5]Note that Bratman does not believe that all goals are intentions.

assume that every single member of a corporation conforms to Bratman's conception of a shared intention, each intending to J and each engaged in achieving the shared corporate goal, we still obtain a notion of corporate intention that is reducible to its individual members. Therefore if we use Bratman's conception of "shared intention" as the state of affairs that exists when we attribute intentions to a corporation we obtain an attribution that is reducible to the corporate members individually. I shall leave the collective moral responsibility implications of his account until later when I come to discuss Bratman's position in relation to Tuomela's account.

- Bratman's Notion of a Shared Intention: An interrelational state of affairs among two individuals that consists of a common goal (which they are both aware of is common) to be realized by coordinating their actions.

Raimo Tuomela (1993, 2000, 2002, 2003, 2007) has also developed a theory of collective intention. He has developed his theory to explicitly deal with corporate intentions, which he believes are attributable to the group members as a whole. Can Tuomela's account of corporate intentionality give us a notion that is not reducible to its members? We shall see. At the base of Tuomela's view of corporate intentions and actions lies his strongest account of collective intentions. Tuomela develops several different views of collective intention that are adapted to several different collective situations of intending. The views differ mainly in the strength of the conditions necessary to obtain the different types of collective intentions; the stronger the conditions the more committed the individual agents are to the collective intention. Tuomela's strongest notion of collective intention is what he calls a full-blown joint intention, which is a stronger notion than Bratman's "shared intention". Tuomela's joint intention rests on his conceptually non-reductive notion of "we-intentions". He has expanded his theory to explicitly deal with corporate intentions (with many people), whereas Bratman's theory is developed for the limited two person case. Tuomela's notion of joint intention relies on explicit or implicit agreements. Agreement-making is a characteristic of members acting within a corporation and therefore he uses this view of collective intentions to expand his theory to cover corporate intentions. I shall now sketch the main features of Tuomela's theory by first considering his theory of a joint intention (two people) and then the expanded view of a corporate intention (with many people):

A joint intention in the two person case can be characterised as follows (Tuomela 2000):

You and I have the joint intention to act together in performing an action X if and only if:

1. X is a collective type action, and this is understood by us. (A collective type action is something that is performed in concert with others. For example an orchestra playing Beethoven's 9th.)
2. (a) I intend to perform X together with you, and on this basis I accordingly intend to participate in the performance of X. (b) You intend to perform X together with me, and on this basis you accordingly intend to participate in the performance of X. (The intention of an individual to perform a collective type action is called a "we-intention").

3. (a) I believe that you will participate in the performance of X. (b) You believe that I will participate in the performance of X. Furthermore, this is common knowledge between us because we have implicitly or explicitly made an agreement to perform X.
4. 2(a) in part because of 3(a). 2(b) in part because of 3(b).

Tuomela says that joint intentions are expressible by locutions like "we will do X". An individual that expresses such a locution is expressing a we-intention. He says "we-intentions are action-generating intentions which have collective content and which are attributed to single individuals in a social context. In contrast, a joint intention is an intention shared by several agents" (Tuomela 2000: 48). A shared we-intention of which the participants are mutually aware is called a joint intention. For a joint intention to exist each agent must we-intend to perform X jointly with others, and this is common knowledge for each agent due to implicit or explicit agreement. Joint intentions are formed when agents jointly decide to perform a joint action. Joint intentions require agreement making, which communicates the desire of agents to participate in the joint action. Such agreements give rise to social commitments and inter-personal obligations of the parties who contribute their part to performing the joint action. It is important to note that the joint intention does not exist in some super-agent, but is rather an interrelation of we-intentions. If the above conditions are satisfied it is then legitimate to attribute the joint intention to the collective.

Tuomela and Bratman's account share the following similarities: The participating agents intend to perform their contribution to "X" in part because of the others intention to do likewise. Furthermore, these conditions are mutually believed by the agents. However, Tuomela's account differs in two important respects. Firstly, his account requires implicit or explicit agreement making. Secondly, his account relies on the non-reductive notion of we-intention.

Tuomela incorporates the necessity of agreement into his account because "information only travels through a physical medium" and thus agreement making is necessary in order for the participants in the joint activity to have the mutual belief of the others participation. What this requirement also entails is that the agents are normatively bound to the participation of the joint activity, because they have expressed a promise (through the agreement making) rather than simply independently intended to contribute to the joint activity.

The second important difference with Tuomela's account is that it is founded on the non-reductive notion of we-intention. Tuomela (2000: 53) says: "My analysis of joint intentions, group-intentions and we-intentions is conceptually non-reductive, although it is ontically individualistic or, better, interrelationistic". For an individual to we-intend he must accept the intention-expression "we will do X". The notion itself is conceived fundamentally as non-individualistic. The existence of the non-reductive notion of "we-intention" is taken to be primitive. Because joint intentions are regarded as a shared we-intention of which the participants are mutually aware, the notion of joint intention is also conceptually non-reductive. However, it is important to keep in mind that it is only the concept of we-intention with regard to its *collective content* that is not reducible to that of intentions predicated upon individuals. In other words we-intentions are not reducible to I-intentions with proper interrelations among individuals. However, metaphysically speaking we-intentions are individualistic because they exist as the mental intentions of individuals and not in the mind of some super-agent.

- A Brief Overview of Tuomela's Notion of a Joint Intention: A "we-intention" is an intentional mental state with collective content of an individual person. A person who we-intends will accept the intention expression "we will do X". A joint intention is an inter-relational state of affairs that consists of several individuals sharing a we-intention and being mutually aware of the others participation in the goal directed activity (joint action). Joint intentions are metaphysically reducible to individual we-intentions with proper inter-relations, but the collective content of each individual's we-intention is not reducible in individual terms.

8.2 Group/Corporate Intentions

Tuomela now uses his account of joint intentions in the two person case in order to explicate his view of corporate intentions that include many collective members. He adapts his notion of joint intentions by supplementing his account with different norms together with characteristic traits found within corporate organizations. Tuomela aims at developing a descriptive account for the conditions under which attributions of actions can be made to social groups. He conceives of social groups as collectives of individuals capable of collective action. Central to this action capability of the collective is the notion of an "authority system" which is a kind of group decision-making system. Tuomela (1993: 17) expresses a simplified version of his thesis for *Group action* in the following way:

> "If a group (with the agents A1,...,An as its members) does something X, then at least some of its members, say A1,...,Am (m < n) must, in the right social and normative circumstances, do something X1,...,Xm, their parts of a joint action (of X or of a joint action X), and in normal circumstances these parts serve to generate or "make up" X. Here, X1,...,Xm will be parts of a joint action of A1,...,Am, who are called the "operative" agents (for action) of the group. This joint action need not be of the type X, but it should be taken as one generating or bringing about a token of X. In the case of intentional group action intentional joint action is required, and therefore shared "we-intentions"... by the agents will be involved".

Tuomela's theory states that collectives such as corporations consist of operative and non-operative members who are engaged in achieving a collective goal through a joint action X.[6] The operative members, those who are actively involved in making decisions and performing actions directed toward the realisation of X are

[6]The difference between operative and non-operative members is that the former are actively engaged in the pursuit of core business objectives, whereas the latter may be regarded as auxiliary

considered to have shared mutually believed and communicated we-intentions, and thus collectively considered to have a joint intention to X. This is all along the lines of the above explicated theory of a joint intention.

The phrase "the right social and normative circumstances" is introduced to account for the three components of "authority-norms", "social norms" and an "authority-system". These notions are to act as the rule-guiding and decision-making cohesive that binds together the intentions of the operative and non-operative members so that collective intentions are attributable to the corporation as a collectively unified whole. These circumstances bind the desires and beliefs of members giving rise to corporate intentions. When the operative members take actions in accordance with those intentions we obtain actions attributable to the corporation. I shall consider these notions below.

Social norms (s-norms) can be society-wide or group-specific and are based on "normative collective expectations". These are norms of behaviour that are acquired through socialization. Social norms are not explicitly stated, but are rather informal in character. An example would be the principle of reciprocity used in mutual gift giving. Authority-based norms (r-norms) are on the other hand explicitly stated and are created through direct or indirect group-authorised agreement making. These norms can also be society wide or group-specific. For example "the law" is society wide and "job description duties" may be group-specific forms of r-norms. Social and Authority based norms may or may not be coupled with sanctions as the case may be.[7]

Social and authority based norms function to help create "the right social and normative circumstances" letting agents know what is expected of them and what they can expect of others. When authority based norms are created by a group for the group (usually by the operative members), these norms are created through agreement making while the social norms are held through mutual belief. Norms such as these within organizations generate a "task-right system" for positions involved within the organization. Task-right systems indicate the right behaviour which is expected of organizational members, for both operative and non-operative members.

Tuomela says that the authority based norms that are created by and for the group can only be created by use of some "authority-system". An authority-system typically involves operative members of the collective representing the other members. Such a system helps create shared we-intentions, binding the operative and non-operative members so that the collective as a whole may be considered to have an intention. The intentions and actions of the operative members

personnel whose role it is to facilitate and aid the realization of the goals of operative members. An example would be a managing director (operative) and his personal assistant (non-operative) who takes care of all administrative work surrounding the MD.

[7]R-norms, when sanctioned, are coupled with r-sanctions imposed by the authority (e.g.: jail sentence or job dismissal), and s-norms, when sanctioned, are coupled with s-sanctions imposed by the social community (e.g.: social disapproval aimed at inducing feelings of shame).

represent the intentions and actions of the entire collective. Tuomela (1993: 18) writes, "[u]nderlying the existence of such authority and the involved possibility of representation is the capability of group members –to speak in Rousseau's terms- to give up their will (with respect to some issues) and thus their 'original' authority and to transfer it to the group via a group-authority system, which 'pools the wills' into a group will". Adopting intentions for a collective through representation is meant to be similar to public policies adopted by governments in a representative democracy. Tuomela (1993: 19) formalizes an intentional group action as it also applies to a corporation as follows:

A group, G, performed an action X intentionally in the (right) social and normative circumstances C if and only if, there were operative agents A1,...,Am of G such that:

1. A1,...,Am, when performing their social tasks in their respective positions P1,...,Pm and due to their exercising the relevant authority system of G, intentionally jointly brought about X.
2. because of (1), the non-operative members of G, as members of G, tacitly accept the operative agents' intentional bringing about of X- or at least ought to accept it.
3. there was a mutual belief in G to the effect that there was at least a chance that (1) and to the effect that (2).

Tuomela's account of a corporate intention attributes intentions to the corporation as a collective whole. The authority-system together with the authority-norms (and other social-norms) binds the intentions of all collective members including the non-operative members. The non-operative members are considered to tacitly accept (or at least *ought* to tacitly accept) the intentions of the operative agents to bring about a joint action. The non-operative agents are thus committed to the joint action, but in a weaker sense than the operative agents because they only display a tacit acceptance. The operative members who act as the representatives of the non-operative members with regard to the intention of the collective must act on a joint intention. Because the representative operative members act on the conceptually non-reductive notion of we-intention, the resulting intention attributed to the corporation is also conceptually non-reductive. Furthermore, the actions taken by the operative members are taken in their roles as representatives for the collective whole. Therefore on Tuomela's account the intentions and actions taken by these operative members may be attributed to the corporation as a collective whole.

Now we may ask, is Tuomela's view of corporate intentions reducible to its members? Tuomela has given an account of collective intentions based on the members of the corporation and their interrelations that are governed by the authority system, authority based norms and social norms. Therefore his account is reducible to the individuals that comprise the organization because we can reduce the corporate intention attribution by reference to the "we-intentions" of the operative members and the structure that binds all members.[8] The intention

[8] I am working on the assumption that the authority based norms and social norms are reducible to the mutual beliefs of the members.

attribution to the corporation may be conceptually non-reductive because it is based on a conceptually non-reductive notion of a "we-intention", but this is only an irreducibility of content of the intention. Tuomela takes "we-intentions" to be primitive for his concept of collective intentionality rather than "I-intentions" as Bratman does. However, nothing crucial hinges on this distinction for the reducibility of the collective intention, because although the content of a "we-intention" may be irreducible to "I-intentions" with proper interrelations, the "we-intentions" reside as intentions in the minds of operative members, thus allowing a reduction in terms of individuals (operative and non-operative) and their structural interrelations.

Tuomela's attribution of corporate intentionality is dependent upon the intentions of its members, but it displays several similarities with French's position (e.g.: 1991a) for whom the corporate intention is separate from the members. Tuomela's notion of an "authority system" can be likened to the way that French's corporate structure synthesises the intentions of members into a corporate intention. The authority system binds the operative and non-operative members through a system of representation so that the collective as a whole may be attributed with an intention. Furthermore, the authority based norms that create the corporation's "task-right system" can be likened to French's Corporate Internal Decision Structure (CIDS) with its positions and lines of authority that defines what counts as acceptable behaviour on behalf of the corporation. These similarities go to show that they are in agreement about the importance of the structural aspect of a group of individuals for unifying them to act purposively. But this is where the similarities end. The most significant difference between their positions is the role the structure plays in the corporate intention attribution. For French the structure that contains the corporate policy stands as a corporate intention on its own, separate from its members. Tuomela on the other hand attributes the corporate intention to the corporate members as a whole through the corporate structure that allows the intentions of operative members to represent the corporate collective (both operative and non-operative members).

- Tuomela's view of corporate collective Action: Operative members of the corporation acting on a joint intention represent the intentions of non-operative members through the authority system (together with authority norms and social norms). The result of the activities of operative members acting on a joint-intention is characterised as a collective action attributable to the corporate collective as a whole.

8.3 Corporate Collective Intentions

If we accept Tuomela's view of corporate intention attributions then one could arguably use it as a basis for expanding it to moral responsibility attributions. Let us first however perform this expansion with Bratman's view of "shared intentions".

For Bratman a collective intention is attributed to a group of individuals if they all have the intention to perform their part of a collective action. The intention attribution amounts to saying "collective Y intends to achieve X", as a short hand for saying "they intend to achieve the collective goal X". This means that each and every member intends this goal when they perform their individual part in achieving the desired collective result. Now, if we simply add the assumption that all members of the collective are moral agents then their individual intentionality will satisfy sufficient conditions for moral agency. Given that the members of the collective then act to realize their intention we may then attribute moral agency to the collective and moral responsibility attributions for the actions they perform. The moral agency attribution to the collective is then a short-hand way of referring to the intentions and actions of each member; and likewise a collective moral responsibility attribution is a short-hand way of referring to the moral responsibility of each and every member. It is as if we are saying "they are morally responsible". This is not however a simple aggregation of moral agents because the intentions of the members are coordinated. The intention of each moral agent to achieve the common goal is in part due to the other members' intention to contribute to that goal and each individual intends the common goal through the meshing of sub-plans (which means to coordinate and bargain for the means by which it is to be achieved).

Nevertheless, such a collective of agents has the same property of an aggregate in that the moral responsibility attribution is distributed to all its members. The structure of such a collective of agents, although limited, ensures that the intentions of the members are aligned. The structure consists of the interrelations of the agents, which are mutual beliefs and coordinated plans, which allows the agents to have shared intentions. Furthermore, the agents must be unanimous in their intentions for there to be a shared intention because a deviation on the part of any member means that there is no shared intention for the collective as a whole. Due to this structure, which insists on unanimous intentions, moral responsibility attributions are distributed to all the members because each member intended and acted in pursuit of the common goal for which responsibility is being attributed to the group. (I shall return to this issue of moral responsibility *distribution* in greater detail after I explore the implications for moral responsibility attribution of Tuomela's position.)

- Attributing Moral Responsibility to a Unanimously Intending Collective: Expanding Bratman's view of a shared intention by adding the assumption that all members of a collective are moral agents, we then obtain a collective that unanimously intends to contribute to the collective goal and thus every single member is morally responsible for the event in question.

We may ask, does the above type of collective satisfy the necessary moral agency condition of possessing an ability to intend? An individual intention and a collective intention (in the above sense) are not metaphysically the same because the former is a mental state while the latter is an interrelation of the intending mental states of individuals. However, the collective case is a plurality of the morally relevant individual case. In other words the collective intention consists of a plurality of mental states. The moral agency attributed is in no way distinct from the constituents. It is merely an attribution by virtue of the unity displayed by the constituents who themselves are moral agents. Along the same lines the collective also has autonomy and action abilities as these are abilities of the members who collectively decide to work in concert for the achievement of the event being attributed. But the collective satisfaction of the moral agency conditions is not really surprising as the moral responsibility attribution to the collective essentially amounts to saying "they are morally responsible".

Although Bratman's concept of a shared intention differs slightly from Tuomela's notion of a joint intention I do not believe that it is possible to reformulate Tuomela's account of *corporate* intentions and actions so as to legitimize corporate moral responsibility attributions.

Toumela (2007) does briefly discuss group responsibility but does not explicitly expand his account of corporate intentions (1993) to cover corporate responsibility.[9] When discussing group responsibility the notion of "group ethos" is central. A group ethos consists of the group's "constitutive goals, values, beliefs, standards, norms, etc." (2007: 32). I take it that the group ethos has a similar normatively binding effect among members with regard to group action as the above mentioned authority system. When a group acts on a joint intention (an interrelation of we-intentions) in accord with the group ethos then the group as a whole, every member, is considered to be responsible for the group action.

When trying to expand the account of corporate intentions (1993) to deal with corporate responsibility my main point of disagreement with Tuomela is that his notion of an authority system is not a legitimate system for representing the intentions of non-operative members in order to attribute an intention to the collective whole. Although the intention attribution that Tuomela is willing to give to the corporation is based on the intentions of its members and their interrelations, I do not believe that the corporate intention legitimately represents *all* those members. Firstly, it seems descriptively false to say that non-operative members tacitly accept the intentions and actions of operative members. In what sense does a janitor in a corporation accept the intentions and actions of the operative members? In what sense is the janitor we-intending or accepting a specific we-intention? It may be the case that there are corporations where auxiliary members feel involved to the extent that they share or accept the we-intentions of the operative members, but in general this is surely not the case. The jobs that non-operative members of an organization perform are unrelated to the core pursuit of business. If operative members decide to make a radical change to the product being sold or the way the product is being sold, it will not have any significant implications for the work of the janitor nor

[9]Tuomela (2007: 248–249) does exemplify his account of group responsibility in terms of responsibility in a corporate context. Terminology here is important. Toumela's (1993) account of corporate intentions regarding the attribution of *intentions* to corporations is divorced from his (2007: 248–249) note on *responsibility* in a corporate context. According to him the attribution of intentions to a corporation is not meant to be connected with attributions of moral responsibility (ref. correspondence with the author). It is not clear to me why these notions are disconnected. Because Tuomela's account of group/corporate intentions is fully developed (while his note on responsibility in a corporate context is not) my discussion here explores the attribution of moral responsibility based on his account of corporate intentions (1993).

the administrative accountant. Therefore non-operative members need not and often do not take any interest in the intentions of operative members and therefore it seems false to say that they tacitly accept the intentions and actions of operative members.[10] It can be argued that the non-operative members tacitly accept the intentions of the operative-members as long as they do not protest or cease to be beneficiaries of the organization by leaving the organization. This is an important point to consider for the distribution of moral responsibility (and I shall return to it later), but my point here is merely that tacit acceptance seems to be descriptively false because non-operative members are often not informed about the intentions of operative members (because they do not need to be) and therefore have no basis upon which to accept those intentions, not even tacitly.[11]

Tuomela does however say that non-operative members tacitly accept *or at least ought to tacitly accept* the intentional actions of operative members. French (1991b) performs a similar move when suggesting that the CIDS is not just descriptive but also prescriptive such that it tells corporate members how they *ought* to act. Arnold (2006: 289) uses this to support a view of corporate collective moral agency on the basis that "[e]mployees should have the appropriate intention, and if they do not, they fail to properly represent the corporation". This cannot be right because it renders any (immoral) intentional act by corporate members that is out of step with the prescriptions of the CIDS as a non-corporate act. The consequence of this is that corporations cannot behave immorally (unless that is part of the CIDS), which negates the purpose of constructing a theory advocating the possibility of attributing corporations with moral blame.[12]

Secondly, in what sense are the operative members *representing* the non-operative members? Tuomela likens the system of representation to a pooling of the wills as with Rousseau, which suggests that the intentions of the non-operative members are somehow being represented. For the non-operative members to be represented the operative members must first of all be their representatives. This would suggest that the operative members are in some way elected on a platform of intentions or that the operative members consult with the non-operative members, perhaps even through a voting procedure before they act. This would be

[10]Tuomela's notion of "tacit acceptance" as applied to the non-operative members has nothing to do with approval. In its weakest form it simply amounts to the non-operative members not acting against the operative members. However, on this interpretation of "tacit acceptance" I am puzzled by how, if at all, the operative members are representing the intentions of non-operative members. I shall turn to the problem of representing the intentions of non-operative members below.

[11]Tuomela's (2007) account of group responsibility allows for various circumstance of dissent among members while still maintaining that the group as a whole is responsible. Such dissent also allows for degrees of responsibility among members but Tuomela does not explicate how this is to be done.

[12]In general it is reasonable to assume that corporate members ought to accept decisions made by the corporate leadership less they wish to seek new employment. But this can only count for decisions that members are aware of. No one can be expected to blindly sign off on the intentions of others, and certainly not be held morally responsible for decisions that they had no idea about.

to misconstrue the hierarchy of authority in corporations as being bottom up rather than top down. Non-operative members are simply not operative. Their intentions are not being represented by anyone. Furthermore, there is no need for them to tacitly accept the intentions of operative members because, whether or not they do, it does not influence the pursuit of the operative members.

Most corporations have a top down hierarchy of authority by which those members at the top decide the goals that other members are to be guided by as they contribute their part to the set goals. Only those members whose jobs are affected by these intentions will have to share these intentions (joint intentions) in order to fulfil their obligations towards their employer, but they will not necessarily have participated in the formulation of those intentions.[13]

Nothing crucial hinges on the participation of decision making of members for the forming of collective intentions. The important point for collective intention attribution is that all members actually share the intention. A group may very well share an intention by being told by one member what they should do collectively. The decision procedure in such a case is dictatorial, but if the members accept it then they can all be said to share the intention and thus the group can be attributed with a collective intention.[14] My contention with Tuomela is that he depicts the authority system as a system of representation that would incorporate the intentions of those not involved in the core pursuit of the collective. Because the non-operative members do not share in the joint intention it is not legitimate to attribute an intention to an entire corporate collective. But what if the corporation is a cooperative such that the members get to vote for those who are going to lead the corporation and represent them collectively? I believe that intention attributions to such corporations are legitimate, but under the special circumstance that the voting rule is one of unanimity. Let me explain.

There is an important difference between the vicarious representation of my lawyer acting on my behalf (as a non-free agent) and the representative of my community acting on behalf of the community (as a free agent).[15] Any act done by my lawyer will be in accord with my desires, while I may very well not even have

---

[13]In *The Philosophy of Sociality* Tuomela (2007: 248–249) provides an example of responsibility in a corporate context that is consistent with this view. This brief note maintains that hierarchical authority relations in a corporation hinder distribution of moral responsibility to organizational subordinates because they lack autonomy in relation to their superiors. "[T]hose higher up in the hierarchy are responsible for those lower in the hierarchy" (2007: 248), with shareholders conceived as the highest hierarchical level. Although I concur that seniority in authority relations is significant for decision-making, and thus responsibility attribution, shareholders have no operative authority in corporations. I have chosen to consider moral responsibility in relation to his more developed account of corporate intentions (1993). Please see footnote 9.

[14]I am assuming that corporate members are free from coercion. If a corporate decision method is dictatorial then members are still free to decide whether or not to accept the dictated directives. Non-acceptance of a directive may imply that a person ceases to be a member of the collective, but the person is still free to choose. I concede that due to incentive schemes and group pressures such decisions may not be easy, but acting ethically is not always easy.

[15]See Sect. 4.2 "Free vs. Non-Free Agents" for an explanation of these concepts.

voted for the representative of my community. There is no necessary connection between my intentions and the intentions of the community representative as there is between me and my lawyer. The community representative may get elected through a decision procedure of majority votes. I may consent to the decision process and participate in it by voting, but it does not mean that my intentions are represented by the representative that gets elected. I may accept the system of representation, but I do not necessarily accept the intentions or actions of the representative.[16] I believe (at most) that the community representative only represents those that voted for him, because they are the only ones that have consented to have him represent them.[17] I consent to him having the position of community representative because I consent to the decision process, but he is not *my* representative. He does not represent me if he does not act according to my desires. But as I have said, the decision method does not necessarily determine whether the members share a common intention or not, because independent of how the decisions are made the members may (or may not) accept to act in accordance with them and thus intend them.

The important point of the decision method is the manner in which it can incorporate the intentions of non-operative members who do not have to accept or act in accordance with the collective decisions. If a corporation consists of only operative members then the method by which decisions are made bears little relevance to whether the members share an intention after the decision has been made, because those members who had different intentions must align with the decision in order for there to be a continued sharing of intentions or otherwise cease to be members. An operative member cannot continue to be considered a member of the collective if he pursues goal Z while the rest of the collective intends to realize collective goal X, because it is the pursuit of the same collective goal that binds the members to have a joint intention. However, the non-operative members of a cooperative may very well vote that the collective pursue goal Z (or vote for a representative that intends to pursue goal Z) and yet have no need to align their intention when goal X is enacted instead of Z. This is because the performance of the tasks of non-operative members does not influence the pursuit of the core business. Operative members who act in pursuit of the core business objectives necessarily intend those actions and must thus align their intentions with the goal that is to be pursued collectively, while non-operative members who can only act vicariously through representatives that they did not necessarily vote for do not have to intend the actions performed by operative members.

[16]Public office may involve obligations to an entire group, but that does not imply that the public official represents the entire group as their *agent*. E.g. Hitler's actions did not represent the intentions of all Germans, and all Germans should not be blamed for those actions.

[17]If I vote for a representative who is candidating on a platform of several intentions I need not desire all those intentions if I vote for him. Nonetheless, if he gets elected I have given my explicit consent to having him represent me through his intentions and actions as stated by his election platform. Furthermore, should I not find any of the candidates to my satisfaction I could hand in a "blank" vote, which under a voting system of unanimity would imply my handing in a veto to the intentions on offer.

It is with regard to the incorporation of the intentions of non-operative members into a collective intention that the decision method becomes important. It is only if a corporation has a unanimous voting procedure that we can legitimately attribute a collective intention to the corporation which incorporates all the members. If the decision procedure is not one of unanimity then a collective intention attribution to a corporation will only be legitimately attributable to the subset of members who do have the intention and not to the collective whole. If the representative for my community (A) intends to declare war on the neighbouring community (B) the intention attribution "community A intends to go to war with B" does not represent my intention because I am not an operative member engaged in the pursuit of war and I voted against the declaration of war (but I am still a member of the community).

- The Decision Procedure of a Collective is not per se of Moral Importance: How a collective decision is reached is not important for the attribution of moral responsibility. What is important is if the members intend and act in pursuit of the decision that is made.[18] However, a decision procedure of unanimity guarantees that all members intend to pursue the collective goal and thus moral responsibility attributions to the entire collective are legitimate.[19]

There is however an important moral difference between me and my community representative and the situation of a non-operative member in a corporation. The difference is that I may be unable to leave my community if I disagree with what is being done, while the non-operative member is a beneficiary of the corporation and has the ability to leave the organization if its goals morally disagree with him. The intuition here is that my inability to leave my community in some sense absolves me from being party to the moral responsibility attribution in a manner that is not applicable to the non-operative member. Although the non-operative member may not have intended the event being attributed to the corporation, one can maintain that if the member was informed of the intention to realize the collective type event then he has a duty to stop supporting and benefiting from his membership by dissociating himself from the organization. Non-operative members, although they are not involved in the core pursuit of business, are involved in supporting and aiding that pursuit. If the non-operative member was informed of the joint-intention of the operative members, then he is still not encompassed by the corporate responsibility attribution Y, but is responsible for the separate but related responsibility attribution

[18]A similar point was made earlier (Chap. 5) with regard to Pettit's premise based decision procedure that could lead to a doctrinal paradox. I said that the decision procedure is not per se of moral importance because whether or not a collective decision agrees with an individual member it is the individual that must decide whether or not to enact the decision.

[19]In order for all corporate members (the electorate) to be held morally responsible for the actions of the representatives (operative members), the representatives must be given a very narrow scope of discretion for their actions. This is because they must qualify as the non-free agents of the electorate in order to for the moral responsibility of their actions is to be transferable to the electorate.

X, which is aiding the pursuit of Y.[20] If informed non-operative members do not wish to be held responsible for X they must leave the organization (or alternatively cease to do their job), because if they help the operative members (which usually is the basis for their employment) then they are aiding Y. In this sense *informed* non-operative members tacitly accept the intentions of operative members.

If a non-operative member is informed or not may vary depending on the event which is being attributed to the corporation. However, one thing we can say in general is that any non-operative member that is employed by a producer of a product or service that is itself considered unethical, for example cigarette manufacturing,[21] will be tacitly accepting and thus aiding the core pursuit of the business. This is unavoidable as the non-operative member will inevitably be aware of the overarching collective goal. Nevertheless, many if not most morally blameworthy corporate acts are not inherent to the core pursuit of business, but are more like illegitimate means to a collective end usually pursued by a subset of operative members e.g. bribery, environmental contamination, or foul marketing practices. It seems likely that non-operative members will be unaware of such behaviour because they need not be aware of such behaviour. The same applies to operative members not engaged in pursuit of the immoral event and to that extent it is only the subset of operative members who were involved that have a joint-intention with regard to the collective type event being attributed.

Morally attributing event Y to the corporation implies that there is an individual or group of individuals that is morally responsible for that event. However, as noted above, many others may be responsible for adjacent events, for example X (the aiding of Y). So although it may be the case that many (perhaps at times everyone) is morally responsible for something relating to Y, it is only a subset of the membership that are morally responsible for Y itself, while others members may be morally responsible for something else. For example, the corporation may be attributed with the responsibility for the event Y of "polluting the river". The moral responsibility for this event lodges with the set of operative members who intentionally acted to pollute the river. There may be non-operative members in the corporation, such as secretaries, who are aware of the intention to pollute the river and whose job it is to aid the operative members. Such auxiliary personnel may then be attributed with responsibility for the related event X of "aiding the polluting of the river".

Some people may employ corporate moral responsibility attributions in the sense of merely saying that everyone within that organization is morally responsible for something relating to Y. However, such an attribution is clearly not the same as

[20]If the corporation has a unanimous voting procedure then non-operative members will necessarily be informed of any collective intention as they will have voted for it. In such a case non-operative members will be morally responsible for the collective type event Y.

[21]It has been argued that employees engaged in the tobacco industry earn more than their equivalent counterparts in other industries because this is meant to help soothe the moral discomfort of being engaged in an industry that manufactures and aggressively markets a product that kills its customers.

holding the entire collective responsible for Y, and further there is no guarantee (and often it will not be the case) that everyone within a corporation is responsible for an event relating to Y.

- Non-Operative Members are Not Responsible for the Joint Actions of Operative Members: Operative members generally do not represent the intentions of the collective whole. Furthermore, even if some non-operative members intentionally aid the pursuit of the joint action of the operative members, then they are merely responsible for the separate event of aiding the joint action and not for the event of performing the joint action itself.

Now, can we reformulate Tuomela's position of corporate intentions in order to accommodate moral agency and responsibility attributions as we did with Bratman? As Tuomela's position stands it does not incorporate the intentions of non-operative members because their intentions are not being represented. Therefore, although we can say that each member is a moral agent we cannot say that each member intends an action that is collectively attributed to the corporation. The purposive unity among all the corporate members is lacking with regard to the moral responsibility attribution. Because it is only the operative members that are acting on a joint-intention the collective as a whole does not have an intention that has the same metaphysically relevant property of individual intentions. Although the joint-intention of operative members is an instantiation of a plurality of the morally relevant mental states[22] it is only a subset of the corporation that displays this characteristic, which means that the attribution of an intention to the collective whole casts its net too wide. The morally responsible collective is merely a subset of the corporate membership.

Furthermore, if we are to attribute moral responsibility in a distributive sense to a collective then I believe it is necessary that all those who are members intend the action, which requires that all members are operative members or that there is a decision procedure of unanimity through which non-operative members act vicariously. Unless there is unanimity of intentions among the members in pursuit of realizing the collective goal, the necessary intention condition for moral responsibility attributions is lacking.

- Attributing Moral Responsibility to a Collective Whole: Expanding Tuomela's account of corporate collective action by adding the assumption that all the members are moral agents does not enable the legitimate attribution of moral responsibility to a collective whole. The reason is that the necessary cohesion of intentions among the members with regard to collective goal is lacking. Not everyone in the corporation intended or acted in pursuit of the collective goal. Furthermore, there is no sense in which operative members represent the intentions of non-operative members. Non-operative members are not

[22]I am assuming that there is no morally relevant difference for any given individual to possess a "we-intention" rather than an "I-intention" as both involve the intentional mental state of an individual to purse and take part in a course of action with certain consequences.

participants in the decision process. However, non-operative members who intentionally aid the collective goal are morally responsible for the separate act of aiding, and those who unintentionally aid the collective goal are merely causally responsible for the act of aiding.

References

Arnold, D. 2006. Corporate moral agency. In *Shared intentions and collective responsibility*, ed. P.A. French and H.K. Wettstein. Boston: Blackwell Publishers.

Bratman, M.E. 1987. *Intention, plans, and practical reason*. Cambridge, MA: Harvard University Press.

Bratman, M.E. 1993. Shared intention. *Ethics* 104: 97–113.

French, P.A. 1991a. The corporation as a moral person. In *The spectrum of responsibility*, ed. P.A. French. New York: St. Martin's Press.

French, P.A. 1991b. *Corporate ethics*. Brace: Harcourt.

Gilbert, M. 2000. *Sociality and responsibility*. London: Rowman & Littlefield Publishers.

Tuomela, R. 1993. Corporate intention and corporate action. *Analyse und Kritik* 15: 11–21.

Tuomela, R. 2000. Collective and joint intention. *Mind and Society* 1: 39–69.

Tuomela, R. 2002. *The philosophy of social practices*. Cambridge: Cambridge University Press.

Tuomela, R. 2003. *The We-mode and the I-mode*, from his webpage. http://www.valt.helsinki.fi/staff/tuomela/papers/Midwest_Studies_paper_Tuomela.htm.

Tuomela, R. 2007. *The philosophy of sociality: The shared point of view*. New York: Oxford University Press.

Chapter 9
Conclusion: Legitimate and Illegitimate Corporate Moral Responsibility Attributions

This section aims to summarize and conclude Part I in the form of a taxonomy of legitimate and illegitimate corporate moral responsibility attributions. I believe we can categorise four types of corporate moral responsibility attributions two of which are legitimate and two which are illegitimate with regard to our concept of moral agency and our moral intuition of fairness.

9.1 Moral Responsibility Attribution to a Collective Whole

The diagram below (Fig. 9.1) depicts moral responsibility being attributed to an entire corporate collective of individuals (in accordance with my moral responsibility expansion of Tuomela's 1993 view of corporate intentions). Some of the members (non-operative) neither acted nor intended the event being attributed to the corporate collective. Because the attribution applies to the entire collective those members who are not morally responsible are nevertheless encompassed by the attribution. It may or may not be transparent who the operative members of the untoward event are, but the attribution of moral responsibility is meant to encompass the collective whole.

The meaning of the word "responsibility" has a close connection with the idea of having to defend one's actions and if the defence is unsatisfactory one is then the legitimate subject of punishment. Lewis (1984: 26) writes, "[b]y far the most predominant tendency is to define responsibility in terms of a "liability to answer" and to incur blame or punishment". This suggests that there is an important sense

D. Rönnegard, *The Fallacy of Corporate Moral Agency*,
Issues in Business Ethics 44, DOI 10.1007/978-94-017-9756-6_9

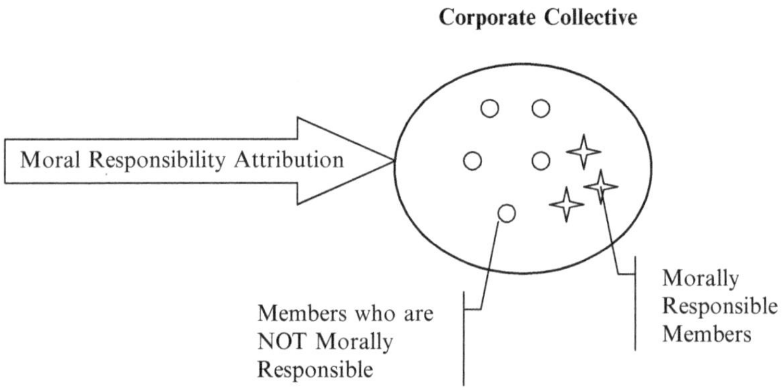

Fig. 9.1 Moral responsibility attribution to a collective whole

in which responsibility ascriptions and punishment go hand in hand; if one is "responsible" then one is "punishable".[1]

To the extent that collective moral responsibility ascriptions to a collective as a whole go hand in hand with collective punishment it becomes clear that whether or not we are willing to grant the legitimacy of such responsibility ascriptions per se, collective punishment is always distributive. Feinberg (1968: 687) has said:

> "One would think that where group-fault is nondistributive, group liability must be so too, else it fall vicariously on the individual members who are faultless. But for all overt unfavorable responses, group-liability is inevitably distributive: what harms a group as a whole necessarily harms its members".

For example if a legal fine is imposed on the corporation this may affect all the members financially. Some may be laid off because of cost cuts while others may forgo bonuses etc.[2] Although collective punishment may have repercussions for all members its direct effect is usually on the financial interests of shareholders who may be as far removed from the morally blameworthy intentions, decisions, and actions as the janitor.

To this extent it becomes clear that a collective responsibility ascription in an undistributive sense is ultimately unfair because it may involve the distribution of liability to the constituents, some of whom are not morally responsible. This is an illegitimate moral responsibility attribution because it goes against our moral intuition of attributing responsibility *only* to those who are morally responsible.

---

[1]The attribution of moral responsibility is not the same as punishment, although the distinction may be negligible when the punishment comes in the form of social stigma.

[2]However the punishment need not be legal. It might be a social sanction in terms of a loss of social status or shunning from the affection of the members of the community.

9.2 Moral Responsibility Attribution to a Corporate Structure

The diagram below (Fig. 9.2) depicts a moral responsibility attribution being ascribed to the corporate entity "itself". This type of corporate moral responsibility attribution corresponds to French's position that the Corporate Internal Decision Structure (CIDS) is the personality of the corporation and possesses moral agency. The CIDS is according to French a proper reference of our moral blame.[3] As I have argued previously the central reason for why this is an illegitimate responsibility ascription is that we are not blaming a moral agent which is a prerequisite for ascribing moral responsibility. A CIDS simply does not possess the relevant autonomy, intention, and action abilities necessary for moral agency.

Our use of language clearly does use corporate names as the subjects upon which we predicate moral responsibility. However, this is a semantic attribution of moral responsibility to corporations. In order to establish that such an attribution refers to a moral agent that is logically distinct from its members requires independent metaphysical argumentation for the possession of the necessary characteristics for moral agency which does not follow from mere semantics. There is simply no vicarious relationship between the corporate entity and its members because the corporation is not a principal in its own right with the relevant ability to have an autonomous intention with which to direct the corporate constituents. The morally relevant sense of an intention is one which the agent is aware of. This

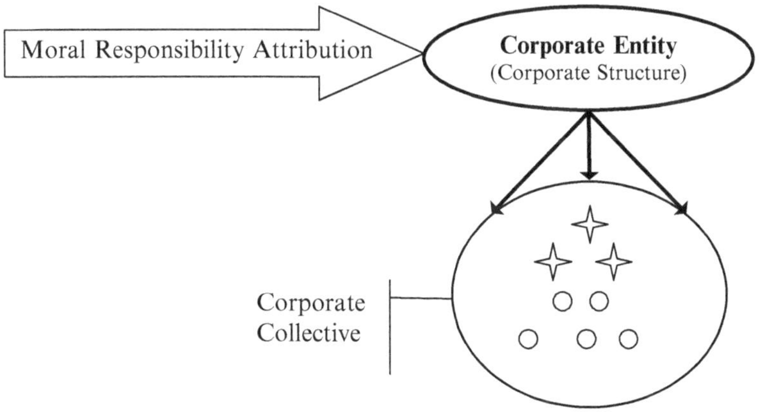

Fig. 9.2 Moral responsibility attribution to a corporate structure

[3]The CIDS, in part, consists of the organization's mission statement, corporate positions, and lines of authority. The CIDS directs and structures the behaviour of members, but the members themselves are not part of the structure. Thus the diagram depicts the corporate structure as sitting on top of and separate from the body of corporate members.

is a property of the intentions of natural people from which the concept of moral agency originates, which suggests that the morally relevant sense of intentions are based on actual mental states rather than a mere functional attribution of such states. The corporation itself does not possess “intrinsic intentionality”. Furthermore, it is useless to attribute moral responsibility to a structure that cannot learn from its mistakes nor appreciate the moral nature of its acts.

French’s position is similar to the manner in which corporations are held *legally* liable for the actions performed by their members. Members act on behalf of the corporation and the corporate legal entity is held liable for their acts. Even if we hypothetically accept the status of the corporation as the principal in a vicarious relationship (type two), then the corporation is still not morally responsible for the acts of its employees; it is merely liable. Moral responsibility is not transferable from autonomous and freely acting members.

9.3 Moral Responsibility Attribution to a Unanimously Intending Collective

The diagram below (Fig. 9.3) shows a corporate moral responsibility attribution being ascribed to a unanimously intending corporate collective. This type of responsibility attribution is in line with my expansion of Bratman’s conception of shared intentions where I add the assumption that all members are moral agents and intend the realization of the collective goal by performing their part. The moral agents are necessarily unanimous because any member who does not share the intention will not be a member of the collective because he is not intending and performing his part in the realization of the collective goal. Unanimity of intentional action can also be achieved if the corporation has a unanimous voting procedure by which the non-operative members act vicariously through the representation of the operative members. This type of moral responsibility attribution is legitimate

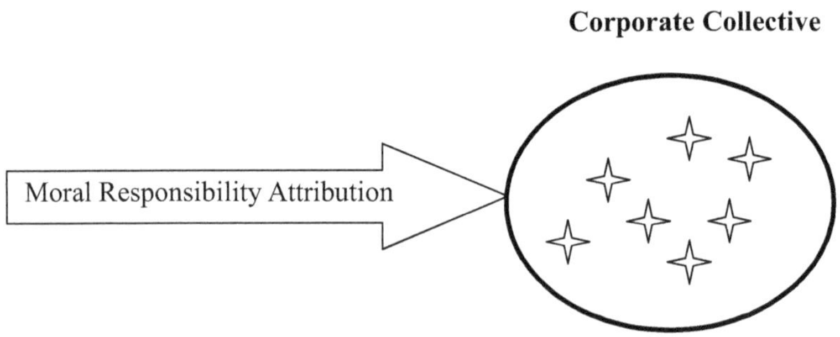

Fig. 9.3 Moral responsibility attribution to a unanimously intending collective

because it ascribes responsibility in a distributive sense to a collective of individuals all of whom intended the collective type event being attributed to the corporation.

The distribution of moral responsibility to the collective is prima facie an equal distribution to each and every member in the sense that each member is equally morally responsible. Michael Zimmerman (1991: 276) says that when we speak of sharing responsibility such talk can often be misleading because it seems "to suggest that the responsibility of each person involved in a group action (or omission) is diminished simply by virtue of the fact that others are also involved and are responsible". There is no prima facie reason why moral responsibility for a group action must sum to one. To believe that that is the case would be to confuse causal with moral responsibility ascriptions; the causes of an event must sum to one (if we disregard over and under-determination), but there is no need for contributions of moral responsibility to sum to one. By equal distribution to each and every member I do not then mean that each member is attributed an equal share of the responsibility; I mean that each member obtains the same amount of responsibility, i.e. each member is fully morally responsible for the event. The reason is that each member intended and acted (some acted perhaps vicariously)[4] in the realization of the collective goal. The action of each member does not need to be a necessary action for the realization of the collective goal, but each member must intend the collective goal.[5]

From the point of view of distributing moral blame there is little difference if each member would have acted to realize the same goal alone or if the members acted collectively. The members have simply chosen to act collectively either to simplify the realization of the goal or because it was not possible to achieve the result alone. Although prima facie the distribution of responsibility is an equal distribution, I also believe that there is some room for judging the wrongfulness of the contributions of the individual agents. Every member is morally responsible for the attributed event Y, but the degree of responsibility may vary. For example, there might be mitigating circumstances for those who argue against the action but go along anyway due to social pressure, or those who had the intention based on erroneous belief etc.

The corporation on this conception, being merely an organized collective of moral agents, does not obtain any moral duties distinguishable from those which the moral agents have as individuals. Moral prescriptions that govern what ought and ought not to be done do not differ for corporations. The moral evaluation of

[4]A decision method of unanimity implies that each member has a veto. Therefore the vote of each member is necessary for the realization of the collective goal.

[5]The actions of non-operative members are not necessary for the realization of the collective goal, but their intention which they contribute though their vote is. It is the operative members that act but the action of each and every operative member need not be necessary for the realization of the collective goal, but may merely facilitate the bringing about of the collective goal. For example if the goal is to push a boulder down a hill only five members may be needed but ten perform the act to make it easier.

the collective action does not differ from if it were done by a single moral agent.[6] We may attribute moral agency and moral responsibility to such an organized collective of moral agents because each and every member fulfils the intention, action and autonomy abilities with regard to the collective action being attributed. There is however no "group moral agent" literally speaking; there is no super-agent over and above the group members. The attribution of moral agency to the corporation may be considered just a short-hand for saying that there is unanimity in the group of moral agents with regard to what they intend together and that they are committed to contributing their part to the realization of the intention. As such a moral responsibility attribution can be ascribed to the group as whole in a distributive sense and it is not unfair to hold all members morally responsible.

What kinds of corporation would qualify for this type of legitimate moral responsibility attribution?[7] The conditions we have seen are that the corporation either only has operative members who all share an intention and perform their part in realizing the collective goal, or they also have non-operative members but these must be represented through a unanimous decision procedure. Without having performed a comprehensive empirical survey over the kinds of corporate structures that exist, I believe that few corporations would qualify that have non-operative members. Corporate authority structures are usually top down rather than bottom up because this is a more efficient manner to direct a large number of individuals in the pursuit of a common goal and thus a voting rule of unanimity that includes non-operative members seems out of the question. Even cooperatives which are bottom up would not opt for a decision procedure of unanimity because this would generally lead to no decisions being made. Therefore realistically we are left with such corporations that consist only of operative members. This will generally imply a restriction on the size of such corporations, because auxiliary personnel are generally required for larger organizations to function efficiently. I imagine that small family businesses or small professional firms such as law firms are typically the kind of corporation that will qualify for this type of corporate moral responsibility attribution.

[6]It might be argued that a structured collective of individuals may have a duty which a single individual may not have. A prerequisite for the validity of moral prescriptions is that an agent is able to perform the prescription. "Ought" implies "can". It may be the case that there is a moral prescription that cannot be realized by a single moral agent in a given situation, but could be realized by a group of people. In such a situation the organized collective of individuals may be considered to have a duty to perform the prescribed act which a single individual would not otherwise have. The duty then applies to each member of the collective (and not to the separate corporate entity).

[7]Technically this type of entity could not be called a "corporation" because the voting rules for incorporated companies are constrained by law and a rule of unanimity would not be allowed.

9.4 Elliptical Moral Responsibility Attribution to a Collective Whole

The diagram below (Fig. 9.4) represents an elliptical moral responsibility attribution being ascribed to a corporation in a distributive sense, but we abstain from distributing blame due to transparency difficulties. This position is much in line with Velasquez's (1983) views. The responsibility ascription is not literally meant to be attributed to the collective whole of individuals, but due to a lack of insight into the dealings of the corporation we use the corporate name when attributing moral responsibility as an elliptical way of referring to those members who are morally responsible.

The action for which the corporation is being held responsible is one that is done by some subset of members in their roles working on behalf of the corporation and not in pursuit of individual goals. Those responsible will be operative members of the firm but not necessarily all operative members. The blameworthy event attributed will be consistent with the collective goal of the operative members (e.g. to profit maximise within the financial services industry), but need not be a goal that is intended or pursued by all operative members.[8] The blameworthy event will be more of an immoral means of realising the collective goal of the corporation than a goal in itself, e.g. dumping chemical waste in the river to reduce costs and increase profits. If we are elliptically attributing moral responsibility to the Example Corporation for polluting the river we are then elliptically referring to the set of operative members who intentionally caused the event. One must believe that someone did what they did on behalf of the corporation, and not in their own private capacity, in order to legitimately use the corporate name as the subject of one's moral responsibility attribution for the purpose of elliptically referring to their

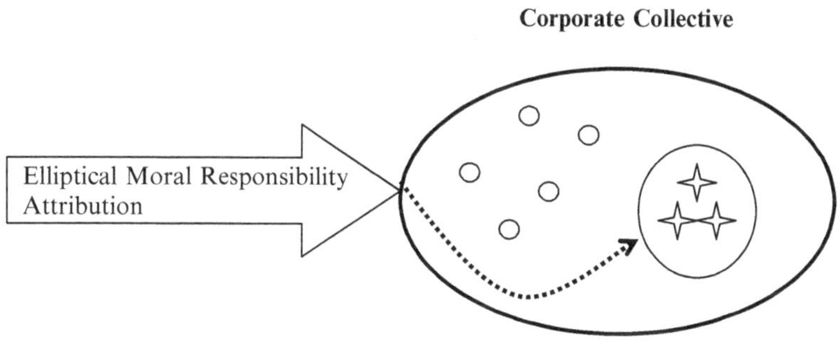

Fig. 9.4 Elliptical moral responsibility attribution to a collective whole

[8]In the case of attributing negligence to the corporation the event will be inconsistent with the corporate goal (because no corporation has a goal to do harm per se), but one must believe that someone in the organization had a duty to prevent the event being attributed.

wrongdoing. This belief is necessary otherwise there is no reason to believe that someone within the corporation is responsible for the event being attributed and there would be no connection between the moral responsibility attribution and the corporation.

An elliptical moral responsibility attribution is legitimate because it is consistent with our moral intuition of only ascribing responsibility to those who are morally responsible. There is no need to attribute moral agency to the corporate collective for the purpose of such a moral responsibility attribution because the attribution is not meant to apply to the group as a whole. The attribution of moral responsibility to the corporation is merely instrumental and carries with it no attribution of metaphysical characteristics for moral agency. Furthermore, it is not legitimate to connect any form of punishment to an elliptical moral responsibility attribution because that would amount to a collective punishment which unfairly affects those who are not responsible. The distribution of responsibility can only come once the corporate veil has been penetrated and we can identify those with whom the wrongful act resides. The corporate structure is instrumental in determining how responsibility is distributed both with respect to identifying those who are responsible and the degree of their responsibility. All those who intended and acted in pursuit of the goal will be fully morally responsible for the event. It may also be the case that we assign moral blame to a member who has a duty to prevent the type of act in question (perhaps because of his position of authority) but did not take action to prevent the act. The structure is instrumental in determining his degree of responsibility by identifying the extent to which he could have known about the intention to perform the act and the degree of influence he could have had to prevent the act.

An elliptical moral responsibility attribution to a collective whole will not only be appropriate for suspected intentional acts but also for negligence if we do not know who has been negligent. Often it will be the role responsibility of a corporate member to prevent a certain type of event from happening. For example, imagine that the produce from a dairy plant unintentionally get contaminated and as outsiders we do not know who is responsible.[9] We might believe that there is someone who has the position of "product safety officer" at the dairy plant that has a positive duty to make sure that equipment is regularly checked and maintained so as not to cause contamination of the dairy products. We might then make an elliptical corporate moral responsibility attribution of negligence until we can identify the responsible member or set of members. Attributions of negligence will tend to be of an elliptical form, because they will tend to lodge with only a subset of members. For example it would seem a bit strange if we attributed negligence to a unanimously intending collective, because we would have to say that the entire collective had a duty to intentionally perform X in order to avoid Y. But organizationally the types of events

[9]We will not know that the contamination is unintentional, but if we are to elliptically attribute negligence to the corporation we must assume that it was unintentional. Such an assumption may be justified because the occurrence of the event of contaminating the dairy products would generally not be consistent with the corporate agenda.

that one aims to *prevent* are usually assigned to roles having to do with safety rather than being something that the collective as a whole has a goal to pursue.

This concludes my discussion on the moral status of the corporation and the legitimacy of corporate moral responsibility attributions. Having rejected that the corporation qualifies as a moral agent we can say that a moral responsibility attribution to a corporation itself (or a collective whole) is not legitimate. The corporation's lack of moral agency implies that it is not an end in itself. Only that which possesses intrinsic intentionality can be an end in itself. The corporation does not choose its own ends and we may thus ask for what instrumental ends do we create corporations? More generally we may ask, what is the purpose of the corporate legal form in our society? In Part II I shall explore the role of the corporation in society where I shall in part argue that the status of the corporation is primarily as a *legal* entity rather than the *moral* status we have so far been considering. I will come to suggest that the state ought to primarily enact in law the responsibilities its citizens want corporations to be held accountable for.

References

Feinberg, J. 1968. Collective responsibility. *Journal of Philosophy* 65: 674–688.

Lewis, H.D. 1984. Collective responsibility. *Philosophy* 24: 3–18.

Velasquez, Manuel G. 1983. Why corporations are not morally responsible for anything they do. *Business and Professional Ethics Journal* 2: 1–18.

Zimmerman, M.J. 1991. Sharing responsibility. In *The spectrum of responsibility*, ed. P.A. French. New York: St. Martin's Press.

Part II
The Role of the Corporation in Society

This part takes as its premise the conclusion from Part I, namely that the corporation is not a moral agent. The first section of this part is titled: "The Role of the Corporation in Society: The Descriptive View". This section aims to show that the corporation *is* primarily a legal agent; a creation and manifestation of law. I explore the development of the corporate legal form in the English and American common law systems, which parallel the economic growth of the corporation as a dominant institution in society. In this context we get a chance to survey the influence of the legal debate over the nature of the corporation, which overlaps with the metaphysical debate over corporate moral agency. By exploring the development of the corporate legal form together with the economic effects of legislation we obtain a *description* of the role of the corporation in society. I maintain that corporations are primarily legal agents and that the *role* of the corporate legal form serves as an instrument to further the socio-economic ends of the state, while the *goal* of actual corporations is to be instruments to further the ends of the incorporating parties.

Having analysed the *descriptive* role of the corporate legal form the second section, which is titled: "The Role of the Corporation in Society: The Prescriptive View", aims to explore what role the corporation *ought* to have in society. First, I consider if the corporate legal form ought to be used as an instrument of the state and secondly whether actual corporations ought to primarily be the instruments of the incorporators. That is to say, given that the corporation is a legal instrument, to what use should this instrument be put? I defend the normative assumptions that underlie the use of the corporate legal form as a socio-economic instrument against libertarian objections based on absolute property rights of shareholders.

Having argued that the libertarian position based on absolute property rights is weak and having concluded that the corporate legal form ought to be an instrument of the state, I then explore whether actual corporations ought to primarily serve the interests of incorporators. This will involve a collision between Shareholder Theory and the moral prescriptions of the Corporate Social Responsibility movement. I argue in favour of an idealized version of Shareholder Theory whereby stakeholder concerns are explicitly accounted for in legislation. I maintain that the prescriptions of CSR are difficult to uphold without an illegitimate reliance on corporate moral agency. I suggest that the issues that CSR wishes to tackle are better addressed through public initiatives and legal enactments by governments.

Finally, I discuss the division of role responsibilities between the state and private corporations. I come to suggest that the public/private divide falls neatly into the distinction between the corporate legal form on the one hand and actual corporations on the other hand. In other words the public realm consists of the corporate legal form, the *role* of which is regulated by the state, while the private realm consists of actual corporations that are free to decide on the best means to realize their private *goals* within the boundaries of the law. I also maintain that the market is a zone of moral exception where it is acceptable to act purely out of self-interest while playing within the rules of the law. In fact the underlying market justifications of competition and efficiency demand this zone of moral exception.

The normative force of my argument is that society should primarily enact in *law* the responsibilities it wants corporate *legal* entities to be held accountable for in accordance with citizen's normative preferences. Actual corporations can then pursue the interests of incorporators within the constraints of the law.

The structure of the argument is as follows: The corporation is not a moral agent. Because the corporation is not a moral agent it is not an end in itself with moral rights that we need to take into consideration. The corporate form is as a matter of description a legal fiction created by the state that has a role to further its socio-economic ends. In a democracy the ends of the state are a reflection of the desires of its citizens. Legislation is the primary means by which the state manifests the public's preferences regarding public policy; thus if the public desires that corporate legal entities behave in a certain manner then the state ought to enact legislation that regulates corporate behaviour in such a manner. Actual corporations can then focus on pursuing the goals for which they were created under the constraints of the law while contributing to social welfare as a producers, employers, and tax payers.

Chapter 10
The Role of the Corporation in Society: The Descriptive View

The aim of this section is primarily descriptive in order to show that the corporate form is a legal creation of the state to serve the socio-economic goals of government. I shall look at the development of the corporate legal form from the first companies granted Royal Charter in the fifteenth century to the modern corporate legal form of today. The legal and economic development of the corporation reflects the role it has played in society and helps us understand the role the corporation plays in our society today. Interestingly, the evolution of corporate law is paralleled by a legal debate over the nature of the corporation which is reminiscent of the debate over corporate moral agency. The legal debate is primarily between three different positions; those who regard the corporation as a legal fiction, those who regard it as a nexus-of-contracts, and those who regard it as a real entity in a metaphysical sense. The influence of this debate on legislation shows the practical importance of the metaphysical status that we deem the corporation to have. I will be defending the view of the corporation as a legal fiction against both the views of the corporation as a nexus-of-contracts and the corporation conceived as a real entity.

This section shall look at the origins of the corporate legal form and the development of four of the most important and distinguishing legal features of the modern corporate form. These features are the shareholder primacy norm, the separation of shareholders from the corporation, the transferability of corporate shares, and finally the limited liability of shareholders (Kraakman et al. 2004).

This section will be focusing on the legal development of the corporate form primarily in English law because the modern corporate form is by and large an English development. I will also to some degree be looking at the development of American corporate law because the US adopted the English law of corporations without change at the end of the American Revolution (1784). American law also provides important legal developments that contribute to the legal fiction vs. real entity debate and the eventual legal reification of the corporation into a legal person.

D. Rönnegard, *The Fallacy of Corporate Moral Agency*,
Issues in Business Ethics 44, DOI 10.1007/978-94-017-9756-6_10

10.1 The First Corporations

The first corporations were craft guilds and trading companies to which the English crown granted Royal Charters in the fifteenth century (Blumberg 1993). The chartering of a company was known as "incorporation" because it united the members into one body under the charter. The monarch would call upon a guild or company to perform a public task, such as building a bridge, and would grant it a Royal Charter throughout the duration of the task. The granting of Royal Charter often carried with it several privileges that were written in the charter for each company. These privileges were granted because the corporation was thought to be contributing to the public good and because it sometimes assumed public responsibilities as part of its operations. For example a charter could confer the privilege of monopoly status stating that company X had the sole right to trade goods Y in territory Z. A legendary example is the English East India Company which was granted Royal Charter in 1600 to trade in the East Indies and eventually ended up governing large parts of India. A Royal Charter often brought with it the benefit of transferable shares and limited liability. This was in contrast with partnerships that did not allow the free transfer of one's stake in the company and held each partner legally liable to the full extent of their wealth.

With the growth in power of the English Parliament (in relation to the monarch) it eventually also became possible to obtain a charter through a Special Act of Parliament, which essentially could confer the same rights and privileges as a Royal Charter. It is however important to point out that Royal Charters and charters through a Special Act of Parliament were by no means commonplace. During the entire eighteenth century there were only about a dozen charters issued for corporations in England (Blumberg 1993).

Joint stock companies emerged in the sixteenth century as a form of partnership,[1] but started growing in numbers in the eighteenth century when charters were exceptionally difficult to come by. Up until the eighteenth century and for much of the nineteenth century the term "company" was used as an abridgement of "joint stock company" and denoted an association of a particular economic type rather than a particular legal status (Ireland 1996). Griffiths and Taylors (1949: 3) write: "These companies were treated in law as partnerships, and whilst the capital holdings of the members was transferable, their liability for the debts of the company was unlimited". In the eighteenth century joint stock companies were the type of association that would usually seek a charter, but they were unpopular because they were often associated with fraud and consequently few charters were granted.

It is important to point out that English corporation law and English company law (the law applicable to Joint Stock Companies) were separate legal domains towards the end of the eighteenth century. As mentioned, Joint Stock Companies

[1] In 1688 there were only 15 joint stock companies in England.

were unincorporated associations and were treated legally as a form of partnerships. However, because incorporation was so rarely granted, Joint Stock Companies became the common mode of economic association, which consequently led to modern English business law developing as company law rather than corporate law (Blumberg 1993). As we shall see the Company Acts that were made between 1844 and 1862 laid down the fundamental pillars of the modern corporation as we know it today and it was done as a legal augmentation of the Joint Stock Company (not the chartered corporation).[2] For one, the 1844 Joint Stock Companies Act provided for general articles of incorporation, which meant that any association of individuals could now become incorporated by a simple act of registration, eliminating the need for a Royal Charter or a Special Act of Parliament. Nowadays virtually all UK enterprises are incorporated by registration under the Companies Acts and generally one would assume that the layman's use of the term "corporation" is a reference to such a registered entity. One should note that corporations that are created by Royal Charter or a Special Act of Parliament are not subject to the provisions of the Companies Acts, although the rights and duties governing such corporations are often similar in content. The 1844 Joint Stock Companies Act says "this Act shall not extend to any Company incorporated or which may hereafter [be] incorporated by Statute or Charter".

Although there have been several influential corporations pre nineteenth century, there were not very many and they did not have the all-pervasive economic and social influence that they have in most of our societies today. The big rise of the corporation started with the Industrial Revolution in England at the end of the eighteenth century. As we shall see, the Industrial Revolution sparked a demand to start Joint Stock Companies and the growth of these companies in turn created pressure to augment the legislation governing such companies resulting in a succession of Companies Acts between 1844 and 1862.

Before we go on to follow the economic and legal development of the Companies Acts we shall briefly look at the positions in the legal debate over the nature of the corporation that will later help us explicate the motivations for legislation reform.

10.2 The Legal Debate About the Nature of the Corporation

There are three main theories in law about the nature of the corporation that have come in and out of fashion depending on legal and economic developments. These are called the Legal Fiction Theory, the Nexus-of-Contracts Theory, and the Real Entity Theory. These theories have no official standing in law, but they have been used time and again to justify court rulings.

[2]The Acts between 1844 and 1856 are generally referred to as the "Joint Stock Companies Acts" while the 1862 Companies Act and onwards are referred to as the "Companies Acts". When referring to the Acts collectively, both prior and after 1862, I will simply be using the term "Companies Acts".

The Legal Fiction Theory essentially says that the corporation is merely an abstract creation of law, which is granted to an association of individuals. The corporation is an artificial legal entity with an existence distinct from the incorporating members and it exists entirely at the discretion of the state. When Chief Justice Marshall delivered the opinion of the court in the 1819 case of Dartmouth College v. Woodward (17 U.S. 518), he delivered perhaps the most famous articulation of the Legal Fiction Theory. He said:

> "A corporation is an artificial being, invisible, intangible, and existing only in contemplation of law. Being the mere creature of law, it possesses only those properties which the charter of its creation confers upon it either expressly or as incidental to its very existence. These are such as are supposed best calculated to effect the object for which it was created . . . The objects for which a corporation is created are universally such as the government wishes to promote. They are deemed beneficial to the country, and this benefit constitutes the consideration, and in most cases, the sole consideration of the grant".

The Legal Fiction Theory was dominant during the early eighteenth century, especially considering that incorporation was only possible through a grant from the state (or the monarch) that usually limited them to a purpose of a public nature. For this reason the Legal Fiction Theory is closely associated with the Concession Theory which focuses on the idea that the corporation is a grant from the state.

The dominance of the Legal Fiction Theory faded after the introduction of general incorporation statutes towards the mid-nineteenth century in England and America. General incorporation statutes established a procedure for creating corporations, which seemed to reduce the importance of the state in granting incorporation. Michael Phillips (1994: 1065) says: "As a result, during the latter part of the nineteenth century some theorists began to use partnerships analogies to describe the corporation, thereby characterizing it as an aggregate formed by private contracting among its human parts". This development led to what has come to be known as the Nexus-of-Contracts Theory, which essentially characterises the corporation *as if* it were a web of interrelating private contracts among all the members of the corporation. Advocates of this theory often have Libertarian leanings and promote the theory as part of their belief in inviolable private property rights and the unrestricted freedom of individuals to consensually contract with one another. Although Nexus-of-Contracts advocates realize that all corporations are incorporated either under general incorporation statutes or as a grant from the state/monarch, they regard the process of incorporation as a shorthand way of obtaining a contractual situation that otherwise could and would be achieved through the private contracting of individuals. This theory stands in stark contrast with the Legal Fiction Theory that characterises the corporate legal form as essentially a concession from the state.

The Real Entity Theory first started appearing at the end of the nineteenth century when the German legal theorist Otto von Gierke published his organic theory of the corporate personality in 1887. He argued that the corporation and group activity in general was "real". The main tenet of the Real Entity Theory is that corporations are real, naturally occurring beings, with characteristics that are distinct from their individual members. Adherents maintain that corporations are social organisms that possess a will and a life of their own and therefore may be the proper subject of moral and legal rights as much as natural persons. Similar to the Nexus-of-Contracts theory, the Real Entity Theory rejects the notion that the corporation is a creation or grant from the state. However, for the Real Entity Theory those rights are not derived from the rights of the individual members, but are owed to the corporation itself as a separate organism. Advocates of this view often maintain that the corporation ought to be granted the same legal rights as natural persons by virtue of having similar capacities.

It is easy to see how this legal debate over the nature of the corporation parallels the metaphysical debate over corporate moral agency in Part I. The Real Entity Theory shares similarities with Peter French's advocacy of corporate moral agency. For instance, both views regard the corporate entity itself as possessing metaphysical capacities of agency that are separate from the corporate members. Both views regard these capacities as being sufficient to give rise to rights and duties. French's corporate moral agency view regards these capacities as giving rise to *moral* rights and duties, while the Real Entity Theory regards the capacities primarily as a justification for conferring *legal* rights and duties.

The Nexus-of-Contracts Theory shares similarities with the moral individualist position that denies that corporations or collectives have the relevant characteristics that would qualify them as moral agents. The theory regards the corporation as an aggregate web of contracts with all members. Like the position of moral individualism, any rights or duties that ought to be attributed to the collective are so conferred only by virtue of the capacities and actions of the individual members.

Finally, the Legal Fiction Theory is compatible with both of the above views simply because it does not make any metaphysical commitments. The Legal Fiction Theory is a manifestation of legal positivism, which maintains that the law is merely a man-made artefact. The Legal Fiction Theory has nothing to say about the metaphysical characteristics of natural persons or collectives. It merely maintains that mankind may create (through the proper legal procedures) any type of legal entity and confer upon it whatever rights and duties it desires. A legal personality, whether attributable to a human agent or a corporation, "is an artifact of legal rules, not human evolution. In this sense, all legal persons are artificial" (Cane 2002: 147). Marmor (2004) explains that for the legal positivist the conditions of legal validity are determined by social facts, for example an act of legislation or a judicial decision. The legal positivists also maintain that "there is a conceptual separation between law and morality, that is, between what the law is, and what it ought to be" (Marmor 2004: 42). Nevertheless, that is not to deny that moral justifications may often influence the content of the law.

Having explicated the main legal theories concerning the nature of the corporation, I shall now look at the economic and legal development of the corporation, with special focus on the Company Acts 1844–62 in England. I will specifically be looking at the emergence of some of the most distinguishing legal features of the modern corporate form. I shall look at the development of the shareholder primacy norm, the separation of shareholders from the corporation, the transferability of corporate shares and last, but by no means least, the limited liability of shareholders.

These legal developments occurred in step with economic developments that will help us understand the economic effects of legislation as well as the socio-economic role the corporation plays in society.

10.3 The Shareholder Primacy Norm

Corporate law says that directors have a fiduciary duty to make decisions on behalf of the corporation that further the interests of the shareholders. This part of a director's fiduciary duty is usually referred to as the shareholder primacy norm. The term "fiduciary" comes from the Latin "fiducia" meaning "trust". A fiduciary duty used to only be attributed to trustees who held legal title over some property and administered it for a beneficiary. Directors do not hold any legal title over the corporation, however "during the early nineteenth century the Chancery Court extended the fiduciary duties it had imposed on trustees to other persons who acted in a representative capacity, such as agents and directors of companies. The extension was by analogy and the court referred to these persons as "trustee"" (Pennington 1987: 34).

The shareholder primacy norm was implicitly active in the 1844 Joint Stock Companies Act,[3] but was operative in the courts considerably prior to then. For example, Gordon Smith writes with regard to American law: "Although creation of the shareholder primacy norm did not occur until the 1830's... the ground work for adoption of the norm was laid well before that time" (Smith 1998: 304).

[3]The Joint Stock Companies Act of the 5th of September 1844 is formally known as "An Act for the Registration, Incorporation, and Regulation of Joint Stock Companies". The Act does not explicitly refer to the primacy of the interests of shareholders but it does make certain provisions that together amount to the same: Firstly, section 25, says that the company is only empowered to pursue aims for which it was formed (ultra vires doctrine). Secondly, section 25 also says that the shareholders have unlimited liability; the shareholder shall "be and continue liable as he would have been if the said Company had not been incorporated". Section 28 says that the company director must "hold in his own Right at least One Share in the Capital of the Company". Section 29 says that the director must not have any personal interest in company contracts or else "be precluded from voting or otherwise acting as a Director". These four points in concert amount to prescribing that the efforts of directors and in turn the corporate members are to be primarily directed to satisfying the interests of the shareholders. The fact that the director must be a shareholder implies that the director is in part working in his own interest when he is working for the shareholders. Furthermore, he will be careful not to incur excessive debt in his decision making because all his personal assets, as well as the assets of other shareholders, are accessible in the event of bankruptcy due to unlimited liability. Furthermore, the director may not enter into contracts where he has a personal interest that prevents him from making decisions that are of personal benefit rather than benefit the shareholders as a whole. Finally, the doctrine of ultra vires implies that the director cannot enter the company into legally binding contracts that are not in accord with the purpose for which the incorporators created the company. These restrictions on the company director protect the interests of shareholders and implicitly keep the company focused on satisfying shareholder interests.

The shareholder primacy norm (SPN) says nothing with regard to the content of a director's fiduciary duty; it merely points out who is meant to be the beneficiary of the duty. The fiduciary duty of the director is to act in good faith for the benefit of all shareholders. This is a general duty, but in particular it requires directors not to put themselves into a position where their duty to the company and their own personal interests conflict. An example would be if a director stood to benefit directly from a contract entered into by the company. Another important part of the fiduciary duty is for directors not to exceed the powers of authority conferred upon them. Such a transgression is called ultra vires (Latin meaning: "beyond [their] power"), and directors may be held liable for any loss that the corporation incurs as a consequence of their transgression.

The shareholder primacy norm has become of contemporary importance due to the flourishing advocacy of Corporate Social Responsibility (CSR). Many CSR advocates regard the shareholder primacy norm as one of the biggest obstacles hindering directors and managers from considering the interests of other corporate stakeholders besides shareholders (Boatright 1994; Campbell 2007; Dodd 1932; Evan and Freeman 2003; Hinkley 2002; Phillips et al. 2003; Testy 2002). They argue that corporate managers are legally bound not to consider the interests of stakeholders such as employees, customers, or society at large, if those interests conflict with the interests of shareholders. Such a norm would among other things rule out philanthropic donations that cannot be shown to contribute to the corporation's bottom line. For most of the nineteenth and twentieth century this analysis was probably correct. Nowadays, as we shall see, in practice corporate directors and managers have a considerable discretion as to how they use corporate funds.

Today when most people think of the shareholder primacy norm they think of it as a norm to the benefit of shareholders at the expense of everyone else. Conflicts of interest between shareholders and other stakeholders may be called "horizontal conflicts" and are the type of conflicts that are the main concern for the advocates of CSR.[4] However, the shareholder primacy norm did not evolve out of horizontal conflicts of interest but out of minority oppression cases, i.e. cases where a shareholder majority tries to force a corporate decision at the expense of (or contrary to the desires of) a minority. One of the most famous articulations of the norm comes from the minority oppression case Dodge v. Ford Motor Co in 1919. Henry Ford was a majority shareholder and wanted to force the Dodge brothers to sell him their share of the company. To this end Ford, who was also the director of the company, refused to pay any dividends on the company's shares saying that he would reinvest all the profits back into the corporation. This is a classic "squeeze-out technique". In delivering the opinion of the court (in favour of the Dodge Brothers) Chief Justice Ostrander (170 N.W. 668) said:

> "A business corporation is organized and carried on primarily for the profit of the stockholders. The powers of the directors are to be employed for that end. The discretion

[4]Conflicts of interest between managers and the corporation have been dubbed "vertical conflicts" and are the main concern of principal-agent conflicts as part of corporate governance.

of directors is to be exercised in the choice of means to attain that end, and does not extend to a change in the end itself, to the reduction of profits, or to the non-distribution of profits among shareholders in order to devote them to other purposes".

This articulation of the shareholder primacy norm shows that directors and managers have an obligation to further the interests of *all* shareholders, and that their interest is assumed to be profit. The shareholder primacy norm was not initially intended to be a norm conferring primary importance to the interest of shareholders versus other stakeholders, but rather to confer equal rights to all shareholders. However, the norm has important implications for horizontal conflicts of interest because the fiduciary duty to primarily pursue corporate profits, which makes all shareholders claims equal, has the consequence of juxtaposing the interests of shareholders with everyone else.

Dodge v. Ford is often cited by advocates of shareholder primacy. However, Lynn Stout (2012) suggests that it is widely misunderstood. First, it is not a case about a public corporation: "It was a case about the duty a controlling majority shareholder (Henry Ford) owed to the minority shareholders (Horace and John Dodge) in what was functionally a closely held company—a different legal animal altogether" (Stout 2012: 26). Second, Justice Ostrander's remark was just that; as Stout (2012: 26) observes: "This remark . . . was what lawyers call "mere dicta"—a tangential observation that the Michigan Supreme Court made in passing, that was unnecessary to reach the court's chosen outcome or "holding". It is holdings that matter in law and create binding precedent for future cases."

In principle it would seem that the shareholder primacy norm significantly restricts directors' efforts to furthering the interests of other stakeholders. However, Gordon Smith (1998: 280) says that the "application of the shareholder primacy norm to publicly traded corporations is muted by the business judgement rule". The business judgement rule is the presumption that directors have not breached their duty of care, i.e. that they have acted in good faith when exercising their abilities to further the interests of the company as a whole. The rule is called the "business judgement rule" because it relieves the court of any duty to make evaluations of the business judgement of a director.[5] For example, if the board of directors decide to donate a million pounds of corporate resources to the Tsunami Relief Fund of the Red Cross, shareholders may try to sue the directors personally for breaching the shareholder primacy norm; that is to say for using corporate funds in a manner that does not further shareholder interests. But the business judgment rule relieves

[5]A consequence of the business judgment rule is that directors' fiduciary duty becomes a negative duty to not act in bad faith. The fiduciary duty of directors seems at first glance to be a positive duty to pursue the interest of shareholders. However, courts do not sanction directors for not pursuing profitable opportunities that are open to the company, but rather for acting in bad faith with regard to the opportunities they do pursue. The courts quite rightly find that it is not their place to make judgments about the merits of directors' business strategies; that issue is up to the market and the shareholders to decide. (Directors may however be held legally liable for negligence for the losses incurred by the corporation if they are found to breach their duty of care, i.e. a breach of a positive duty to avoid harm to the corporation.)

the court from considering whether or not a one million pound donation to the Red Cross is a good business decision (it may be depending on the publicity spin that results), and instead only considers if the director exercised his abilities in good faith to further the interest of shareholders.

Many decisions in business do not have direct economic returns, for example philanthropic donations or improved working conditions for employees. Such decisions can usually be rationalized as having indirect benefits such as improved brand image or employee productivity and thus they may well be in the interest of shareholders. With the business judgement rule in place it becomes incredibly difficult for a judge to evaluate if a director acted in bad faith. A decision may have a large direct cost for a corporation, but whether or not it was indirectly profitable may be difficult to measure. Moreover, even if it is determined that the decision was not profitable it is very difficult to evaluate if the decision was made in bad faith, because most business decisions can be rationalized to seem reasonable at the time they were made. Gordon Smith (1998: 288) writes: "Although it is possible for shareholders to prevail on claims that the board of directors violated the shareholder primacy norm, such cases are extremely rare".

Stout (2012: 30) suggests that the 1986 case, Revlon, Inc. v. MacAndrews & Forbes Holdings, is the only significant modern case "where a Delaware court has held an unconflicted Board of Directors liable for failing to maximize shareholder value". But she adds that this case ruling, while often cited by advocates of shareholder wealth maximization along with Dodge v. Ford, is also misunderstood, and is the exception that proves the rule. Revlon's Board planned to take Revlon private, thus "it is only when a public corporation is about to stop being a public corporation that directors lose the protection of the business judgment rule and must embrace shareholder wealth as their only goal" (Stout 2012: 31). In contrast, Stout cites the 2011 case of Air Products, Inc. v. Airgas, Inc., wherein the Delaware court ruled in favour of the Airgas board of directors, which had refused a takeover offer from Air Products at $70 a share when Airgas was trading at $40–50 a share. As a memorandum from law firm Skadden (2011: 3) explains, the judge "was "constrained" to follow Delaware Supreme Court precedent, holding clearly that a law-trained Court must not substitute its business judgment for that of the board."

Stout (2012: 31) observes as follows:

> The business judgment rule thus allows directors in public corporations that plan to stay public to enjoy a remarkably wide range of autonomy in deciding what to do with the corporation's earnings and assets. As long as they do not take those assets for themselves, they can give them to charity; spend them on raises and health care for employees; refuse to pay dividends so as to build up a cash cushion that benefits creditors; and pursue low-profit projects that benefit the community, society, or the environment. They can do all these things even if the result is to decrease—not increase—shareholder value.

A fairly recent UK development occurred with the Companies Act of 1985, where Section 309 makes a slight augmentation to the shareholder primacy norm. It states that directors must take into account the interests of employees when performing their functions for the company and that this duty is to be regarded as a fiduciary duty owed to the company. This requirement is expanded on in the UK Companies Act of 2006, stating that corporations are further required to take into account the interests of other stakeholders such as suppliers, customers, the community, and the environment. The acts do not give employees or other stakeholders the right to challenge decisions of directors if they feel that their interests have not been taken into account. This means that now the fiduciary duty of directors need not be exclusively to the benefit of shareholders as the shareholder primacy norm would suggest. But, because employees do not have a right to challenge the decisions of directors this legal development would seem to indicate that directors still have a primary fiduciary duty to shareholders, although they are now also at liberty to take into consideration the interests of employees.

Similar developments have happened in America where over half the states in have adopted non-shareholder constituency statutes that allow managers to consider the effects of their decisions on employees, suppliers, customers and communities generally in the context of corporate takeovers (Smith 1998). Pennsylvania was first to adopt such a statute in 1983, states such as New York and Nevada have followed suit (Delaware, however, has not). These statutes do not *require* managers to consider the interests of non-shareholders, but they make explicit that managers are not prohibited from doing so.

The American Law Institute's (1994: 55) Principles of Corporate Governance also provides considerable latitude for managers to act beyond the apparent dictates of the shareholder primacy norm. Section 2.01 states: "Even if corporate profit and shareholder gain are not thereby enhanced, the corporation, in the conduct of its business: (1) Is obliged, to the same extent as a natural person, to act within the boundaries set by law; (2) May take into account ethical considerations that are reasonably regarded as appropriate to the responsible conduct of business; and, (3) May devote a reasonable amount of resources to public welfare, humanitarian, educational and philanthropic purposes." This consensus document has been regularly cited and relied upon by U.S. courts.

Another possible restriction on directors' liberty to pursue non-shareholder interests is the doctrine of ultra vires. Courts have in the past tried directors for pursuing opportunities that are claimed to be ultra vires, i.e. outside of the scope for which the corporation was created and thus outside the contracting powers of directors. Companies incorporated and registered under the Companies Act must have a constitution which calls the corporation into legal existence. This Memorandum of Association defines the purpose for which the corporation is formed.[6] It used to be the case that any corporate action that was deemed to be outside the purpose of the corporation as defined in the Memorandum of Association would be ultra vires and consequently invalid. For example the donation to the Red Cross could be construed as an act outside the scope for which the corporation was created. However, the ultra vires doctrine was in a long time decline since the beginning of the twentieth century in both American and in England. Morton Horwitz (1989: 24) writes: "Before the Civil War... the ultra vires doctrine was

[6]The constitutional document may also be a charter from the Crown or a Special Act of Parliament.

strictly applied by American courts... By 1930, the ultra vires doctrine was, if not dead, substantially eroded in practice". In England the ultra vires doctrine also gradually declined. For example the 1948 Companies Act allowed corporations to change their Memorandum of Association to get around ultra vires restrictions. This decline culminated in the 1989 Companies Act which states:

> "The validity of an act done by a company shall not be called into question on the ground of lack of capacity by reason of anything in the company's memorandum."

Advocates of both the Real Entity Theory and the Nexus-of-Contracts Theory claim that their theory helps explain the demise of the ultra vires doctrine. The Real Entity Theory can be regarded as contributing to its demise because of the characteristics it attributes to corporations. The idea is that because natural persons are assumed to be able to pursue whatever they deem good, and corporations are regarded as having many of the same characteristics as natural persons, it therefore seems unreasonable that the corporation should be restricted to act in a manner that is dictated by its Memorandum of Association.[7] On the other hand the Nexus-of-Contracts Theory helps explain the demise of the ultra vires doctrine by maintaining that the rationally contracting members of the corporation would choose to dismiss the doctrine on the grounds that they would accept ultra vires acts because such acts could benefit the corporate members. On the other hand the Legal Fiction Theory does not take any specific position on the demise of ultra vires. The theory regards the corporation as a creation of the state and thus it may choose to abolish the ultra vires doctrine if it no longer suits its purposes. The theory is consistent with the demise of ultra-vires although it does not specifically advocate it. Either way, one thing is clear, and that is that the ultra vires doctrine is no longer in effect.

Not only is the ultra vires doctrine dead but we have seen that the shareholder primacy norm has been augmented to allow for non-shareholder interests. Furthermore, to top it off, the business judgment rule makes the shareholder primacy norm virtually unenforceable. We may then ask if there anything left to consider with regard to CSR fears that corporate directors are bound to primarily satisfy the interests of shareholders. I believe that CSR advocates are correct in pointing out the importance of shareholder primacy norm, but not as a *legal* norm. There are good reasons to think that directors and managers follow the shareholder primacy norm, not because they are legally bound to do so, but because they believe they ought to do so. In other words the shareholder primacy norm is alive as a *social* norm.[8]

---

[7]This would seem to give rise to an "is-ought" problem for the Real Entity Theory. If the corporation is as a matter of legal fact unable to make any ultra vires acts it is difficult to see how one can also maintain that the corporation is able to pursue any purpose it desires. Is the Real Entity Theory describing the corporation as a social organism with many of the same characteristics of natural persons or is it prescribing that it ought to be attributed with such characteristics?

[8]Anderson (2000: 170) defines a social norm as "a standard of behaviour shared by a social group, commonly understood by its members as authoritative or obligatory for them". Cialdini and Trost (1998: 152) specify that they "guide and/or constrain social behaviour without the force of laws".

Business schools all over the world teach their students as part of the "Theory of the Firm" that corporations exist to maximise profits. Students are taught that profit maximisation is the purpose of the corporation in society and that it is the duty of directors to pursue this end on behalf of shareholders as their agents (Gentile and Mary 2004; Ghoshal 2005). West (2011) affirms that this is not only true of business schools but also of law schools. Dobson (1999: 69) states that students "will have drummed into them that the ultimate objective of all activity within the firm is the maximization of shareholder wealth". Consequently when these students get jobs in the corporate world they are working on an implicit assumption of shareholder primacy in their business decisions.

One might hypothesize that business schools perpetuate the shareholder primacy norm because they incorrectly believe it is the current state of law. This might well be part of the reason. However, I believe a more significant reason is that business school professors conceive of *homo economicus* (economic man) as the most basic building block in the economy- the rationally self-interested person in the sole pursuit of wealth. This means that shareholders are also presumed to be rationally self-interested and will thus demand the greatest possible return on their investments. This description of human motivation is clearly too simple, but by and large it is correct in assuming that currently most investors, most of the time, are merely looking for a return on their investment. Because shareholders have the legal power to elect and dismiss the board of directors, there is a very real sense in which the members of the corporation are the agents representing the interests of the shareholders; if they do not they will be out of a job.[9]

The fiduciary duties imposed on managers in common law are due to early judicial depictions of their relationship with shareholders as one of trust (e.g. Berle 1931, 1932). Managers were considered trustees for the shareholders who were the owners of the corporation. However, as we shall see, the corporation was legally separated from its shareholders in the mid-nineteenth century and considered to own itself, whereas shareholders were considered to own shares as a separate form of property (Pickering 1968). Despite the legal separation of the corporation from its

[9]Fundamental to the teaching of shareholder value maximization in business schools is the principal-agent model of the corporation, which has its origins in Jensen and Meckling's (1976) Theory of the Firm. Stout (2012) explains at length how this standard view is ill-founded. First, it assumes shareholders own corporations; whereas, in fact, corporations are independent legal entities that own themselves and shareholders own shares of stock, which amount to a contract between the shareholder and the corporation providing the former with rights under certain limited circumstances. Second, it posits that shareholders are residual claimants, receiving profits left over after the company's various contractual obligations have been met; whereas, it is up to the board of directors to decide whether (if any) profits are to be distributed as dividends to shareholders (the idea of shareholders as residual claimants has its origins in bankruptcy law and is incorrectly applied to the public corporation that is a going concern). Third, is the assumption that shareholders are principals who hire directors and executives to act as their agents; whereas, as a matter of corporate law, corporations are controlled by boards of directors, not shareholders.

shareholders in terms of ownership, important features of the structure of corporate law that came with the earlier depiction remained, both in terms of fiduciary duties and more importantly in terms of voting rights of shareholders.

It is this right of shareholders to vote for the board of directors that self-enforces the shareholder primacy norm and not the legal existence of the norm itself. Therefore, as long as shareholders have the right to vote for the board of directors, and as long as they remain self-interested, and as long as the government does not pass legislation forcing the rights of non-shareholders to be taken into the account, then the shareholder primacy norm will continue to be an operative prescription for directors.[10]

Corporations that donate one percent of their profits (or more) are very rare and considered exemplary by many. The reason they are so rare is not because directors are prohibited from making donations, as some CSR advocates would like to maintain, but because directors want to please shareholders and keep their jobs. The view among business scholars is that directors act as agents on behalf of the shareholders is derived from the perception that shareholders are the owners of the corporation. The idea is that owners of a company will employ a manager or director to run the company on their behalf. This characterisation of the power relationship between directors and shareholders is fairly accurate in practice, but legally speaking directors are the agents of the corporation itself and it is merely their fiduciary duty that is owed to the shareholders. (As we shall see in the next section this is due to the legal development of the separation of the corporation from the shareholders in the nineteenth century, which implies that shareholders do not hold legal title over the assets of the corporation but merely own shares as a separate form of property.)

Pre nineteenth century few corporations were publicly held. That is to say few were listed on the stock market with publicly transferable shares. Rather, the overwhelming majority of corporations were closely held, meaning that even though they had transferable shares they were rarely traded and they were held by a small number of shareholders. This helps explain the early commitment to the shareholder primacy norm. Early development of corporate law began in relation to these smaller corporations that were often family owned, which usually meant that directors and managers were also the main shareholders of the corporation. Consequently a director's duty to further the interests of shareholders was essentially a matter

---

[10]It has been suggested by some that the right to vote should be revoked from shareholders to enable managers to dispose of corporate funds with less focus on the bottom line. However, this suggestion ignores the genesis of corporations. If incorporation implies that shareholders lose control of the company then few if any entrepreneurs or investors would choose to make use of the corporate legal form. Moreover, if directors and managers no longer need to answer to shareholders then there is no primary stakeholder to hold them accountable to goals of financial performance. With less incentive to pursue profits, corporations will be less profitable which further diminishes the incentive for shareholders to incorporate. Although corporate managers might make more use of corporate funds for philanthropic ventures, removing shareholder voting rights may have negative consequences for the corporation's role as an efficient producer of goods and services.

of self-interest. But now, with the rise of the public corporation, with separation of ownership and control, shareholder voting rights for the board serve to keep managers focused on shareholder's interests.[11]

Finally, what do the legal theories of the nature of the firm have to say about the shareholder primacy norm? The Legal Fiction Theory would not seem to have a strong leaning one way or the other. It regards the law as merely an artefact of mankind and it is easy to associate this view with a form of legal instrumentalism, because arguably mankind creates legal artefacts in order to further certain ends. For example, if we assume that the government believes that the role of the corporation in society is to be an efficient producer of goods and services, then arguably the shareholder primacy norm is in line with economic theory that advocates profit maximization for the efficient allocation of resources in society. However, if you are a CSR advocate you may believe that the role of the corporation ought to be as an organization that aims to satisfy the interests of all corporate stakeholders. If that is the case then clearly the shareholder primacy norm is not instrumentally beneficial to furthering that end. Nevertheless, the shareholder primacy norm emerged in the early nineteenth century when the industrial revolution was in full swing and notions of CSR were far from corporate agendas.

The Real Entity Theory does not per se have anything specific to say with regard to shareholder primacy because the entire point of this theory is to advocate that the corporation has rights of its own that are distinct from those of the corporate members. However, the Real Entity Theory might advocate corporate rights that can be in conflict with the shareholder primacy norm. If the corporation has rights that are in no way motivated by the rights of the members then it is by no means clear that corporate rights are subordinate to the rights of members. It would not be unreasonable for the Real Entity Theory to advocate something like the "corporate primacy norm", in which case the interest of furthering the aims of the corporation (set out by the corporate charter) are primary and presumably the varying interests of the members are secondary. In my view it is simply inconceivable that a corporate collective can be real in such a distinct sense that it has rights that are separate from the corporate members.

The Nexus-of-Contracts Theory, which depicts the corporation as a web contracts among all the members, seems to say that directors have a contractual duty to

[11]Long ago, Berle and Means (1932) argued that shareholders of corporations with dispersed shareholdings had lost their de facto control to corporate managers because of diluted voting power. In this context it should be acknowledged the threat of dismissal / non-reelection of board members is real but rarely happens in practice in large public corporations (Benz and Frey 2007). However, in these large organizations there are usually other incentive structures in place that aim to align shareholder interests with those of top management; for example, the issuing of shares or stock options and payment of bonuses tied to corporate financial performance. Voting rights matter even in this context because it is common practice for shareholders to approve top management's remuneration by voting. The legal power of shareholders to vote for the board of directors and their remuneration helps perpetuate the SPN as a social norm, not as a principle of law likely to be upheld in court.

work in the interest of those stakeholders that have contracted for such a fiduciary duty, whether it be shareholders or other stakeholders. However, it does seem likely that the contracting parties would consent to the shareholder primacy norm. This is because the shareholders are in a particularly dominant position compared to other stakeholders and are likely to obtain a contract that allows their interests to be primary. The shareholders are in a dominant position because without them there would be no corporation. If we assume rational self-interest, then the story of corporate genesis according to the Nexus-of-Contracts Theory goes as follows: one or several persons decide that they wish to engage in a certain economic activity to further their financial aspirations; next they each contribute their share of starting capital; then finally (for simplicity) they start to collectively contract with employees to engage in the enterprise.[12] It is at the discretion of the shareholders to decide who works for the corporation. Clearly the point of the Nexus-of-Contracts Theory is that every employee may try and negotiate whatever employment contract they please, but given that any offer of employment is at the discretion of the employer then clearly shareholders are in a dominant position to negotiate a shareholder primacy clause into the contracts. For a corporation to be started there must be an incentive for rationally self-interested investors to part with their money, and it seems unlikely that this will be the case unless the corporation is created to further the financial interests of the investor.

Although the Nexus-of-Contracts Theory would seem to advocate the shareholder primacy norm neither it nor the Real Entity Theory can have influenced the actual emergence of the shareholder primacy norm because they did not appear until the second half of the nineteenth century. The shareholder primacy norm however was firmly in place at the beginning of the nineteenth century and if it was influenced by any theory at all it would have to be the Legal Fiction Theory, which indeed is consistent with the shareholder primacy norm.

- Summarizing remarks: The shareholder primacy norm is the part of directors' legal fiduciary duty that obliges them to primarily consider the interests of shareholders in their decision-making. Directors are allowed to consider the interests of other stakeholders, but do not have a duty to do so. Furthermore, the shareholder primacy norm is virtually unenforceable due to the business judgement rule and thus does not lend credence to the view of CSR advocates that the norm legally hinders managers from considering the interests of all stakeholders. However, the norm is still very much alive as a social norm because it is perpetuated in business schools and directors find it in their best interest to please shareholders because they have sole voting rights for the board of directors. The legal theories of over the nature of the corporation would seem to have had little influence on the development of the shareholder primacy norm because only the Legal Fiction Theory existed at the time and although it is consistent with the norm it does not explicitly advocate it.

[12]Recall that the Nexus-of-Contracts Theory does not regard legal incorporation as necessary for creating a corporation; the legal act of incorporation is merely a shorthand way of obtaining a contractual situation that can be obtained through the private contracting of individuals.

10.4 The Separation of the Corporation from the Shareholders and the Emergence of the Corporate Share as an Autonomous Form of Property

In law the corporation is considered as a completely distinct entity from the shareholders who incorporate the company. As we shall see this has led to the important legal development of corporate shares being regarded as property in their own right, which in turn has influenced the popularity and economic importance of the corporate legal form.

The most famous rendering of the separation of the corporation from its shareholders was given in 1897 in Solomon v. Solomon & Co Ltd when Lord Macnaghten stated: "The company is at law a different person altogether from the subscribers to the memorandum; and, though it may be that after incorporation the business is precisely the same as it was before, and the same persons are managers, and the same hands receive the profits, the company is not in law the agent of the subscribers or trustee for them."

The corporation conceived as a separate legal entity was already in place several decades before Solomon v. Solomon Co. Ltd. Nowadays, it is often assumed that the complete separation of corporation and shareholder is a direct consequence of the act of incorporation. This was however not the case in the late eighteenth century and only developed towards the middle of the nineteenth century. Paddy Ireland (1996: 45) writes: "while incorporation had very important legal consequences, for many years [early nineteenth century] a complete separation of company and members was not among them." Interestingly Ireland also mentions that the legal development of the corporation as a separate legal entity was also followed by a similarly linguistic development. The corporation nowadays is usually referred to in the singular "it", but in the early nineteenth century when shareholders were still regarded as forming the corporation it was referred to in the plural "they".[13] Up until the 1856 Joint Stock Companies Act corporations were referred to in the plural and said that persons "form themselves into an incorporated company" with the implication that the persons *were* the company and thus made *of* them. It was not until the 1862 that corporations were said to be made *by* people and not *of* people (Ireland 1996). The 1862 Companies Act clearly indicates that the corporation is to be regarded as a completely distinct legal entity and this was rendered 25 years before Solomon v. Solomon & Co. Ltd.

---

[13]This can help explain why people often refer to the corporation in the singular in their responsibility attributions. It is not that the corporation is a moral agent, but rather that they have adopted the legal singular usage referring to the separate legal entity. This may mean that they are not making a moral responsibility attribution at all, but a legal responsibility attribution, or it may mean that they are making a category mistake by attributing moral responsibility to a legal agent.

Lee v. Lee's Air Farming Ltd (1961) is an interesting case to illustrate the corporate status as a distinct legal entity. Lee was the sole director, the main employee and the controlling shareholder of Lee's Air Farming Ltd in New Zealand. Lee's role as an employee was as a pilot. Following Lee's accidental death his widow brought a claim against the company. The question before the court was if Lee could be considered as a "worker" for the purposes of the New Zealand Workers' Compensation Act of 1922. It was ruled that Lee's duties as director were owed to the corporation itself and that Lee's contract of employment as a pilot was with the corporation itself. These were considered two separate contracts with the corporate entity and therefore Lee was not considered to be controlling himself as a director. Rather, it was deemed that legally speaking Lee was being controlled by the corporation through its director, and consequently Lee's widow's claim was successful (Pickering 1968). The example shows how an incorporated one man company is at law nevertheless a completely distinct legal entity from its only member who is at once director, employee and shareholder.

Alongside the legal development of the corporation as a separate entity was the development of the corporate share as property in its own right. The first development to this end was that the corporate share ceased to confer any right to the assets of the corporation. The court's decision in Bligh v. Brent (1837) set the tone that the shares of a corporation did not constitute a direct interest in the corporation's assets. This meant that shareholders had no legal title to any of the corporation's assets and had no right to control how those assets were to be used. For example; imagine that you have inherited the controlling stake of shares in a large corporation that has been in your family for generations. One of the assets of the corporation is a piece of land that you would like to use to build a house on. Legally you would have no right to make any use of that land unless you bought it or rented it from the corporation. Justice Walton put the point clearly with the following truism: "The property of the company is not the property of the shareholders; it is the property of the company" (Pickering 1968: 497).

The fact that shares no longer constituted a right to the corporation's assets was important with regard to the transferability of shares. It meant that the identity of the shareholders was of considerably diminished importance, because they could not make claims on corporate assets, which facilitated the transferability of shares to new shareholders. As we shall see later, the granting of limited liability to joint stock companies in 1855 also greatly helped to reduce the significance of the identity of the shareholders and thus assist the transferability of shares. These two developments together with the growth of a proper share-market meant that shares were rapidly becoming commodities that could be easily bought and sold. This in turn made corporate shares considerably more attractive to investors and further helped contribute to the spread of the corporate form. By the mid-1850s corporate shares were becoming liquid assets. It was this trading of shares that above all else "established shares as an autonomous form of property, independent from the assets of the company" (Ireland 1996: 68). Once shares were being readily traded and they no longer conferred any rights to corporate assets it was fairly uncontroversial for shares to be regarded as legal property in their own right, which they clearly were by the 1860s. A corporate share is now itself a form of legal property that primarily confers a right to vote for the board of directors and a right to receive dividends if the boards so decides.

The separation of the corporation from its shareholders led to a greater independence and empowerment of directors and managers. This in turn led progressive thinkers in the mid-twentieth century to regard corporate boards as possessing a great deal of autonomy from the shareholders. This postulated autonomy led to the development of different positions advocating the dawn of a new "socially responsible" corporation. The hope was that a corporation would emerge that would aim to satisfy a variety of different interests and not merely those of the shareholders. These hopes never materialized, but they are still resonating in the CSR movement of today.

At first sight the empowerment of management makes it seem plausible that the corporation could try to satisfy several different stakeholders simultaneously without giving primacy to shareholders. On closer inspection the separation of the corporation from its shareholders further entrenches the shareholder primacy norm. The central reason for this is that the greater autonomy of management only stretches to the running of the business and the disposal of corporate assets. The shareholders still have sole voting rights and therefore still have decision-power over who sits on the board of directors. Furthermore, when the corporation is a separate legal entity and the corporate share is regarded as property in its own right, then shareholders mainly have the privilege of receiving potential dividends. Previously shareholders might have had an interest in the actual assets of the corporation or how it was run, but a consequence of downgrading shareholder rights is that the interest in holding corporate shares becomes primarily financial. Therefore it seems reasonable that investors are unlikely to hold shares unless they are afforded primacy among stakeholders. With a shareholder primacy norm in place the separation of corporation and shareholders merely grants managers the autonomy of choosing the *means* to realize the *ends* chosen by the shareholders.

Although the establishment of the corporation as a separate legal entity has empowered directors it has only provided managerial autonomy with regard to the daily running of the business corporation. Directors are still faced with mostly self-interested shareholders and therefore the concerns of shareholders remain a considerably more dominant focus for corporate boards than do the prescriptions of the CSR movement.

What do the legal theories about the nature of the firm have to say about the corporation as a separate legal entity? The Legal Fiction Theory does not prescribe that the corporation ought to be regarded as a separate legal entity from the incorporators, but it is clearly consistent with such a view. Furthermore, the Legal Fiction Theory does easily lend itself to the interpretation that the corporation is a separate entity altogether from the corporate members. If the corporation is a fiction then obviously there is a sense in which it is separate from the members who are real natural persons.

The Real Entity theory on the other hand is very clear about its prescription to recognise the corporation as a separate legal entity. Because the theory puts forward the view that the corporation is a naturally occurring being it advocates that the corporation should be legally recognized for what it is; a being in its own right capable of having rights and duties. Morton Horwitz (1989: 45) says that "one of the major organizing premises of the natural entity theory was to posit the existence of a sharp distinction between the corporate entity and the shareholders". This separation is important to the advocates of this theory in order to maintain that the legal rights and duties that are conferred upon the corporation are in no sense derivative from the members. These rights and duties are possessed and exercised by the corporation itself as a distinct moral and legal person.

The Nexus-of-Contracts Theory poses a contrast with the Real Entity Theory as it seems to argue against regarding the corporation as a separate legal entity. It regards the act of incorporation as shorthand way of obtaining a contractual situation equivalent to that which could materialize through the private contracting of individuals. This position regards the legal rights and duties of the corporate legal entity as derivative from the rights and duties of the contracting parties, which suggest that the corporation should not be regarded as a separate legal entity from the shareholders.

It is only the Real Entity Theory that explicitly advocates the separation of the corporation from its shareholders; however it cannot have influenced this separation as it did not exist at the time. At the time of the explicit articulation of this separation in the 1862 Companies act the Legal Fiction Theory already existed and the Nexus-of-Contracts Theory was gaining ground. If any theory influenced the separation at all it would have been the Legal Fiction Theory because it implicitly lends itself to the interpretation of a separation of a fictional corporate entity from the shareholders who are real persons.

- Summarizing remarks: The corporation is an entirely separate legal entity from its members, which has led to corporate shares as being regarded as property in their own right. These legal developments have greatly contributed to the transferability of shares, which in concert with the development of stock-markets has led shares to become readily traded commodities. Although the separation of the corporation and shareholders led to a greater autonomy for directors this was primarily an autonomy of decision-making pertaining to the daily running of the business. In other words directors have the autonomy of choosing the *means* but not the *ends* of the business enterprise. This implies that in practice managers do not have the discretion to dispose of means that do not further the ends of the shareholders. The theories over the nature of the corporation do not seem to have had a strong influence on the separation of the corporation from its shareholders because only the Real Entity Theory explicitly advocates such a separation and it did not exist at the time.

10.5 The Limited Liability of Shareholders

Nowadays all UK corporations registered under the Companies Act are granted limited liability. This means that the liability of the shareholders is limited to the value of their shares, so that a person who purchases a share in a corporation does not stand to lose more than the value of his share. In other words if the corporation incurs large debts, for example due to making poor investments or due to being sentenced with a large fine, the creditors cannot access the personal wealth of the shareholders to cover these debts. So to speak, the debts of the corporation are not the debts of the shareholders, they are the debts of the corporation.

Limited liability is by many considered the most important feature of the corporate legal form. In particular it is one of the most significant distinctions between the corporate form and a legal partnership where the shareholders have unlimited liability. However, limited liability was a relatively late characteristic to be attributed to corporations. When tracing the evolution of limited liability it is important to distinguish between on the one hand corporations chartered by the Crown or incorporated by a Special Act of Parliament, and on the other hand joint stock companies incorporated under general incorporation statutes.

Corporations chartered by the Crown or incorporated by a Special Act of Parliament could be granted limited liability but it varied from one corporation to another. Nevertheless, with the passage of time limited liability became progressively more associated with the act of incorporation and by the late eighteenth century "it became increasingly accepted that where the charter was silent, shareholders had the benefit of limited liability" (Blumberg 1993: 9).

The Joint Stock Companies Act of 1844, which introduced general incorporation statutes for companies, did not confer limited liability upon incorporation. It was not until the Limited Liability Act of 1855 and the Joint Stock Companies Act of 1856 that limited liability was conferred to joint stock companies upon incorporation. The years between 1844 and 1855 were characterised by a long political struggle regarding whether or not the state should grant limited liability to joint stock companies. Phillip Blumberg (1993: 15) says that "the political struggle over limited liability involved joint stock companies, not the handful of existing corporations that already had such protection".

The issue of limited liability caused controversy both in England and in America. In England it created heated debates in parliament and in America it was debated state by state. However, England's adoption of limited liability in 1855 came three decades after it was generally adopted in America (Blumberg 1993). So what was all the fuss about?

Joel Bakan (2004: 12) writes: "On both sides of the Atlantic, critics opposed limited liability on moral grounds. Because it allowed investors to escape unscathed from their company's failures, critics believed it would undermine personal moral responsibility". Thorstein Veblen was also of the opinion that a policy that removed the liability of individuals for the consequences of their actions was central to the controversy over limited liability (Blumberg 1993). People were concerned that if anyone and everyone could start an incorporated company with limited liability through a simple act of registration this would lead to people making decisions without concern for negative consequences because their liability was limited. Although this concern has proved to be legitimate under certain circumstances,[14] by and large these fears have been unfounded. This is probably because *limited* liability does not mean that there is *absence* of liability as some seem to mistakenly think. Shareholders are liable to the extent of the entire value of their shares. Shareholders not only wish to keep the value of their shares but they also wish for the share value to increase. The self-interest of shareholders should bring them to demand corporate investment decisions that are expected to be profitable. This by itself means that corporations will strive to retain and increase the value of shares rather than make decisions that may be harmful to others, which in turn may damage share-value through litigation or loss of customers.

A complaint that is often levied against limited liability is that a great share of the risk of business failure is shifted onto creditors because they may not get paid in the event that the corporation is declared bankrupt. This is usually referred to as a negative externality[15] of the rule of limited liability. This rests on a misconception because there is no externality. Voluntary creditors (e.g. banks, bond holders, and suppliers) are compensated for the greater risk that the corporation might default on its payments *prior* to any such potential default, therefore there is no externality. Easterbrook and Fischel (1985: 102) write: "The creditors assume some of the risk of business failure, just as they would if they were "insurers" as well as creditors. The legal rule of limited liability is a shortcut to this position, avoiding the costs of separate transactions". The general idea is that because creditors are exposed to a greater risk of payment default they will demand a higher rate of return on their credit to compensate for the extra risk they assume.

Despite some heated opposition to limited liability, it eventually emerged in the UK in 1855 as a political reaction to rapid industrialization that was taking place at the time. Limited liability proved to bring with it several benefits to shareholders and the economy as a whole. Six of the major benefits are[16]:

1. <u>Lower Cost of Monitoring Managers:</u> It is in the interest of shareholders that their managers do not make poor decisions that might put the corporation into debt. With unlimited liability corporate debt is a serious threat because the shareholders may lose not just their corporate shares but also their personal wealth. With the rapid progress of industrialization in the nineteenth century more companies were becoming incorporated. Furthermore, as the corporations

[14]It is generally accepted that an incentive problem occurs when a corporation is near insolvency. This is because the closer the corporation is to being insolvent, the less the corporation is worth, and therefore due to limited liability the corporation has "nothing to lose" in making very risky decisions.

[15]An externality is a cost or benefit of a decision that falls onto a third party that plays no part in the decision made.

[16]The following points are inspired by Easterbrook and Fischel (1985).

were becoming ever larger, those running and those owning corporate shares were increasingly becoming different groups of people. This meant that the shareholders were incurring significant monitoring costs to make sure that poor decisions that might endanger their personal wealth were not made. The introduction of limited liability significantly reduced the costs of monitoring shareholders because now, although managers might still make poor decisions, those decisions could not affect the personal assets of shareholders.

2. Removal of the Cost of Monitoring other Shareholders: Without limited liability the identity of the other shareholders was of financial importance. The reason is that in the event of corporate bankruptcy, creditors would turn on the assets of the shareholders to regain the payments they were due. This meant that it was important to know the personal wealth of one's fellow shareholders, because the wealthier the other shareholders were the less likely it was that one would have to shoulder the debt burden on behalf of other shareholders that could not pay. The introduction of limited liability meant that the personal wealth of other shareholders became irrelevant because creditors could no longer make any claims on the personal wealth of shareholders. In turn this meant the removal of the cost of monitoring other shareholders to make sure that they did not sell their shares to people with little wealth.
3. Facilitates Pricing of Corporate Shares: Without limited liability the price of corporate shares depends in part on the personal wealth of the current and prospective shareholders. This is because the personal wealth of the existing shareholders influences the risk of investment that a new shareholder incurs upon his purchase. Limited liability makes corporate shares into homogenous commodities because the market price of a corporate share is the same irrespective of who owns them. This makes shares more easily transferable by reducing information gathering costs that would be required for each purchase, which in turn helps the stock market to be more responsive.
4. Increased Performance Feedback: By helping to make the identity of the shareholder irrelevant limited liability facilitated the free transfer of shares. The free transfer of shares is an integral part of a stock market's ability to be responsive to corporate investment decisions and to set an "accurate" share price based on the valuation of market players. Corporate shares that are publicly traded transmit information to the managers through the share price about how well the corporation is perceived to be doing.
5. Enables the Diversification of Risk: Nowadays it is common for shareholders to reduce the risk of investing in the stock market by holding a market portfolio[17] of shares. This eliminates the industry specific risk of a shareholder's investment and leaves only the general market risk. This is only possible with a rule of limited liability. With unlimited liability a diversified portfolio would mainly serve to increase rather than decrease the risk incurred by the investor, because if

[17]A market portfolio of shares is a portfolio that mirrors the proportions of all the shares in the market.

any one of the corporations went bankrupt the investor could stand to lose all his personal wealth. Under a rule of unlimited liability investors are therefore unable to avoid investment risk that could have been avoided under a rule of limited liability.

6. Gives Managers the Incentive to Make Efficient Allocation of Resources: Some investments that managers expect to be profitable may be dismissed as too risky under a rule of unlimited liability. For example, some positive net present value investments[18] may bankrupt the corporation if they go wrong. Therefore shareholders would not wish such investments to be made because it could result in claims on their personal assets. Positive net present value investments are regarded as an efficient allocation of resources and consequently to pass up on such an investment would be a social loss. However, with a rule of limited liability the personal assets of shareholders are out of reach from creditors and therefore rational shareholders would endorse risky positive net present value investments.[19]

The corporation as a completely separate legal entity from the corporate members emerged at about the same time as that of limited liability in the mid-nineteenth century. As previously mentioned, this was a time of rapid industrialization when due to the size of corporations it was becoming increasingly common to have a functional division between professional managers running the firm and shareholders supplying the necessary investment capital. The division of the functions of management and investment influenced the call for a separate corporate entity with limited liability and vice versa. As I have noted above, this functional separation implies monitoring costs for shareholders. The introduction of the rule of limited liability helped remove some of these costs. Furthermore, it was probably not a coincidence that the corporation as a separate legal entity emerged in concert with limited liability. It is difficult to consistently maintain that the corporation is a completely separate legal entity from the shareholders if the courts at the same time are accessing the personal wealth of shareholders for debts incurred by the corporation. In other words, it seems inconsistent to hold onto the view that the assets of the corporation are the assets of the corporation, if one also maintains that the debts of the corporation are the debts of the shareholders.

The rule of limited liability is now an accepted and ingrained characteristic of the corporate form having been available through a simple act of registration for a century and a half. The rule generally protects the personal assets of shareholders from any claims that might arise out of debts incurred by the corporation. However,

[18]The net present value of an investment is the discounted sum of all expected future revenues and costs of the investment.

[19]Arguably a risk neutral rational investor would not pass up on a positive net present value investment irrespective of the risk and possibility of having claims made against his personal assets. However, it seems reasonable to assume that real investors are not risk neutral about their personal assets in a way that they might be about their shareholdings. People tend to regard their shareholdings as assets disposable for speculation while personal wealth is needed for living.

over the years there have been several rare occasions when the courts have gone behind the veil of incorporation and held shareholders personally liable. There are no general or well established rules for when courts may "pierce the corporate veil", but one situation in which courts have disregarded the limited liability of shareholders is when it has been intentionally abused. This has almost always involved close corporations where there is often considerably less functional separation between management and investment. Close corporations are usually characterised by a dominant shareholder who is also the director of the corporation. When the dominant shareholder and the director are the same person then limited liability does not afford any extra advantage in the reduction of monitoring costs. Furthermore, the incentive for directors to engage in overly risky activity is considerably greater in close corporations. If a director is also the main shareholder he stands to gain handsomely if one of the risky investment decisions pays off, but potential losses are limited by limited liability if the investment goes wrong. On occasion when the courts have deemed that overly risky investment decisions have been made by deliberately abusing the protection of limited liability, they have decided to pierce the corporate veil and allow access to the personal assets of the shareholders.

What do the theories about the nature of the corporation say about limited liability? Blumberg is of the opinion that the theories about the nature of the firm did not influence the development of limited liability. He writes: "The universal adoption of limited liability in the legal systems of the industrialized world rests on relatively modern legislative enactments reflecting politico-economic values, not on fundamental jurisprudential concepts of the nature of the corporation as a legal unit" (Blumberg 1993: 7).

Contrary to Blumberg's view Horwitz maintains that the Real Entity Theory was of significant importance for the justification of conferring limited liability on the corporate legal form (Phillips 1994). This is because the Real Entity Theory argues that the corporation has an existence that is independent from the corporate members, which then contributed to the idea that the liability of the corporation should be distinguished from the liability of shareholders.

Both the Nexus-of-Contracts Theory and the Legal Fiction Theory are also consistent with the rule of limited liability, although they do not imply limited liability as the Real Entity Theory does. Easterbrook and Fischel (1985: 89) write: "The liability of 'the corporation' is limited by the fact that the corporation is not real. It is not more than a name for a complex set of contracts among managers, workers, and contributors of capital. It has no existence independent of these relations". This characterisation of the corporation sounds very much like the Nexus-of-Contracts Theory, which suggests that the corporation has limited liability because the contracting parties (corporate members and creditors) can deliberately create such a clause in their contracts.

The Legal Fiction Theory is also consistent with the rule of limited liability, because it is closely related to legal instrumentalism. If one regards the corporate legal form as an instrument of the state then it should confer limited liability upon incorporation if it helps to further certain politico-economic goals of the state. Furthermore, the Legal Fiction Theory easily lends itself to explain how it is possible on occasion for the courts to disregard the limited liability of shareholders. Martin Wolff (1938: 507) writes: "The fiction formula further makes it easy to reject some undesirable consequences of legal personality... It is sometimes necessary to 'disregard the corporate fiction'". The rule of limited liability can be disregarded because the corporate legal form as an instrument exists to further the ends of the state and therefore the rule of limited liability can be overridden when the rule no longer serves its purpose.

Although the Real Entity Theory would seem to advocate a rule of limited liability Horwitz is most certainly wrong in maintaining that the Real Entity Theory had a significant influence on bringing about the rule. This is because the theory did not emerge until half a century after the rule's establishment in 1855. At this time the Legal Fiction Theory had long existed and the Nexus-of-Contracts Theory was emerging. The rule of limited liability is consistent with both these theories but neither explicitly advocates it. However, if any theory was of influence it would have been the Legal Fiction Theory seeing as the political debate surrounding limited liability regarded whether or not to *grant* corporations limited liability. (The descriptive dominance of the Fiction Theory over the Nexus-of-Contracts Theory will be further discussed in Sect. 11.1, with specific focus on the granting of limited liability).

- Summarizing remarks: The emergence of limited liability as part of general incorporation statutes came into effect only after much heated debate in both England and America. The rule of limited liability implies that the liability of shareholders is limited to the value of their shares. It was feared that such restrictions on liability would lead to grossly irresponsible behaviour. Although such fears did hold some substance, the many economic benefits of limited liability were of greater importance. In particular limited liability helped to turn the stock market into a truly liquid market.

  The rule of limited liability implies that creditors end up bearing a greater risk of business failure, but this is not an externality because they are compensated upfront for this risk in terms of a higher rate of return. It seems reasonable that creditors should bear this risk rather than shareholders if we are to regard the corporation as a separate legal entity. Therefore it is probably not a coincidence that the corporation as a separate legal entity emerged at the same time as limited liability. The debts of the corporation belong to the corporation itself, and if it cannot pay, this risk should be borne by those who gave it credit.

  Although the Real Entity Theory would advocate a rule of limited liability the theory did not exist at the time the rule was established. If any theory was of influence it would have been the Legal Fiction Theory because the political debate pertained to the *granting* of limited liability to corporations.

10.6 The Reification of the Corporation (and the Legal Influence of the Theories About the Nature of the Corporation)

In both American and English law the corporation is regarded as an artificial *person* and accorded many of the same legal rights as natural persons. As we shall see this personification of the corporation has been influenced by the theories about the nature of the corporation. This has subsequently led to a reified conception of the corporation in law that has led to misguided legislation and court rulings for not adequately appreciating the difference between corporate persons and natural persons.

The landmark case in America for the personification of the corporation occurred with the 1886 case of Santa Clara County v. Southern Pacific Railroad. The case presented the question of whether the Equal Protection clause of the 14th Amendment to the Constitution barred California state law from taxing corporate property differently from individual property. An important issue in the case centred on whether the Equal Protection clause referring to "person" was applicable to the corporation. The first section of the 14th Amendment says:

> "All *persons* born or naturalized in the United States, and subject to the jurisdiction thereof, are citizens of the United States and of the State wherein they reside. No State shall make or enforce any law which shall abridge the privileges or immunities of citizens of the United States; nor shall any State deprive any *person* of life, liberty, or property, without due process of law; nor deny to any *person* within its jurisdiction the equal protection of the laws" (emphasis added).

During the proceedings the court announced: "The court does not wish to hear arguments on the question whether the provision of the 14th Amendment to the Constitution, which forbids a state to deny any person within its jurisdiction the equal protection of Laws, applies to these corporations. We are all of the opinion that it does" (source: Blumberg 1993: 36).

It is interesting to note that the Real Entity Theory has not had a prominent role in extending 14th Amendment rights to the corporation. Santa Clara was decided in 1886, which meant that the ruling was made a year before Otto von Gierke published his work on the corporation as a social organism and well over a decade before the Real Entity Theory emerged as an influential theory. What exactly the motivation was for the decision is difficult to say as no justification was given for regarding the corporation as a "person" for the purposes of the 14th Amendment. The court merely announced that it did not wish to hear any arguments regarding the applicability of the 14th Amendment to corporations because it had already decided that it was applicable. In modern times many legal scholars have erroneously assumed that the Real Entity Theory was the driving force behind the ruling because the theory perceives the corporation as a person.

Nevertheless, we can get an indication of the driving force for the decision from John Norton Pomeroy who was acting as council on behalf of the corporation, Southern Pacific Railroad. He said that the central argument for applying the 14th

Amendment to corporations was that it would protect the *property rights* of the shareholders and not specifically to protect the abstract entity called the "corporation". Pomeroy declared that the provisions of state and federal constitutions apply "to private corporations, not alone because such corporations are 'persons' within the meaning of that word, but because *statutes violating their prohibitions in dealing with corporations must necessarily infringe upon the rights of natural persons.* In applying and enforcing these constitutional guarantees, *corporations cannot be separated from the natural persons who compose them*" (source: Horwitz 1989).

Pomeroy is clearly expressing an adherence to the Nexus-of-Contracts Theory, which merely regards the corporation as an aggregation of the contractual relations of its constituent members. What affects the corporation affects every member. Adherence to this view is hardly surprising seeing as the Nexus-of-Contracts Theory was dominant in the second half of the nineteenth century after the establishment of general incorporation statutes but before the emergence of the Real Entity Theory.[20]

- Santa Clara (1886): The court extended 14th Amendment rights to the corporation with regard to the Equal Protection clause and thus for the first time acknowledged the corporation as a "person" under the constitution. It seems plausible that the court relied on the Nexus-of-Contracts Theory as a justification for their decision.

Interestingly (and ironically) the 14th Amendment was ratified in 1868 three years after the end of the American Civil War in order to confer equal status before the law to all the newly freed slaves. However, it soon came to be used for the benefit of protecting corporations. The Santa Clara case was ground breaking in that it set a precedent for regarding the corporation as a person for the purpose of the constitution. Only 2 years later in 1888, in the case of Pembina Consolidated Silver Mining and Milling Co. v. Pennsylvania the court held that the corporation qualified as a "person" for the purpose of the Equal Protection *and* the Due Process clause of the 14th Amendment.

Although nowadays the corporation has many of the same legal rights of natural persons there are certain areas that are regarded as decidedly personal where the constitutional protections differ for corporations. For example, the self-incrimination clause of the 5th Amendment is not applicable to corporate persons in American law. A consequence of this is that corporations may be forced to make

[20]Although the Nexus-of-Contracts Theory probably was the motivating force for the *Santa Clara* ruling it was not well thought through. By the time of Santa Clara, limited liability had already been conferred upon incorporation for several decades and the corporation was clearly established as a separate legal entity from the shareholders. The Nexus-of Contacts Theory as the primary *justification* for regarding the corporation as a "person" under the 14th amendment is problematic because it is inconsistent with the corporation's limited liability and legal status as a separate entity. If "corporations cannot be separated from the natural persons who compose them", then one should also bite the bullet and hold that the debts of the corporation ought to also be the debts of the shareholders.

potentially incriminating documents available to the state prosecution. In the 1906 case of Hale v. Henkel Justice Brown speaking for the majority made use of the Legal Fiction Theory when he said:

> "[T]he corporation is a creature of the State. It is presumed to be incorporated for the benefit of the public… It would be a strange anomaly to hold that a State, having chartered a corporation to make use of certain franchise, could not in the exercise of its sovereignty inquire how these franchises had been employed, and whether they had been abused, and demand the production of the corporate books and papers for that purpose" (source: Blumberg 1993: 38).

- Hale v. Henkel (1906): The court ruled that the self-incrimination clause of the 5th Amendment is not applicable to corporations. The Legal Fiction Theory formed the basis of the courts justification as it is deemed that the corporation is a creation of the state and thus the state may legitimately demand to know how the corporate instrument has been used.

Blumberg highlights that self-incrimination in English law is quite different. He says: "Although there is, of course, no written English constitution, there are fundamental rights, comparable to the American Bill of Rights, guaranteed by the common law… The English cases conclude that under common law the privilege against self-incrimination is a fundamental civil right of corporations as well as human beings" (Blumberg 1993: 39).

In 1978 the case of First National Bank of Boston v. Bellotti came before the court. The problem was if a Massachusetts Statute restricting the use of corporate political expenditures to influence *referenda* was unconstitutional. In other words, the point of contention was if corporations should be allowed to use corporate funds to support a political position (yes or no) in referenda. At the heart of the case stood the question of whether or not the constitutional free speech protection of the First Amendment was applicable to corporations. However, the majority opinion of the court shifted the issue from the rights of corporations per se to the type of speech acts that the First Amendment was meant to protect.

The majority opinion by Justice Lewis F. Powell "shifted the issue from whether corporations have or ought to have First Amendment rights coextensive with those of natural persons to an issue of whether the statute 'abridges expression that the First Amendment was meant to protect'… Instead, Justice Powell simply identified the speech involved as political speech, a type of speech clearly within the meaning of the concept of speech as that concept is used in the First Amendment" (Flynn 1989: 147). A consequence of construing the issue in this manner is that the First Amendment is merely concerned with the type of speech it is meant to protect in the market place of ideas rather than protecting the right of a certain source of ideas to employ free speech.

The court held that the Due Process clause in the 14th Amendment, which includes the right of "liberty" of persons, also incorporates the free speech clause of the First Amendment. Thus the court ruled that the Massachusetts Statute violated the guarantee of free speech under the First Amendment. The case thus reversed the courts long held policy of denying First Amendment rights to non-media business corporations. Once again the corporate person had been conferred the same rights as natural persons under the constitution.

A point of contention during the proceedings in Bellotti was whether or not the First Amendment embodies a standard of equality that can be imposed to guarantee the free exchanges of ideas. The idea is that corporate *wealth* might constitute an unfair advantage in the "market place of ideas" for the purpose of winning votes. Justice Powell when writing for the majority rejected that the First Amendment contained such a notion of equality. However, dissenting Judges Byron R. White, William H. Brennan and Thurgood Marshall forcefully opined to the contrary. They quite rightly said:

> "Corporations are artificial entities created by law for the purpose of furthering certain economic goals. In order to facilitate achievement of such ends, special rules relating to such matters as limited liability, perpetual life, and the accumulation, distribution, and taxation of assets are normally applied to them... It has long been recognized, however, that the special status of corporations has placed them in a position to control vast amounts of economic power which may, if not regulated, dominate not only the economy but also the very heart of our democracy, the electoral process... The State need not permit its own creation to consume it... Such expenditures may be viewed as seriously threatening the role of the First Amendment as a guarantor of a free marketplace of ideas" (source: Bowman 1996: 157).

Bellotti employs a theory of the political "market place of ideas" that is analogous to a competitive economic marketplace where the laws of supply and demand determine the winner and losers. Scott Bowman (1996) points out that a problem arises because efficiency is the main arbiter among actors in the economic sphere, while reasons are meant to separate winners from losers in the political marketplace. A consequence of this is that the analogy breaks down when the actors have vastly different means to express their political points of view, because financial wealth rather than reasoned arguments will tend to determine the outcome of the debate. The court ruling in favour of conferring First Amendment rights to corporations results in treating corporations as natural persons. This approach ends up simply ignoring the disproportionate power corporations have in influencing an election process.

Similar to the *Santa Clara* case the *Bellotti* case was not justified on the basis of the Real Entity Theory as one might think. Instead the *Bellotti* decision was made on instrumental grounds for protecting political speech in the market place of ideas, irrespective of the source of those ideas. This instrumental justification is consistent with the Legal Fiction Theory, which deems that the state may restrict the actions of corporations if allowing such action does not further the desired ends of the state. The Legal Fiction Theory is consistent with *any* instrumental justification, which explains why it was also employed by the dissenting Justices in *Bellotti*. Both the Justices for and against the ruling desired a functioning political marketplace of ideas as part of the electoral process, but they differed as to whether or not conferring First Amendment rights to corporations was the bests *means* to attain that *end*.

- Bellotti (1978): The court ruled that the corporation was to be extended First Amendment freedom of speech rights with regard to *referenda*. The court held that the First Amendment did not contain a notion of equality with regard to the *wealth* of actors that might constitute an unfair advantage in the market place of ideas.

Bellotti only addressed the issue of corporate political expenditures to influence *referenda* and not the issue of corporate speech in *candidate* elections. This issue was addressed in Federal Election Commission v. Massachusetts Citizens for Life, decided in 1986. In this case the court upheld the provision that prohibited corporations and unions from directly making contributions or expenditures to *federal* elections. Justice Brennan speaking on behalf of the majority said:

> "The resources in the treasury of a business corporation... are not an indication of popular support for the corporation's political ideas. They reflect instead the economically motivated decisions of investors and customers. The availability of these resources may make a corporation a formidable political presence, even though the power of the corporation may be no reflection of the power of its ideas" (source: Bowman 1996: 160).

- Massachusetts Citizens for Life (1986): The court held that First Amendment speech rights were *not* applicable to corporations for the purposes of *federal* elections. The justification was based on the fact that corporate economic *wealth* is not per se a reflection of the political opinions of investors and customers.

Only 4 years later, in 1990, Austin v. Michigan State Chamber of Commerce was decided. The court upheld restrictions on the spending of corporations in candidate elections for *state* governments. Bowman (1996: 161) says: "Austin stands for the proposition that the political marketplace is not self-regulating and can be regulated in the public interest when free trade of ideas is threatened by massive aggregations of corporate wealth". The court invoked the Legal Fiction Theory to reach its conclusion. The rationale was that the state confers a unique structure with privileges to the corporation, which facilitates the accumulation of wealth, and thus the state may legitimately curb corporate powers that may distort the electoral process. Bowman points out that it is not *wealth* per se that is the point of contention, because a billionaire could equally well use his wealth to distort the electoral process.[21] Rather the point is that the state confers several advantages of wealth accumulation for corporations and thus it would be unfair relative to the wealth accumulations abilities of natural persons if corporations could use that wealth in the context of a political campaign.[22]

[21]For example, in the 2004 presidential election billionaire George Soros contributed vast amounts of his personal wealth to counter the re-election of George W. Bush.

[22]Austin says that corporations may not use their resources to contribute directly to an election campaign, but it does not restrict them from establishing a segregated fund to achieve the same goal. This seems a bit strange because it does not in effect hinder corporations in practice from influencing the electoral process.

- Austin (1990): The court held that First Amendment speech rights were *not* applicable to corporations for the purpose of *candidate* elections for *state* governments. Applying the Legal Fiction Theory, the court held that *state conferred corporate privileges* for wealth accumulation constituted an unfair advantage in the market place of ideas.

Bellotti conferred First Amendment rights to the corporate person with regards to *referenda*, but because *Massachusetts Citizens for Life* and *Austin* denied corporations the protection of the First Amendment in federal and state candidate elections one may until recently legitimately doubt the extent of free speech rights for corporations. There would appear to be no material difference between these three cases and thus the rulings seem inconsistent. I can see no good reason why corporations should have the right to influence referenda but not state and federal candidate elections. The arguments that apply to restricting corporate free speech rights ought to apply equally to all elections that are part of a democracy's electoral process.

This blatant inconsistency was resolved (in the wrong direction) by the Supreme Court in 2010 with the ruling in Citizens United v. Federal Election Commission, which held that First Amendment rights to free speech apply to corporations for the purposes of independent political expenditures. As mentioned (see Chap. 1) the ruling formally relied on the Nexus-of-Contracts Theory arguing that corporate free speech rights are necessary for protecting the free speech rights of corporate members (defined as shareholders), while the dissenting judges argued that the majority opinion implicitly assumes the Real-Entity Theory. Nevertheless, the ruling in *Citizens United* seems to hold an incredibly shareholder centric view of the political process. For one, why does it only consider shareholders as members of the corporation? If the argument centres on the free speech rights of corporate members then why not include corporate employees? Secondly, why are shareholders' political rights infringed by not allowing corporate political expenditure? They are not only shareholders, they are also citizens, and as such they have the same rights and opportunities for political speech as other citizens (that do not own shares). Thirdly, and perhaps most importantly, corporations are at law entirely separate legal persons from the shareholders and there is legally no necessary connection between shareholder's rights and corporate rights.

If corporations were truly moral agents, then not only should they be granted all the constitutional protections afforded to natural persons (who are also moral agents), but importantly every American corporation should be afforded the right to vote in every election open to the citizens of the United States. However, corporations are not moral agents, and my aim is to argue that they are primarily legal persons. Being the latter but not the former is an essential difference. It is by virtue of citizens possessing the capacities for moral agency that they are afforded their constitutional rights and privileges. If something or someone does not possess autonomy, intentionality or the ability to act, then there is nothing there for rights to protect. What value is the right to freedom of speech for something that cannot intend nor communicate? A corporation, being merely a legal person, does not have the fundamental capacities that could be used to justify that it too should have the privileges of natural persons under the constitution. Furthermore, given the legal separation of the corporation from its members, it is difficult to see how shareholder's political rights are infringed by disallowing corporate political speech. Whether or not the corporation is afforded constitutional rights and privileges ought to be a matter for the state to decide in its representative capacity of helping to further the ends of its citizens. Representatives of the state should be asking themselves the following question: is conferring such and such a right to the corporate legal form a good *means* of furthering the *ends* of our citizens?

As we have seen, on several occasions the courts have relied on the Real Entity Theory and the Nexus-of-Contracts Theory to motivate their decisions to confer rights and privileges to corporations. Blumberg (1993: 31) writes: "In the process of constitutional construction, theories of the corporate personality inevitably played a role in determining the extent to which corporations could invoke constitutional provisions and obtain constitutional rights". These theories, especially the Real Entity Theory, contributed to a reified conception of the corporation. Part I of this book will hopefully have convinced you that the corporation does not possess the necessary capacities for moral agency and consequently the Real Entity Theory is false. The Nexus-of-Contracts Theory is also descriptively false as it is openly phrased as a counterfactual. Recall that it says that it is possible to represent the corporate legal form *as if* it were a nexus-of-contracts. It says that the corporate form is just a short-hand process of obtaining the contractual relations that individuals would privately contract, were it not the case that the state had already conferred them. The fact of the matter is that the corporate form is not a web of contracts and individuals did not create such a web to mimic the rights and privileges of incorporation. If they actually could, they also would, and thus the constitutional rights of corporations would be of little importance as they could then contractually create those rights for themselves anyway. (The descriptive shortcomings of the Nexus-of-Contracts Theory will be discussed in greater detail in Sect. 11.1).

Misguided legal theories lead to both misguided legislation and misguided court rulings. Corporations are neither real entities nor a nexus-of-contracts, and to portray them as such leads to legislation that reifies the corporation in such a manner that it will confer legal rights to corporations that there is no good reason for them to have.

When judges use language in a certain way, for example when they speak of a corporation as an "organism", "a set of contractual relations", or as an "artificial being", this has normative significance that stretches beyond the individual court case. Warren Samuels (1989: 127) says that the judicial affirmation of the corporation as a person "is a linguistic means of establishing nominative premises functional for subsequent legal reasoning and choice". This would seem to suggest that the personification of the corporation in law has helped to conceptually reify the corporation in the minds of judges. Therefore, even though *Santa Clara* was not influenced by the Real Entity Theory, the decision to regard the corporation as a person should have helped the Real Entity Theory's rise to dominance at the end of the nineteenth century. Blumberg seems to concur with Samuels when he writes:

"First, in the law, concepts have a life of their own because of their influence over the thinking of judges and their usefulness in justifying conclusions... Second, the use of a particular language has a cultural force of its own. Identification of the corporation as a "person" may start as a metaphor, but its usage gives rise to an association between the attributes of a person and those of the corporation" (Blumberg 1993: 47). Thus, the use of a certain theory about the nature of the corporation reinforces itself and prescribes its further use each time it is drawn on in judicial decisions.

Recent and important court rulings towards the end of the twentieth century, such as *Massachusetts Citizens for Life* and *Austin*, have not made use of a reified conception of the corporation. However, in the growing field of business ethics and the ever expanding CSR movement the dominant position is to regard the corporation as a moral agent. Therefore, to the extent that such concepts start to gain acceptance again in the legal domain there should be a heightened concern today for a backlash to a Real Entity Theory permeating political and legal thought. Although *Citizens United* (2010) did not explicitly rely on the Real Entity theory, the dissenting judges did seem to think that it was implicit.

A very good way to exemplify the category mistake that occurs when judges equate the status of natural persons with that of corporate persons is to look at cases where a corporation is set against a person in a court case. John Flynn highlights the case of Adair v. United States in 1908, set at a time when the Real Entity Theory was firmly established. The case involved the application of the courts fixed concept of contracts, which is regarded "as a freely bargained and consensual relationship between two persons of equal bargaining strength" (Flynn 1989: 141). An important issue in the case was how this concept of contracts was to be applied to legislation restricting the right of an employer to fire employees for union activity. Flynn (1989: 42) writes: "[T]he Court took no note of the difference between an individual human person doing so [firing an employee] and a powerful and far-flung corporate person doing so. The concept of corporate personhood was so entrenched in the minds of the judges as to prevent the issue of whether contracts by corporate persons should be treated differently from contracts by natural persons from even being thought of, let alone from being raised as a fact that ought to be considered".

The *Adair* case is a good exemplification of how judges come to regard the corporate legal person in a reified from, influenced by the contemporary popularity of the Real Entity Theory and previous references by other judges to the corporation as a "person". To misconstrue the status of the corporation in this way inhibits judges from appreciating the important differences between corporations and natural persons and might therefore lead to unfair rulings and precedents against natural persons.

- Summarizing remarks: Ever since the *Santa Clara* case of 1886 the status of the corporation as a person for the purpose of the protections of the American constitution has been an important topic of legal debate. By establishing the corporation as a person for the purposes of the 14th Amendment to the Constitution, *Santa Clara* set a precedent both as a matter of law and in terms of the prescriptive use of judicial language. This in turn helped confer more constitutional privileges upon corporations similar to those of natural persons. Some of those privileges were aided by the Nexus-of-Contracts Theory and some were conferred by judges in court rulings that relied on a reified conception of the corporation influenced by the Real Entity Theory. These descriptively false legal theories have helped to influence misguided and unfair legislation and court rulings. Important recent court rulings towards the end of the twentieth century, such as *Massachusetts Citizens for Life* and *Austin*, have not made use of a reified conception of the corporation. Nevertheless, most recently, *Citizens United* (2010) explicitly relied on the Nexus-of-Contracts Theory (and according to the dissenting judges implicitly relied on the Real Entity Theory). There should be a heightened concern today for a backlash to reified conceptions of the corporation, especially with the growing advocacy of corporate social responsibilities based on an erroneous conception of corporate moral agency.

10.7 The Corporation as Socio-economic Instrument

The aim of this section is to analyse and summarize the discussion so far through the perspective of the *role* that the corporate legal form has played as an instrument in the process of industrialization and economic development of nations.

Let us start at the beginning of the industrial revolution. It is generally acknowledged that the industrial revolution began in the third quarter of the eighteenth century in Britain and was characterised by a widespread replacement of manual labour by machines. One might say that it was technological innovation that sparked the industrial revolution. Examples of the most important innovations in Britain at the time were the steam engine and the spinning frame. Several different social, political and legal conditions were also present to enable and encourage that these innovations be used for productive and commercial purposes. For example, Britain had a stable political system with a stable rule of law, which reduced the risk that the sovereign might arbitrarily seize private property. Furthermore, the security of private property and the existence of patents for innovations meant that investors could plan long term investments that are crucial for economic growth. Britain also pursued an economic policy that was comparatively unregulated. In 1776 Adam Smith published his ground breaking book "An Inquiry into the Nature and Causes of the Wealth of Nations", which greatly helped to advocate a free-market approach to economic policy. The British free-market approach allowed new ideas and innovations to prosper with comparatively little interference or regulation.

The immediate economic changes that the industrial revolution brought were not only the manner in which production was carried out, but also where it was carried out. Industry drew synergy benefits from concentrating in one place, which led to a rapid urbanization and expansion of the cities as people moved in from the countryside looking for employment. The combination of the political, legal and innovative climate thus led to a brisk expansion of commercial activity on a scale of mass production.

The economic success of Britain attracted a lot of attention and several European countries tried to follow suit. However, the most successful imitator came from the other side of the Atlantic in the form of Britain's ex-colony, America, which had newly gained independence. America was quick to follow in Britain's footsteps and jumpstarted its own industrial revolution.

Now, where does the corporation fit into this story of economic change and growth? In Pre nineteenth century Britain and America there were very few corporations and they did not have the pervasive economic and social influence that they have in society today. Recall that at the start of the industrial revolution corporations only existed as companies that had been granted Royal Charter or been created through a Special Act of Parliament. These Charters and Acts were very difficult to come by. The Industrial Revolution therefore sparked an increased demand to start Joint Stock Companies as a form of association in which recourses could be pooled and commercial enterprise carried out. As we shall see the growth and success of these companies in turn created pressure to augment the legislation governing such companies resulting in the Companies Acts 1844–1862.

Ronald Coase is one of the few economists that have specifically written about why companies exist in economic terms. His theory will help us understand why the growth of Joint Stock Companies during the industrial revolution put such economic pressure on granting general incorporation statutes and limited liability. Coase's (1988: 14) theory can be put quite briefly as: "In the absence of transaction costs, there is no economic basis for the existence of the firm". Transaction costs are in the words of Carl Dahlman "search and information costs, bargaining and decision costs, policing and enforcement costs" (Coase 1988: 6). Coase (1988: 7) explains: "The fact that it costs something to enter into these [economic] transactions means that firms will emerge to organize what would otherwise be market transactions whenever their costs were less than the costs of carrying out the transactions through the market". That is to say, people come together to form a company in order to reduce the transaction costs that exist in the market.[23] The absence of economic transaction within a company in effect implies that internal company transactions involve a suppression of the price mechanism.

The need to suppress the price mechanism indicates that there is a cost involved in using it. One of these costs is the very act of finding out what the relevant prices are. Another important cost is the making of contracts with all parties that are to be involved in an enterprise. In the market each owner of a factor of production must make a contract with every other factor of production owner in a nexus of cooperative production. In this economic sense the company is a cost efficient way of eliminating the nexus-of-contracts that otherwise would need to be bargained as independent market transactions.

However, there is another cost within the market that is all-important if there is to be a need to establish a company. That cost is uncertainty. For example, in order

[23] A consequence of this is that the theoretical ideal of a perfect market (characterised by an absence of transaction costs) would not have any companies.

to make long-term investments one needs to be able to plan that certain factors of production will be available in the future. Very short-term contracts of independent labour will thus be inadequate to plan future production. This will prompt the need to employ labour in order to guarantee a continuity of labour with the required skills.

With uncertainty in the picture the primary cost of production becomes how to coordinate the different factors of production. To make this coordination possible long-term contracts are extremely helpful and thus we observe the desire to form companies that encompass this contractual state of affairs. As Coase (1988: 41–42) puts it: "A firm, therefore, consists of the system of relationships which comes into existence when the direction of resources is dependent on an entrepreneur".

Now, I have maintained that the company's economic raison de être is founded on reducing transaction costs.[24] The pressure on the state to create general incorporation statutes and grant limited liability towards the middle of the nineteenth century can be viewed in terms of reducing transaction costs. At the start of the industrial revolution it was possible for virtually any group of people to start a Joint Stock Company. This in itself created many economic benefits for reducing transaction cost. The Joint Stock Company, however, had practical limitations particularly with regard to pooling pool funds for investment.

The 1844 Joint Stock Companies Act provided for general articles of incorporation and allowed shares to be transferred without the express consent of all the co-partners. This by itself increased the transferability of shares and thus reduced the cost of anyone wishing to transfer a share in a Joint Stock Company. This enabled newly formed corporations to obtain funds for the commencement of an enterprise far easier than was the case when the Joint Stock Company was considered a form of partnership and thus the potential transfer of shares required the consent of all the co-partners. Many of the companies being formed under the industrial revolution were very capital intensive and thus this new legislation helped companies obtain more capital.

Although the 1844 Joint Stock Companies Act was a manifest improvement for pooling resources it still had limitations. Without limited liability investing in a Joint Stock Company was very risky for investors as their personal wealth was accessible in the event of bankruptcy. This meant that in practice only people of great wealth, who could also participate in the management of the company, would be willing to part with their financial resources. Industrialisation meant that companies were growing larger and needed further capital to expand and so the pressure to confer limited liability upon incorporation increased. In Britain this was finally granted with the Joint Stock Companies Acts of 1855 and 1856. This presented

[24]Interestingly Adam Smith thought that corporations were inefficient in comparison with sole traders and disliked that companies like the East India Company were granted monopoly status in their Royal Charters. He acknowledged that corporations could be useful for banking, insurance, and public utilities that required vast amounts of financial capital and management skill, but otherwise he considers them to be inefficient for ordinary competitive enterprise. This conviction was probably a reflection of his over-reliance on the market mechanism and a disregard for transaction costs.

a significant decrease in the risk of investment and thus decreased the transaction costs for companies for the further pooling of resources. Now corporations were able to solicit more financial resources from a wider public to finance the capital intensive investments of the mass producing industrial revolution.

Limited liability was by no means an essential component of the industrial revolution, shown by the fact that English industry expanded enormously during the first 100 years of the revolution without it (Blumberg 1993). However, by the middle of the nineteenth century Britain had come to a point in its industrial development were limited liability was sorely needed if its economic growth was to continue. As mentioned, Limited liability also provided a host of other benefits. Among the most important being that it firmly cemented the separation of the corporation from the shareholders, which allowed the corporate share to develop into a form of property in its own right. Without this development we may never have seen the liquid stock markets of today.

The corporate legal form is a contract that confers upon an association of people the status of a legal person with primarily the following attributes: Limited liability, a separation of shareholders and corporate entity, a shareholder primacy norm, shares as an autonomous form of property, and perpetual life. These attributes serve macro and micro economic ends and are all consistent with the Legal Fiction Theory.

It seems clear to me that the Legal Fiction Theory is descriptively dominant. The Real Entity Theory is false because the corporation does not possess the metaphysical characteristics for moral agency it attributes to the corporation. The Nexus-of-Contracts Theory is primarily false because it counterfactually describes the corporation *as if* it were a web of contracts when it is actually one grand encompassing legal form. Furthermore, both these theories are historically incorrect when they deny that the corporate form is a state creation. The corporate form was first created by the state and corporations are still granted corporate status by the state through general incorporation statutes. This point is further reinforced by the fact that corporate law in most countries stipulates charter revocation clauses, which grants the state the power to terminate the existence of a corporation if it is not deemed to serve the public good. It is only the Legal Fiction Theory that maintains that the corporate legal form is *granted* to associations of people. It is only the Legal Fiction theory that places the state in such a position of dominance as to revoke a corporation's license to operate if it does not serve the public good.

In the context of the industrial revolution we can see how the corporate form was instrumental for reducing transaction costs for companies and enabling the pooling of capital for industrial investment. It was in fact the state that conferred the legal rights and privileges of incorporation upon associations of individuals. These rights were not created by self-contracting individuals nor were they moral rights owed to the corporation as a social organism. Rather it was the state that after many years of heated political debate decided that it was in the economic interest of its citizens to allow for general incorporation statutes and limited liability. In this sense conferring legal rights and privileges upon the corporation is done instrumentally, as a *means* to furthering the socio-economic *ends* of its citizens. Therefore, the corporate form conceived as a bundle of legal rights and privileges granted to associations of people is an instrument for the socio-economic ends of the state.

Having analysed the influence of the corporate legal form on the economic activities of a nation, we should make sure to notice the distinction between the *corporate legal form* on the one hand and *actual corporations* that are actors in the market on the other hand. I have argued that the corporate legal form is *descriptively* an instrument of the state, and next I shall also go on to argue that the *role* of the corporate legal form *prescriptively* ought to be an instrument of the state. I will in addition maintain that the *goal* of actual corporations ought to primarily be as instruments of the incorporating parties pursuing their own ends within the legal restrictions set by the corporate legal form and industry regulation.

References

American Law Institute. 1994. *Principles of corporate governance: Analysis and recommendations*. St. Paul: American Law Institute Publishers.

Anderson, E. 2000. Beyond homo economics: New developments in theories of social norms. *Philosophy and Public Affairs* 29(2): 170–200.

Bakan, J. 2004. *The corporation*. London: Constable.

Benz, M., and B.S. Frey. 2007. Corporate governance: What can we learn from public governance? *Academy of Management Review* 32: 92–104.

Berle, A.A. 1931. Corporate powers as powers of trust. *Harvard Law Review* 44: 1049–1074.

Berle, A.A. 1932. For whom are corporate managers trustees: A note. *Harvard Law Review* 45(7): 1365–1372.

Berle, A.A., and G. Means. 1932. *The modern corporation and private property*. New York: Macmillan.

Blumberg, P. 1993. *The multinational challenge to corporate law: The search for a new corporate personality*. New York: Oxford University Press.

Boatright, J.R. 1994. Fiduciary duties and the shareholder-management relation: Or, what's so special about shareholders? *Business Ethics Quarterly* 4(4): 393–407.

Bowman, S. 1996. *The modern corporation and American political thought: Law, power and ideology*. Pennsylvania: Pennsylvania State University Press.

Campbell, J.L. 2007. Why would corporations behave in socially responsible ways? An institutional theory of corporate social responsibility. *Academy of Management Review* 32(3): 946–967.

Cane, P. 2002. *Responsibility in law and morality*. Oxford: Hart.

Cialdini, R.B., and M.R. Trost. 1998. Social influence: Social norms, conformity and compliance. In *The handbook of social psychology*, vol. 2, ed. D.T. Gilbert, S.T. Fiske, and G. Lindzey, 151–192. New York: McGraw-Hill.

Coase, H. 1988. *The firm the market and the law*. Chicago: University of Chicago Press.

Dobson, J. 1999. Is shareholder wealth maximization immoral? *Financial Analysts Journal* 55(5): 69–75.

Dodd, M.E. 1932. For whom are corporate managers trustees? *Harvard Law Review* 45: 1145–1163.

Easterbrook, F., and D. Fischel. 1985. Limited liability and the corporation. *University of Chicago Law Review* 52: 89–117.

Evan, W.M., and R.E. Freeman. 2003. A stakeholder theory of the modern corporation: Kantian capitalism. In *Ethical theory and business*, ed. T.L. Beauchamp and N.E. Bowie. London: Prentice Hall.

Flynn, J.J. 1989. The jurisprudence of corporate personhood: The misuse of a legal concept. In *Corporations and society: Power and responsibility*, ed. W.J. Samuels and A.S. Miller. London: Greenwood.

Gentile, Mary C. 2004. *Corporate governance and accountability: What do we know and what do we teach future business leaders?* The Aspen Institute Business & Society Program.

Ghoshal, S. 2005. Bad management theories are destroying good management practices. *Academy of Management Learning and Education* 4: 75–91.

Griffiths, O., and E.M. Taylors. 1949. *The principles of company law*. London: Textbooks.

Hinkley, R. 2002. How corporate law inhibits social responsibility. *Business Ethics: Corporate Social Responsibility Report*. Jan/Feb.

Horwitz, M.J. 1989. Santa Clara revisited: The development of corporate theory. In *Corporations and society: Power and responsibility*, ed. W.J. Samuels and A.S. Miller. London: Greenwood.

Ireland, P. 1996. Capitalism without the capitalist: The Joint Stock Company share and the emergence of the modern doctrine of separate corporate personality. *Journal of Legal History* 17: 41–73.

Jensen, M., and W.H. Meckling. 1976. Theory of the firm: Agency costs, managerial behavior and ownership structure. *Journal of Financial Economics* 3: 305–360.

Kraakman, R.R., P. Davies, H. Hansmann, G. Hertig, K.J. Hopt, H. Kanda, and E.B. Rock. 2004. *The anatomy of corporate law: A comparative and functional approach*. New York: Oxford University Press.

Marmor, A. 2004. The rule of law and its limits. *Law and Philosophy* 23: 1–43.

Pennington, R.R. 1987. *Directors' personal liability*. London: Collins Professional and Technical.

Phillips, M.J. 1994. Reappraising the real entity theory of the corporation. *Florida State University Law Review* 21: 1061–1123.

Phillips, R., E.R. Freeman, and A.C. Wicks. 2003. What stakeholder theory is not. *Business Ethics Quarterly* 13(4): 479–502.

Pickering, M.A. 1968. Company as a separate legal entity. *Modern Law Review* 31: 481.

Samuels, W.J. 1989. The idea of the corporation as a person: On the normative significance of a judicial language. In *Corporations and society: Power and responsibility*, ed. W.J. Samuels and A.S. Miller. London: Greenwood.

Skadden. 2011. Air Products & Chemicals, Inc. v. Airgas, Inc. *Skadden Newsletter*, February 16. Available at: http://www.skadden.com/newsletters/Air_Products_Chemicals_Inc_v_Airgas_Inc.pdf. Accessed 14 May 2013.

Smith, D.G. 1998. The shareholder primacy norm. *The Journal of Corporate Law* 23: 277.

Stout, L. 2012. *The shareholder value myth: How putting shareholders first harms investors, corporations and the public*. San Francisco: Berrett-Koehler Publishers, Inc.

Testy, K. 2002. Linking progressive corporate law with progressive social movements. *Tulane Law Review* 76: 1227–1252.

West, D.M. 2011. *The purpose of the corporation in business and law school curricula*. Governance Studies at Brookings: http://www.brookings.edu/~/media/research/files/papers/2011/7/19-corporation-west/0719_corporation_west.pdf

Wolff, M. 1938. On the nature of legal persons. *Law Quarterly Review* 54: 494–505.

Chapter 11
The Role of the Corporation in Society: The Prescriptive View

In this section I shall broadly speaking be exploring three areas relating to the purpose the corporation *ought* to have in society. First of all I shall consider whether or not the corporate legal form ought to have a *role* as an instrument of the state. I have so far argued that the corporate legal form descriptively speaking is such an instrument, but I shall look more closely at the libertarian position that maintains through a nexus-of-contracts perspective that it ought *not* to be used as such an instrument.

Secondly, having argued that the corporate form nevertheless ought to be used as an instrument of the state, I shall take issue with the Corporate Social Responsibility movement with regard to how the instrument ought to be used. In other words, ought actual corporations to be instruments whose primary *goal* is to further the interests of the incorporating parties or ought it to serve the interests of a broader group of stakeholders? I shall argue in favour of an idealized version of Shareholder Theory whereby managers should focus on shareholder interests, while stakeholder concerns are explicitly accounted for in legislation. I will maintain that many of the prescriptions that the CSR movement advocates are very difficult to uphold unless one also illegitimately relies on the corporation qualifying as a moral agent. I will argue that the issues that CSR wishes to tackle are better addressed through public initiatives and legislation by government.

Thirdly, and finally, I shall juxtapose the social role of government against the goal of corporations to demarcate a distinction between a public and private sphere of social activity. In this context I shall also look at the justification for our use of the market in society and how this bears on the moral responsibilities of managers. I shall also consider the justification for state legislation that frames the space of acceptable behaviour within the market.

Given the instrumental role of the corporate legal form in society I will come to suggest that the citizens of a democratic state should through representative government enact in law the duties they require corporations to fulfil. In other words,

D. Rönnegard, *The Fallacy of Corporate Moral Agency*,
Issues in Business Ethics 44, DOI 10.1007/978-94-017-9756-6_11

the normative force of the argument is that citizens ought to *primarily* make calls for *legal enactments* to hold the corporate legal instruments accountable to their preferences.

11.1 Ought the Corporate Legal Form to Be Used as an Instrument of the State?

If the corporation is an instrument then it is *not* an end in itself. It is merely a means to some end. I have suggested that descriptively the corporate legal form *is* an instrument for the ends of the state. One might also endorse this state of affairs and formulate it as a prescription; i.e. that the corporation *ought* to be an instrument of the state. This is contrary to the Real Entity Theory because the theory regards the corporation as a social organism with the attributes for moral agency and thus the corporation *is* an end in itself. However, the prescription that corporations ought to be an instrument of the state is also contrary to the Nexus-of-Contracts Theory. This is not because the theory disagrees with the corporation functioning as an instrument, but rather because it ought not to be an instrument of the *state*. Underlying the Nexus-of-Contracts Theory is the idea that the corporation ought to merely be a commercial instrument for furthering the ends of the contracting parties. I shall suggest that actual corporations are indeed the instruments of the incorporating parties, but that the corporate legal form, which regulates corporations, is an instrument of the state.

Blumberg (1993) points out that this nexus-of-contracts perspective is driven by a libertarian ideology. Libertarians advocate a position of minimalist government that has a very limited right to interfere in the affairs of its citizens. In general, the contracts made by freely contracting parties are seen as a private activity where the state may not interfere. Therefore, conceiving of the corporation as a nexus-of-contracts together with the underlying libertarian ideology, we obtain a prescriptive theory which says that the corporation ought to be merely an instrument for the ends of the contracting parties and denies that it may be used for the instrumental ends of the state.

Specifically with regard to corporate contracting the right that inhibits state interference is the libertarian advocacy of absolute property rights. The connection is that the Nexus-of-Contracts Theory, which regards the corporation as an aggregation of its members, does not accept the complete separation of corporation and shareholders. This lack of separation between corporation and shareholders is used to justify the rights of the corporation with reference to the rights of the incorporators. Corporate shares are regarded as shares of corporate assets and not as property that is entirely distinct from the corporation. Because libertarians, such as Nozick (1974), advocate absolute property rights this acts as a justification for why the state may not interfere in the affairs of the corporation as this would be a breach of the shareholders' property rights. If property rights are absolute then the private web of contracts that constitutes the corporation are also inviolable because the contracts pertain to the managing of property.

The Nexus-of-Contracts Theory is at once both a descriptive and a prescriptive theory. These two aspects need to be distinguished. It is prescriptive because it is based on a libertarian ideology that says that corporations ought to be used merely as instruments for the incorporating parties. It is also a descriptive theory in that it says that the corporate legal form may be regarded as the equivalent of individual contracts negotiated among all the members of the corporation. On the face of it this description seems rather uncontroversial because it does not say much more than that we can represent an equivalent contractual situation to the corporate legal form if we construct a web of contracts among individuals. However, note that this description assumes the prior existence of the corporate legal form. It assumes the truth of the antecedent in the following conditional: If we have a corporate legal form *then* it can be represented as a web of contracts among individuals. The Nexus-of-Contracts Theory also makes another assertion. It says that if the corporate legal form were not conferred by the state *then* private contracting parties would create the equivalent contractual situation by themselves. This is however a far more contentious proposition. It not only involves representing the corporate legal form in terms of a web of contracts but it also makes the claim that actual contacting parties could and would create an equivalent contractual situation in the absence of a state grant.

I shall in this section primarily take issue with the prescriptive aspect of the Nexus-of-Contracts Theory, but in order to do this I will also confront the validity of the descriptive claim as this will be helpful in evaluating the libertarian position.[1] Let us start with the descriptive claim that in the absence of a state grant people could and would form associations resembling a web of contracts that collectively would be equivalent to the corporate legal form conferred by the state.

11.1.1 The Problem with the Descriptive Claims of the Nexus-of-Contracts Theory

I shall consider two separate questions. Firstly, could a corporation exist without the state? Secondly, assuming the existence of a libertarian state, could and would the corporate legal form evolve without a state grant?

The first question essentially amounts to asking if a corporation could exist in the "state of nature".[2] It is highly unlikely that this is possible and libertarians

[1]When I speak of "libertarianism" as a political theory I broadly have in mind the libertarianism advocated by Robert Nozick in *Anarchy, State and Utopia* because this work is considered to be one of the most influential libertarian theories of the twentieth century.

[2]The "state of nature" is a hypothetical scenario of human existence at a time before states and societies based on co-operation developed.

are likely to agree because although they do advocate a minimalist state they do believe that the state does serve a legitimate purpose. Its role is to maintain the background institutions that are needed to ensure personal security and to protect the system of free exchanges. This is primarily achieved through two institutions; firstly, the legal system that exists to enact laws and administer justice, and secondly, the police that exists to enforce the law. These institutions are seen as forming the main components of the minimalist state and that is why libertarians like Robert Nozick are said to advocate the "Night Watchman State". For a corporation to exist as a web of contracts it is necessary to have both a situation of personal security that allows for trade to occur among individuals and for there to be a third party guarantor of the contractual relations in which the associating parties enter. If it is not possible to trade because people fear for their lives when they come into contact with each other, then clearly there is no incentive nor possibility to associate for commercial purposes. Furthermore, unless there is some third partly, like a state, to administer justice and enforce contracts, then there is little to keep people to their contractual commitments and little to keep the nexus-of-contracts together whenever those contracts are not self-enforcing. Therefore the corporation could not exist without the state (or its functional equivalent) to provide a legal system to enforce laws and contracts with its "monopoly of force".

- The corporation is dependent on the existence of a state: Without a state to provide an environment with a minimum level of personal security there can be no trade. And without a state to provide a legal system for the enforcement of contracts the nexus-of-contracts could fall apart.

Secondly, assuming that we do have at least a minimal state, could and would the corporate form evolve though private contracting if it were not conferred by the state? It seems fairly certain that people could, as they indeed have through history, band together in associations for commercial purposes. But what we need to answer is whether such a concerted band of people could contract together the attributes that we today associate with the corporate legal form. The legal attributes of the corporate form such as the shareholder primacy norm, perpetual life, and shares as an autonomous form of property could all be contracted among the associating parties. These are contractual relations that only affect the contracting parties and therefore it is not essential that these contracts are agreed to by third parties if they are to serve their purpose. These private contracts will have legal force as long as the state allows them and enforces the contracts. This should not be a problem because I am assuming that a minimal state is in place and therefore it has virtually no right to intervene in private contracts, merely a duty to enforce those contracts. Furthermore, one might even imagine the private contracting parties creating a separation of shareholders from the corporate legal entity. Such a separation is descriptively inconsistent with a nexus-of-contracts description of the corporation as an aggregation of the contractual relations of the members, but it is still conceivable that the contracting parties purely as a point of law decide to separate the corporate fiction from the shareholders because it serves their purposes. So far so good for the libertarians.

The main problem that arises for libertarians is to convincingly maintain that limited liability could be privately contracted. Limited liability is the attribute that is financially most important to the incorporators and it is also the attribute that has the biggest macro-economic effects, therefore it is imperative that libertarians can account for the potential private genesis of limited liability. Easterbrook and Fischel (1985: 93) write: "If limited liability were not provided by law, firms would attempt to create it by contract". This proposition is often stated but never scrutinized. First we must ask: *Could* private contracting parties really contract limited liability? Secondly, would they have sufficient incentive to do so?

Technically, it could be possible for companies to privately contract a truncated version of limited liability, but not one that extends to all potential creditors. What a company can do and what some in fact tried to do, prior to the granting of limited liability through general incorporation statutes, was to contract limited liability with each and every business relation. That is to say, they tried to contract limited liability with all external relations of the company such as customers and suppliers. However, the act of getting all your business relations to contractually accept that your liability is limited falls short of limited liability with regard to all potential creditors. Some potential creditors have no contractual relation with the company at all. These people fall under the heading "the general public". If a company is legally responsible for proprietary or physical harm towards a member of the general public then there is no contractual relation to limit the liability of the shareholders. Hence, potential creditors may still make claims on the personal assets of shareholders because the company cannot *completely* limit its liability.

Secondly, would companies try to contract limited liability? I have already said that there were some attempts prior to the granting of limited liability through general incorporation statutes. Therefore clearly there is an incentive for individual companies to obtain a truncated version of limited liability. This incentive is primarily one of financing. Companies in capital intensive industries require large amounts of financial capital. This is much easier to obtain in terms of issuing shares if a company's liability is *completely* limited. Recall (Sect. 10.5) that limited liability reduces the risk of investment for shareholders because their personal assets are not accessible to creditors and this further has the effect of reducing the monitoring costs of shareholders. Not only do shareholders have to monitor the company managers less, but there is less need to monitor other shareholder because their personal wealth is no longer of consequence in the event of bankruptcy. Furthermore, this turns the company's shares into homogenous commodities with a single price irrespective of the identity of the shareholder. This consequently means that shareholders need not care to whom other shareholders sell their shares. Thus limited liability makes shares much more easily transferable. This transferability together with a reduction of investment risk and monitoring cost makes investing in shares more attractive and accessible to more people. Consequently limited liability is very helpful for a company to obtain large amounts of financial capital when issuing shares. In order to reap the lion's share of these benefits the liability of the shareholders needs to be *completely* limited. If this is not the case then it no longer holds that shareholders personal assets are shielded from creditors' claims and thus it no longer holds that shares are homogenous commodities and further the transferability of the shares is eroded. As a result, without *completely* limited liability the significant financing advantage of limited liability has essentially disappeared. Because it is only possible to *privately* contract a truncated form of limited liability this suggests that a significant incentive to attain limited liability for the company members is lacking for it to become a widespread phenomenon.

The reason an individual company cannot privately contract complete limited liability is that it cannot have a political mandate to make a contract with the general public. The corporation is not a political organization and it has not been granted the authority to represent the public. Corporate members merely represent the interest for which the corporation was formed. If a corporation were to have a role as a political organization then it would seize to be a goal directed enterprise and instead become an organization for the realization of the varying interests of its constituents.

The state does have such a political mandate to represent the public. It can put into effect a contractual state of affairs applicable to all citizens for the benefit of the general public through legislation. For example, Justice Marshal held in the case Dartmouth College v. Woodward (1819) that a corporation is a contract between the *public* and the persons acting as trustees for the corporation (Goedecke 1976). However, the state itself requires a mandate from its citizens in order to have the authority to make decisions on their behalf (beyond enforcing private contracts and personal safety). Therefore, if the state is to grant a contract to corporations limiting their liability with regard to the public this requires that the citizens confer powers upon the state that are beyond the minimal. Therefore, not only is it the case that private parties cannot contract complete limited liability, but if complete limited liability is to be granted by a state, then the state must also have powers beyond the minimal advocated by libertarians.

- The corporate form *could* not and *would* not exist without a state grant: Private contracting parties *could* only contract the equivalent of a truncated corporate legal form. Complete limited liability is not obtainable through private contracting because a company does not have a political mandate to contract with the general public. Only a state, beyond the libertarian minimum, is in a position to make such a contract. In the absence of a contract with the general public a company cannot limit its liability with regard to them. Without complete limited liability the lion's share of the benefits of limiting liability are lost. Therefore the incentive to seek a truncated form of limited liability is curtailed and consequently few *would* seek such a contract.

The preceding descriptive discussion acts in support of the view that the corporate legal form is a grant from the state. Not only have I shown that the corporate form could not completely evolve as a nexus-of-contracts, but I have also suggested that the crucial attribute of limited liability must be granted by a state with powers beyond the minimal. I shall now move on and take issue with the prescriptive aspect of the Nexus-of-Contracts Theory with regard to its libertarian underpinnings that object to the corporate legal form being used as an instrument of the state.

11.1.2 The Problem with the Libertarian Prescription for Absolute Property Rights

Irrespective of the correctness of the descriptive content of the Nexus-of-Contracts Theory, libertarians would still argue that the corporate form (or its libertarian truncated counterpart) ought not to be used as an instrument of the state but merely for the ends of the incorporating parties. As was mentioned earlier it is primarily the libertarian advocacy of absolute property rights that underscores the corporate legal form as merely the instrument of the incorporators.

For many libertarians absolute property rights are founded on the belief that property rights have a natural justification together with the view that a moral agent can only obtain a positive duty[3] with explicit consent. The concept of consent is of paramount importance to libertarians and underpins their conviction for inviolable negative rights of non-interference. Essentially the libertarian state may not do anything to or for its citizens without their explicit *consent*. As we shall see one of the main problems with the libertarian political ideology is its dogmatic defence of negative rights at the expense of positive rights.

Milton Friedman, a noted libertarian, supported very strong property rights (although not going as far as calling for absolute property rights). His main argument is instrumental on the grounds that economic freedom "promotes political freedom because it separates economic power from political power and in this way enables one to offset the other" (Friedman 1962: 9). In other words, private property is the cornerstone of economic freedom which in turn is also necessary for political freedom because only then can empowered dissent against the government exist. This instrumental justification for economic freedom is also consistent with his view on the nature of property rights. Friedman regards property rights as a "complex social creation" that is defined by government. As such property rights are created by us to serve instrumental purposes, although for Freidman those purposes are very fundamental.

Nozick, on the other hand, decided that he would try and establish property rights as fundamental in and of themselves. Nozick, who started off with strong socialist political views, became inspired by Friedman and Hayek and later came to write Anarchy, State, and Utopia, which is arguably the most influential libertarian text of the twentieth century. I shall take his political theory as the paradigmatic libertarian defence of the minimal state and absolute property rights.[4] By considering his theory

[3]A positive right is a right to receive help. It requires an action on behalf of a duty holder for the benefit of the positive right holder. In contrast a negative right is a right of non-interference. It requires a duty holder abstain from activity in relation to the negative right holder.

[4]Please note that I do not mean to say that libertarian property rights are absolute in the sense of trumping all other rights in society, for example the right to corporal liberty. Property rights are negative rights, i.e. they are a right of non-interference with one's property. Negative rights are often consistent with one another. However, negative rights may often conflict with positive rights to receive help. For example the positive right of someone who is starving to receive food from

of entitlement I shall lay bare the weakness with the libertarian prescription against the states instrumental use of the corporate form.

Nozick starts his book *Anarchy, State, and Utopia* by saying: "Individuals have rights, and there are things no person or group may do to them without violating their rights. So strong and far-reaching are these rights that they raise the question of what, if anything, the state may do" (Nozick 1974: ix). He later goes on to say: "The minimal state is the most extensive state that can be justified. Any state more extensive violates people's rights" (Nozick 1974: 149).

In order for Nozick to maintain that people have strong private property rights that may not be infringed upon he gives us two arguments: one for justice in initial acquisition (self-ownership argument) and one for justice in transfer the of holdings (consent argument). In other words one justification for why we may legitimately come to own something that was previously unowned and one justification for the legitimate transfer of ownership. Let us look at each justification in turn.

Firstly, Nozick's entitlement theory of distributive justice relies on the premise that individuals can in the first instance legitimately acquire holdings. That is to say that people can legitimately acquire previously unowned things that then become holdings that they are entitled to. In effect libertarianism advocates the view that the concept of property may exist in a state of nature and is not a social creation.

For Nozick the argument that establishes property rights in original acquisition is not primarily that we mix our labour with unowned objects (as was argued by John Locke), but rather that we own ourselves (in body and mind) and therefore we own everything that flows from these natural endowments. This argument is usually referred to as the self-ownership argument. It says that when we labour we add value to external objects through our natural endowments, and because we own our natural endowments we also come to have property rights over external objects. However, Nozick (in agreement with Locke) holds that it is not sufficient that we improve external objects with our natural endowments in order to yield absolute property rights over those objects if the appropriation of unowned objects might worsen the situation of those who do not have the opportunity to appropriate.[5] Nevertheless, Nozick believes that this condition is usually met. The idea is that even though all natural resources may already have been appropriated by people throughout history, those being born now need not be worse off because the ownership of property has beneficial economic consequences for all. Private property rights are said to allow the productive members of society to gain, which in turn creates labour opportunities for all, which leaves "enough and as good as" for others. Will Kymlicka (1990)

someone else will conflict with a food owner's right of non-interference with his food. Libertarians regard property rights to be *absolute* in the sense that they trump all non-contractual *positive* rights that might interfere with their property. In effect, libertarians argue against the existence of positive rights. Rawls (1999) and other liberals hold that positive rights are necessary to make the negative rights meaningful. For example, the liberty to pursue one's own destiny is vacuous unless one has some means (income and wealth) with which to pursue it (Nagel 1995).

[5]This statement is equivalent to the weak Lockean proviso, and in Nozickian terms is known as the "enough and as good as" proviso.

explains that property rights enable markets, and markets are efficient and give synergies, making people that cannot acquire property initially better off that if there were no property rights. For Nozick the concept of self-ownership together with the "enough and as good as" proviso are sufficient to yield absolute property rights that may not legitimately be violated by the state.

In response to this we may first ask if property rights are natural? Why does self-ownership entail the ownership of external objects? Nozick interprets self-ownership as implying absolute property rights over body, mind and external objects. But why does owning myself imply the ownership of external objects? The problem is one of interpretation. External objects are external to my person and therefore there is no similar sense in which I have a right to objects as I have a right to my person. Nozick needs to show us why we can move from owning our natural endowments to owning external objects. Nozick must answer why anything we do confers *absolute* rights to external objects?

Is there any inherent value to holding rights over property? Would anything fundamental to human existence be lacking without private property? As has been mentioned the crucial point for justice in original acquisition is that it should not worsen the condition of others (those living and those who are yet to be born), i.e. the "enough and as good as" proviso. To this Nozick answers that the economic synergies associated with the institution of private property are of such magnitude as to make those not able to originally acquire property (because all property is already owned) better off than if private property rights did not exist. But this argument avoids the problem of justifying the original appropriation and instead serves as a justification for the legitimate transfer of holdings. This is a utilitarian argument for property rights. Property rights are being justified due to their socially beneficial consequences, rather than as a fundamental right of individuals who initially appropriate objects external to themselves. Jonathan Wolff (1996: 158) says: "It is part of the argument that individuals should hold property, but it is less important how they come to hold that property . . . the issue of justice in transfer takes priority over the issue of justice in initial acquisition". Therefore the "enough and as good as" proviso does not establish property rights as fundamental because they are viewed as merely instrumental for obtaining desirable consequences.

To establish private property rights as natural or fundamental is very problematic. Wherein lies the inherent value of such rights? However, it is very simple to give property rights a utilitarian justification, for example along the lines of Nozick's "enough and as good as" proviso. Clearly the existence of property rights has very beneficial economic consequences. Without private property there would be little or no incentive for homo-economicus to be productive as such production would not result in a proprietary reward. This instrumental description of property rights lends itself to suggest that private property rights are a *social creation* justified in relation to its instrumental benefits.

- <u>The self-ownership argument fails to establish property rights for initial acquisition</u>: The self-ownership argument is weak because it fails to make the link between self-ownership and property ownership. Furthermore, the "enough and as good as" proviso misses the point because it supports a utilitarian view of transfer of property rights rather than property rights in initial acquisition.

Let us now consider Nozick's view of justice in transfer of holdings. He believes that if some property is legitimately appropriated in initial acquisition then the only manner in which that property can be justly transferred is with the *consent* of the owner. Any non-consensual transfer coerced by the state or otherwise amounts to theft.

Nozick (1974) believes that any interference by the state to create a certain pattern of wealth distribution among citizens will be unjust. For example, he asks us to imagine that we live in a society where income and wealth is distributed according to our favourite pattern, say "each according to their need", in which case our society will have a distribution D1. If we allow *consenting* adults to engage in free exchanges then this pattern will be upset (because free exchanges do not follow an intentional pattern) leading to a distribution D2. This leads to the question: If D1 is just, then is not D2 also just as it has come about through the free exchanges of consenting adults? Nozick maintains that it would be a restriction of personal *liberty* and a violation of people's rights if the state intervened to *redistribute* income back to the original distribution D1 because each individual is entitled to their holdings.

Nozick goes as far as to say "taxation of earnings is on par with forced labour". He reasons that because part of your earnings are taken in the form of taxation, then part of the time you are working is for free, which is meant to be equivalent to "forced labour". Nozick adheres to the Kantian dictum that people should always be treated as ends in themselves and never as means. High earners, he says, are used as mere means for those who earn less because income is redistributed from the well-off to the less well-off. This is meant to add to the argument for absolute property rights, because if property rights are not absolute then people may be used as mere means without their *consent*.

Nozick uses these examples to show us that a just distribution is one that results from consensual exchanges and that upholding wealth patterns involves violating property rights. However, Kymlicka (1990) points out that Nozick's example is deceptive. The reason is that a society, which distributes resources according to our favourite pattern, need not distribute absolute property rights to those resources. It is precisely the legitimacy of such rights that is at stake. Therefore Nozick is not putting forward an argument for absolute property rights, but simply stating in a rhetorical manner that they are absolute.

Furthermore, the "enough and as good as" proviso is meant to guarantee that latecomers (those who come after all resources have been originally appropriated) are meant to have access to the benefits of resources indirectly through labour opportunities. This however entails that latecomers become means for those who have already appropriated resources, because proprietors use individuals as labour (means) in order to further their own financial ends. Latecomers do not have the opportunity of originally appropriating resources; they can only labour for their own subsistence.[6] This in turn undercuts the self-ownership argument that adheres to the Kantian dictum of always treating people as ends and not merely as means. Moreover, Nozick emphasises the importance of actual consent in order for individuals to gain obligations, however it would seem that latecomers never give their consent to the initial appropriators to acquire property. Wolff (1991: 101) says that "appropriating property inflicts new duties of non-interference upon people, imposing new obligations. Unless one insists that no one can appropriate property without the consent of all those affected by the appropriation, these obligations will often be imposed upon people without their consent". Thus it would seem that Nozick's consent argument falters on its own premise.[7]

- The consent argument for transfer of holdings fails to establish absolute property rights: Nozick's consent argument against patterned distributions of wealth maintains that absolute property rights have been violated if the state redistributes income. However, it does not justify that property rights are absolute because the central issue is if the state also distributes such property rights. Libertarians would object that justice in initial acquisition of holdings is possible and thus property rights are not a social creation to be distributed by the state. In that case the entire burden of justification for absolute property rights falls on the weak self-ownership argument for justice in initial acquisition. It is difficult to find a good argument for why self-ownership by itself should lead to the *absolute* ownership of external objects.

Nozick states that "taxation of earnings is on par with forced labour" because part of the earnings gained through labour are taken by the state without the *consent* of its citizens. This argument is only strong if we assume that actual consent is necessary in order to obtain any positive duties or obligations towards others. G.A. Cohen (1995) points out that we have many non-contractual moral obligations to one another without having been asked if we want an obligation. Consent is not the only premise for obligations. Most people would agree with the moral intuition that we do not only have duties of non-interference but also some positive moral duties to help those in need. It may therefore be said that taxation does not entail treating net tax contributors as means because they already have a duty to help those in need.

Nozick appeals strongly to our moral intuition for negative rights but seems to ignore our intuition for positive rights. He tries to establish property rights as absolute thus making them inviolable to moral duties to help others. Nagel (1995: 143) says: "It is far less plausible to maintain that taking some of an innocent man's

---

[6]It is this condition of having to sell one's labour that Carl Marx was alluding to with the phrase "wage slavery".

[7]It may further be argued that transactions or transfers based on consent need not be fair. For example, if the power relations between two people (or groups) are grossly uneven, then the weaker party may consent to an agreement that is unfair. It may be said that the weaker party is being used by the stronger party. This is exemplified by the development of trade unions during the industrial revolution in order to balance the overwhelming power positions of employers.

property is an impermissible means for the prevention of serious evil, than it is to maintain that killing him is impermissible. These rights vary in importance and some are not absolute". Scanlon (1976: 7–8) goes on to say, "it may be true, as Nozick claims, that there is a continuum of interferences extending from taxation to forced labour, each foreclosing a few more options than the preceding. But the fact that there is such a continuum does not mean that we are indifferent to any two points along it". Nagel (1995: 146) renders this point vivid when he says, "there is a big difference between suddenly expropriating half of someone's savings and attaching monetary conditions in advance to activities, such as taxation". Nozick argues that property rights are so strong that they are absolute, but on further reflection it would seem that taxation is not so much of a personal infringement as he makes it out to be. Furthermore, if property rights are not absolute and property may in part be appropriated by the state for social welfare, then it is not much of a stretch to claim that the corporate legal form may be used as an instrument of the state for the welfare of society as a condition that is attached in advance of such activities.

Nozick's entitlement theory advocates very strong private property rights and rests on justice in initial acquisition. It is however hard to maintain any justice in initial acquisition and Nozick's self-ownership argument is very weak. It is difficult to answer why anything I do to an unowned object should exclude somebody else's liberty to use it. Without such a justification Nozick's entitlement theory has little or no foundation. If property rights are neither natural nor fundamental, we need an explanation for why other matters of justice cannot take precedence and justify redistribution of income or the instrumental use of the corporate legal form. For it may be said that redistribution through taxation and other state interventions serve to increase liberty rather than restrict it, because redistribution increases the income and opportunities of those in need thus granting them choices they otherwise would not have.

Now, the libertarian nexus-of-contracts view prescribes that the corporate legal form ought not to be used as an instrument of the state because of the absolute property rights of shareholders, which precludes any interference by the state. Not only is there no natural foundation for property rights but I have also tried to suggest that not all interference by the state requires actual consent. That is to say that not all interference by the state is a violation of private negative rights because there are important positive rights to consider as well. Citizens may have positive duties to help those in need because as moral agents we may have duties that arise irrespective of consent. I shall now go on to briefly advocate the instrumental use of the corporate legal form by the state.

If property rights are not absolute and people have positive duties to help others, then this allows for the possibility of the state to institutionally uphold the positive rights of citizens by making use of the property of citizens through taxation. In the same way we may regard the use of the corporate legal form as an instrument to help further the welfare of citizens.[8] Not only does this mean that the state may tax the corporate legal entity, but it may also regulate its behaviour as is deemed socially desirable. For example, labour laws, product safety law, and legislation for restricting pollution are all examples of ways in which the state may impose constraints on the corporation for the welfare of its citizens. As we have seen through the evolution of the corporate legal form during the industrial revolution it brings with it considerable macro-economic benefits for industrial growth. As Lord Shaw of Dunfermline said when speaking about the corporation: "It is a creation of law convenient for the purposes of management, of holding of property, of the association of individuals in business transactions" (source: Pickering 1968). Despite the great benefits of corporate economic activity, industrial growth may also bring with it several unwelcome side effects, which the state may try and curb through legislation.

Viewed in this way the primary purpose for the existence of the corporation is its ability to contribute positively to economic growth through the production and efficient allocation of resources. This is the primary reason for the state grant of general incorporation statutes. In this sense the very decision of the state to grant incorporation is itself an instrumental use of the corporate legal form by the state for the purpose of promoting economic growth. The corporate legal form is granted by the state to the incorporating parties so that they may use the corporation as their economic instrument. Aggregated across the economy these instances of economic activity promote economic growth. The corporate legal form itself, which regulates actual corporations, is the instrument of the state. The state may try and use the corporate legal form for other purposes than economic growth, it is after all its own creation, but it should be wary to use it for other purposes if it still wishes it to perform its primary function well. Therefore, it seems reasonable that the state's primary interference in corporate affairs should be to curb the unwelcome ills that may result from business activity when using the corporate form.

If you are of a libertarian disposition I hope the preceding arguments against absolute property rights and the nexus-of-contracts prescription have convinced you. Either way we must accept that in the world today there are no libertarian states. For the purposes of proceeding with the discussion we should acknowledge that all democracies are part of a spectrum of welfare states, which means that absolute property rights do not exist anywhere. In other words, all democratic states have to a greater or lesser extent a role to help the less fortunate citizens in society. This generally involves some form of redistribution of resources, which is only possible if property rights are not absolute. If property rights are not absolute then the private nexus-of-contracts that is claimed to constitute the corporation are not inviolable either. Thus the state may interfere, and does interfere, with regard to how private resources are used, which opens the door for taxing and regulating the corporate legal form.

[8]The corporation and its assets is no longer the property of shareholders, legally speaking, but it once was, so justifying this instrumental use of the corporate legal form by the state seems necessary.

- Summarizing remarks: This section has taken issue with both the descriptive and the prescriptive aspects of the Nexus-of-Contracts Theory. Descriptively I first maintained that the existence of the corporation is dependent on the existence of a state in order to minimally provide a legal system and uphold contracts. Without a state to provide these functions not only could there be no trade but the corporate web of contracts would fall apart. Secondly, I have argued that the corporate form could not and would not evolve as a web of private contracts because the attribute of limited liability with respect to all potential creditors cannot be contracted privately. In conjunction these two arguments show that the descriptive claim of the Nexus-of-Contracts Theory is false. Irrespective of the descriptive falsity of the theory, libertarians might still prescribe that the corporation ought not to be used as an instrument of the state. The normative basis for this prescription is their belief in absolute private property rights. I have argued that such inviolable rights to property are without foundation. It is difficult to find any natural justification for private property rights in initial acquisition, which first needs to be established before the issue of the just transfer of ownership may be tackled. If we nevertheless postulate the existence of private property then libertarians maintain that no transfers of property are legitimate without actual consent. I have argued that this position seems excessively dogmatic because it grants inviolable negative rights of non-interference without any consideration to positive rights to help those in need. Therefore, not only is it the case that the corporate form could not exist without a state grant, but there is no robust foundation for absolute property rights to justify that the state may not make instrumental use of the corporate legal form. The descriptive and prescriptive weakness of the libertarian nexus-of-contracts position leaves the door wide open for advocating that the corporate legal form ought to be used as an instrument of the state for the welfare of its citizens.

The libertarian position against the instrumental use of the corporation by the state is interesting philosophically but is not an important issue in practice because there are no libertarian states in the world. In contrast the movement advocating the greater social responsibility of corporations has been steadily growing since the 1960s. Pickering (1968: 509) writes: "There has been a tendency to deal with the company more and more as an end rather than as a means; or as being itself a participant in business instead of a mere business medium". People have come to attribute moral duties to the corporation itself for which it is meant to be responsible. This has contributed to the CSR movement that is now an important topic of discussion in boardrooms around the world. In the following section I shall take issue with the CSR movement and analyse its philosophical underpinnings.

11.2 The Wrong with the Corporate Social Responsibility Movement

The aim of this section is to analyse the philosophical foundations of the prescriptions associated with the Corporate Social Responsibility movement. First, I shall explicate what the CSR movement entails and in conjunction highlight its philosophical foundations. Secondly, I shall take issue with the prescriptions of the CSR movement, in part by explicating Milton Friedman's (1970) famous position that "the social responsibility of business is to increase its profits", which stands in stark contrast with many CSR prescriptions. A major point of contention between CSR advocates and Friedman's position is the legitimacy of the shareholder primacy norm. Therefore, I shall finish by evaluating the rationality of this norm which prescribes the primacy of shareholder interests.

11.2.1 The Philosophical Foundations of the CSR Movement

Corporate Social Responsibility is defined in many different ways. Buchholz and Rosenthal (2002: 303) provide a broad definition saying that "in general it means that the private corporation has responsibilities to society that go beyond the production of goods and services at a profit. It involves the idea that a corporation has a broader constituency to serve than stockholders alone". In other words the CSR movement at least contains a prescription for corporations to pursue ends that go beyond merely pursuing the interests of shareholders. At a minimum CSR is concerned with good business judgment that acknowledges that managers must mind the interests of several different stakeholders in order to obtain a concerted effort to achieve business goals. This business oriented view of CSR has become known as "Strategic CSR". However, to call this CSR is merely a renaming of good business strategy and most proponents of CSR wish to say something more than this. They wish at least to say that stakeholder interests should weigh into managerial decision-making in a way that is not necessarily connected to the corporation's bottom-line. In other words, the interests of stakeholders matter in themselves and not just instrumentally as part of achieving corporate goals. Let us call CSR that is not solely concerned with business success "normative CSR".[9]

There is an important distinction to point out which is rarely made. The distinction is one between a business ethics stream of CSR on the one hand and

[9]The term "responsibility" in CSR does not in the first instance refer to legal responsibility. This would make the concept of CSR redundant (because it would be simpler and clearer to refer to corporate legislation). The term "social" is ambiguous but clearly indicates that the responsibility is (at least in part) directed towards society, implying a wider group of stakeholders than merely shareholders. It seems reasonable to conclude that such a non-legal responsibility should be regarded as a *moral* responsibility (whether borne by the corporation or its members).

a legal stream of CSR on the other hand.[10] The business ethics stream is closely associated with Stakeholder Theory and Social Contract Theory that give rise to ethical prescriptions often to be manifested in voluntary codes of conduct for business (normative CSR). On the other hand, the legal stream of CSR focuses on changing the legal responsibilities of corporations. These legal CSR prescriptions often take the form of advocating legal constraints for corporations, but recent legal CSR advocates are often concerned with changing the corporate instrument itself. Lawrence Mitchell writes: "Instead of regulating the uses to which the tool is put, these commentators look to redesign the tool itself" (source: Testy 2002).

Interestingly, the ethical and legal debates about CSR are very much divorced from one another. This may in part be due to the fact that the two separate streams advocate different means of achieving corporate reform. The business ethics stream primarily advocates voluntary means of reform (beyond legislation) while the legal stream advocates legal enactments in order to augment corporate behaviour. One of the reasons for this separation may be due to the prevailing dominance of regarding the corporation as a moral agent among business ethicists in the normative CSR movement, while lawyers on the other hand regard the corporate form as an instrument of the state and thus advocate legal enactments to regulate the use of the legal tool. It seems that the debate that is currently being conducted in the public domain is concerned primarily with normative rather than legal CSR. It is this normative stream of CSR that is being discussed by businessmen, politicians and activists and it is this stream that I will be referring to as I now take issue with the philosophical foundations of the CSR movement.

As was mentioned, the CSR movement prescribes that the role of the corporation ought to be one that goes beyond merely satisfying shareholder interests. There are two theories that CSR advocates often hold dear and underpin their belief in the prescription that corporations ought to sever a wider constituency than that advocated by the shareholder primacy norm. These two theories are the Stakeholder Theory and the Social Contract Theory. Let us look at these theories in turn.

What has come to be called Stakeholder Theory was first put forward by Edward Freeman in his seminal book "Strategic Management: A Stakeholder Approach" (1984). Stakeholder Theory as put forward by Freeman (and developed by him and others) has descriptive, instrumental, and normative interpretations (Donaldson and Preston 1995).[11] I will here be considering ***normative*** Stakeholder Theory that

---

[10]Buchholz and Rosenthal's (2002: 303) definition of CSR involves "responsibilities to society that go beyond the production of goods and services at a profit". Because corporations are expected to make their profits within the confines of the law, responsibilities beyond generating profits suggests that the responsibilities are beyond legislation. In that case a legal stream of CSR would seem to be a contradiction in terms. The concept of a legal stream of CSR is nevertheless intelligible if conceived as prescriptions to improve corporate legal responsibilities (which may be advocated on moral or instrumental grounds).

[11]Since Freeman introduced Stakeholder Theory it has been further developed by many others. For our present purposes I will let Freeman's views represent Stakeholder Theory as he is undoubtedly most influential in the field.

prescribes that managers/corporations have a moral duty to consider the interests stakeholders (beyond shareholders). Stakeholder Theory is a reaction against what may be called Shareholder Theory, which was famously put forward by Milton Friedman in 1970.[12] Shareholder Theory advocates that the fiduciary duties of managers are owed to shareholders alone, while Stakeholder Theory prescribes that the scope of the fiduciary duties of managers be widened to include all stakeholders. Evan and Freeman write:

> "The very purpose of a firm [and thus the goal of its managers] is to serve as a vehicle for coordinating stakeholder interests. It is through the firm [and its managers] that each stakeholder group makes itself better off through voluntary exchanges. The corporation serves at the pleasure of its stakeholders and none may be used as a means to the ends of another without full right of participation of that decision" (source: Freeman and Werhane 2003).

A stakeholder is anyone who is affected by the activities of the corporation. This not only includes employees and shareholders but also suppliers, customers and the public at large. Stakeholder Theory has a Kantian foundation, which prescribes that each stakeholder has a right not to be treated merely as a means to some end (Evan and Freeman 2003). In order to obtain this state of affairs the theory prescribes that each stakeholder must have a right to participate in corporate decisions in which they have a stake.

It should now be clear that the Stakeholder Theory fits in with the CSR movement because it prescribes that corporations should aim to satisfy interests beyond those of shareholders. But what is the normative justification for this prescription? Thomas Donaldson (1989) has said that one of the problems with Stakeholder Theory is its failure to contain within itself a normative justificatory foundation. However, the Kantian foundation of the theory suggests that its normative justification might be the following: Because humans are moral agents they ought to always treat others as ends in themselves irrespective of whether they are engaged in business or not. For an organization to meet the Kantian dictum of never treating persons merely as means it is argued that those affected by the organization must be allowed to participate in the decision process.[13]

---

[12]The juxtaposition of Shareholder Theory vs. Stakeholder Theory is often referred to as the Friedman vs. Freeman debate, and the conflict between shareholders and stakeholders is more generally known as the "basic debate" in business ethics.

[13]Paas (1996) points out that stakeholder participation rights in decision-making do not follow from Kant's categorical imperative to never treat people "merely as a means to an end". This second formulation of the categorical imperative allows people to treat others as means, but not *merely* as means. This is made clear by the fact that any transaction of a good or service involves using the other party in a transaction as a means to attain the object of the transaction. A carpenter agrees to be a means through which a home owner gets a new porch, and the home owner agrees to be a source of income for the carpenter. Therefore it does not necessarily follow that stakeholders have a right to participate in decisions that affect them, because as is often the case, there is an explicit or implicit agreement that one party will do as requested by the other; i.e. that the carpenter will build the porch and the home owner will pay. What the categorical imperative forbids is that either party does not fulfil their part of the agreement; that would be to use someone *merely* as a means.

Such a justification obviously precludes an organization from merely satisfying shareholder interests. Essentially one might say that the theory prescribes that the corporation ought to be a different tool from the one it is- one that is geared towards satisfying the interests of all the stakeholders.[14] Evan and Freeman (2003: 103) write:

> "The stakeholder theory does not give primacy to one stakeholder group over another . . . A stakeholder theory of the firm must redefine the purpose of the firm . . . to serve as a vehicle for coordinating stakeholder interests".

It should be stressed how fundamentally different this prescription is from Shareholder Theory. It completely changes the purpose of the corporation in society. It does not merely prescribe a dabbling in philanthropy, but rather it prescribes a complete redefinition of the corporate form and its role in society. Evan and Freeman realize how fundamental these changes are and acknowledge that if the Stakeholder Theory is ever to be put into practice then some fundamental changes to corporate law need to occur. In this sense Stakeholder Theory overlaps with the legal CSR movement, which advocates the legal augmentation of the corporate form itself. However, many business ethicists that are advocates of the ethical CSR movement fail to realize how fundamentally different the Stakeholder Theory is from the status quo. Many who claim to adopt a "stakeholder perspective" regard it merely as a prescription for corporations to be more sensitive in their decision-making by considering the interests of other stakeholders than merely shareholders.[15] Stakeholder Theory goes much much further than this. It redefines the corporation as a tool for all the stakeholders and gives them a right to participate in the decision process.

Numerous authors over the years have suggested consideration be given to stakeholders in corporate governance, particularly by the board of directors. These suggestions come in a variety of forms and with various justifications. Galai and Wiener (2008) suggest that management "allocation" of board seats to a broader group of stakeholders, primarily employees, can reduce agency costs for corporations. Chilosi and Damiani (2007) suggest that stakeholder representatives on the board may be chosen by employees or appointed by trade unions or government authorities. Bonnafous-Boucher (2005) presents a "proprietorialist" view where stakeholders are encouraged to buy shares and obtain voting rights as shareholders.[16] Schrenk (2006) suggests that the legal fiduciary duty of board mem-

---

[14]This position might be regarded as a nexus-of-contracts (that includes all stakeholders) with the important attribute that all the contracts are evenly weighted rather than being weighted in favour of the shareholders. In other words that managerial attention should give equal weight to stakeholder interests, including shareholders.

[15]It is common among those who adopt a "stakeholder perspective" to mistakenly believe that they are advocating the Stakeholder Theory, which creates confusion in the CSR debate because they are not.

[16]This suggestion does not so much solve the problem as avoid it. For example it implies that employees, who have a stake in the corporation qua employees, should become shareholders so that

bers should be extended beyond shareholders to encompass a wider constituency of stakeholders.[17] And Evan and Freeman (2003) suggest on normative grounds that stakeholders be given voting membership on the board, and furthermore, that stakeholders should demand voting membership on pragmatic grounds in order to have their interests properly represented (Freeman and Evan 1990). Common to all these conceptions of stakeholder consideration is that none of them articulate how non-shareholder stakeholders (beyond employees) are to be identified, nor how such stakeholders are to vote for their board representatives when such a view is advocated.[18]

The reason why no one has suggested how to operationalize stakeholder voting rights for board representation is that there are significant practical difficulties to be overcome. These difficulties come primarily in two forms. First, how do we identify who the relevant stakeholders are? Are we concerned with relevant stakeholder groups or relevant stakeholder individuals? Are suppliers and customers relevant stakeholders if they make one transaction or should they have a working relationship (multiple transactions) over time? Who should represent society as a stakeholder? Second, how do stakeholders vote for their representatives on the board? Does each member of a stakeholder organization get to vote or does only the organization as a whole get a vote? Is the size of the stakeholder organization important? Should all stakeholders' votes receive equal weight or do some groups have priority interests? Thus, in abstract, the idea of stakeholder representation on corporate boards is appealing; in practice, it is difficult to realize. Beyond the representation of employees (as we see in German corporate governance), it may be that stakeholder consideration at board level must simply rely on a broader conception of the role of the board.

Stakeholder Theory's concern with the participation rights of stakeholders does not necessarily hinge on the corporation qualifying as a moral agent. It is primarily concerned with the moral right of stakeholders not to be treated merely as means, and does not per se hinge on the corporation itself qualifying as the bearer of a moral duty to treat stakeholders accordingly. However, the corporate prescriptions

---

they can have their interests as employees considered qua shareholders. Also, there is no reason why employees' ability to obtain stock stands in any proportion to their stake qua employees.

[17]Extending board fiduciary duties beyond shareholders only makes sense if non-shareholder stakeholders also obtain a legal right to challenge board decisions in the court, like shareholders can. For example, the UK Companies Act 2006, requires directors to consider the interests of a wider group of stakeholders but does not provide stakeholders' legal remedy to challenge board decisions. Charging directors with a duty without corresponding legal stakeholder rights calls into question whether stakeholder have their interests represented in practice. A reason why the law may not have extended such rights to stakeholders is the sheer difficulty in identifying stakeholder groups (beyond employees) that can be regarded as stakeholder representatives with legitimate claims.

[18]German corporate law provides employees with board representation for corporations above a certain size (number of employees). This is made possible because employees are easily identifiable individuals while other stakeholder groups with more transactional relationships with the corporations do not lend themselves to such easy and relevant identification.

of those who adopt a "stakeholder perspective" do usually rest on a conception of corporate moral agency. Advocating a "stakeholder perspective" becomes a way of articulating that the corporation ought to be more considerate towards the interests of other stakeholders than merely shareholders. When such prescriptions are beyond the requirements of the law they will usually be contingent on corporate moral agency, because then the corporation is said to have a *moral* duty to satisfy stakeholder interests.[19]

- Stakeholder Theory: This theory prescribes that the corporation ought to be a vehicle for organizing and pursuing the interests of all stakeholders affected by the corporation. It prescribes that managerial attention should give equal weight to stakeholder interests. This prescription involves a complete redefinition of the role of the corporation in society from serving primarily as a productive organization for shareholder interests to a vehicle for the primary purpose of organising the interests of stakeholders. Many CSR advocates claim to take a "stakeholder perspective", but by this they often mean nothing more than prescribing that corporations pay more attention to the interests of other stakeholders than merely shareholders. When such prescriptions are beyond the requirements of the law they will usually be contingent on corporate moral agency.

Let us now take a look at Social Contract Theory and how it supports the CSR prescription to satisfy the interests of a wider constituency of stakeholders than merely shareholders. In the context of the corporation's role in society, Social Contract Theory was first developed by Thomas Donaldson (1989). The basis for the theory is that a corporation operates in a society at the discretion of the community on the understanding that the corporation implicitly makes some commitments to that community. Donaldson (1989: 47) asks us to imagine a hypothetical state of nature scenario inhabited by rational individuals "who attempt to sketch the terms of an agreement between themselves and the productive organizations upon which they are considering bestowing status as legal, fictional persons, and to which they are considering allowing access both to natural resources and the existing employment pool… The raison d'être for the productive organization turns out to be its contribution to society tempered by a set of reciprocal obligations existing on both sides of the organization/society divide".

Although Donaldson asks us to imagine a state of nature scenario, he does at least seem to assume some form of minimalist state, because even libertarians tend to agree that corporations could not exist without a state to guarantee contracts and

[19]Note that the advocacy of a "stakeholder perspective" is not necessarily contingent on an adherence to corporate moral agency because some may merely wish to prescribe that managers be more considerate towards stakeholders in their business relationships. However, I am aiming to portray the prevailing view among CSR advocates where an adherence to corporate moral agency does dominate.

personal safety.[20] Furthermore, some form of state is necessary that has a mandate to speak on behalf of citizens in order to confer the legal status and privileges to an organization that Donaldson has in mind. At face value this sounds fairly similar to the Legal Fiction Theory whereby the state grants corporate status to organizations and may thus regulate the corporate instrument through legislation for the welfare of society. However, Donaldson (1989: 47) says: "The point of applying social contract reasoning to business is to clarify the *moral* foundations of productive organizations" (emphasis added). Donaldson is seemingly using the heuristic device of the social contract, not primarily to argue for the legal obligations of the corporation, but the *moral* obligations of the corporation. The corporate commitments to the social contract create corporate moral obligations to society.

One of the main moral duties of the corporation, according to Donaldson, is to abstain from violating minimum standards of human rights and justice in society. This then clearly connects with the CSR movement in that corporate duties to adhere to human rights go beyond a strict adherence to promoting shareholder interests. For a corporation to have moral obligations requires that it is also a moral agent, and Donaldson does indeed advocate corporate moral agency.

The need for corporate moral agency is further noticed in Donaldson's theory through the organization's position as a bargaining party engaged in agreement making between itself and society. The productive organization is regarded as a bargaining party (singular) and not a collective of individuals. The moral obligations that arise from the social bargain are held by the organization itself and not collectively by the individual members. However, how corporations are constituted is not a central part of the theory. The aim of the theory is to establish the role of the corporation in society in terms of moral obligations and thus it is necessarily a premise of the theory that corporations are the type of entities that can have moral obligations.

- Social Contract Theory: This theory aims to clarify the moral foundations of productive organizations through the application of a hypothetical social contract to a state of nature scenario. We are to imagine that rational individuals bargain with productive organisations to reach an agreement on the conditions that must be met for being bestowed with legal status and its associated rights and duties. This is however not an argument in favour of the Legal Fiction Theory, but rather tries to establish the resulting corporate obligations as moral obligations. The theory is premised on the idea that the corporation is a moral agent and the theory itself is mostly a heuristic device to establish the nature of its moral obligations. The social contract theory fits well with the CSR movement because it prescribes that the corporation take into consideration interests beyond those of shareholders on the basis that it has a moral obligation to do so as part of its contract with society.

[20]Please note that I am not saying that Donaldson is a libertarian. I am only saying that even libertarians with their fierce protection of individual rights still concede that a minimal form of government is necessary for society to function.

Most of the prescriptions that are made as part of the CSR movement take the form of advocating greater social responsibility in the sense of broadening the scope of stakeholder interests that corporations ought to take into account in their decision making. For example the debate concerning the use of sweatshop labour by multinationals in underdeveloped countries often centres on whether or not these corporations have a moral obligation towards their employees to improve their working conditions. As mentioned many who are engaged in CSR take a "stakeholder perspective" but do not mean it in the strict sense of Freeman's Stakeholder Theory. They are not advocating a fundamental redesign of the corporation as a tool for all stakeholder interests. Because most CSR prescriptions concern corporate moral obligations to take into account a broader scope of stakeholder interests this seems more consistent with the Social Contract Theory premised on corporate moral agency, rather than the Stakeholder Theory's redesign of the corporate form.

Although it is conceivable for some corporate moral obligations to be viewed as a metaphor for moral obligations of corporate members, this is not the sense of moral responsibility that most CSR advocates have in mind. Moral agency by the corporation itself (as distinct from its members) is by far the dominant position among business ethicists. Furthermore, regarding corporate moral obligations as the obligations of members often becomes very problematic. For example it is difficult to say that corporate members have a collective obligation not to subject employees to sweatshop conditions, because then they are party to the obligation not to subject themselves to such conditions.[21] Therefore it seems reasonable to assume that the philosophical foundation of the CSR movement is primarily based on regarding the corporation *itself* as a moral agent.

11.2.2 Shareholder Theory vs. CSR

Given that the moral foundation of CSR prescriptions are primarily based on an explicit or implicit adherence to corporate moral agency, then presumably the corporation may not also at the same time be an instrument of the state, because as a moral agent it is an end in itself and not a means to some end.[22] Although the corporation may not be an instrument per se, the CSR movement nevertheless seems to prescribe moral obligations to corporations in order that they should be instrumental in solving some social problems. In contrast we shall next look at Milton Friedman's Shareholder Theory (1970) which prescribes that any managerial decision to solve social problems will tend to be a deviation from the corporation's sole responsibility to focus on shareholder interests.

---

[21]This difficulty is not avoided by saying that management has the collective obligation because clearly managers may be wronged like any other employee.

[22]This might seem to be an absurd conclusion, but if corporations truly are meant to be moral agents, the type of entity that has the capacities to be morally responsible, then it should also be regarded as an end in itself. (According to Kant, it is the capacities for moral agency, in particular the autonomy to choose one's own ends, that makes humans ends in themselves.)

Friedman starts off his famous 1970 article titled "The Social Responsibility of Business is to Increase its Profits" by writing:

> "What does it mean to say 'business' has responsibilities? Only people can have responsibilities. A corporation is an artificial person and in this sense may have responsibilities, but 'business' as a whole cannot be said to have responsibilities in this vague sense".

It seems that Friedman is saying that only people can have responsibilities, both moral and legal, while corporations being mere artificial persons created by law may have responsibilities only in the legal sense. Friedman (1970) goes on to say:

> "In a free-enterprise, private-property system, a corporate executive is an employee of the owners of the business. He has direct responsibility to his employers. This generally means to make as much money as possible while conforming to the basic rules of the society, both those embodied in law and those embodied in ethical custom".

Friedman is saying that the sole recipients of the executives' fiduciary duty are the shareholders and this generally means to maximise corporate profits within the constraints of the law and ethical custom. Friedman never clarifies what he means by "ethical custom" nor why the corporation should take it into account. However, one can gather from his views in general that matters of ethics should not act as ethical constraints, but as economic constraints, because breaking the mores of a society may be regarded as offensive and thus bad for business.

According to Friedman if an executive acts in a manner that is "socially responsible" this must mean that he is acting in a manner that is not in the interest of his employers. For example if an executive decided to reduce the environmental pollution of the enterprise (in a manner that increases costs) beyond what was required by law in order to contribute to the social goal of conserving the environment, then this would be contrary to the interests of the shareholders who expect profit to be maximised. Friedman says that such behaviour by an executive is equivalent to him imposing a tax on the shareholders and then deciding how to spend that tax revenue for social purposes.

In this context two issues arise. Firstly, the raising and spending of taxes is a function of government which has a political mandate to intervene in the private affairs of individuals for the social good. However, businessmen are not civil servants and thus do not have the political mandate to impose taxes. If they were they would have to be elected through a political process. Friedman points out that if primarily political rather than market forces are to allocate scarce resources then we have in effect abandoned the capitalist system in favour of socialism. Secondly, there is a practical problem with regard to having corporate executives make decisions pertaining to social welfare. How are they meant to know how to spend corporate funds in accordance with the goals of society? Because executives do not have a political mandate they are not in an epistemic position to be informed about the needs and desires of society and would thus end up spending corporate funds in a dictatorial manner at best is in line with their own perception of the social good.

This might seem to be taking the argument too far. Clearly there are things that any moral person will know is good. For example, it might seem uncontroversial that less pollution is always preferable. But is completely abstaining from pollution really good for society? Plainly the ideal amount of pollution is not zero pollution. In that case there would be no production of goods and services at all. Managers are not in an epistemic position to determine the ideal level of pollution for society because it involves an aggregate of all industry actors as well as the pollution preferences of citizens. Those mandated with the role of overseeing pollution are in an epistemic and normative position to make such decisions.

Any deviation by executives from satisfying the interests of shareholders is for Friedman on par with illegitimate taxation and therefore the duty of executives is merely to pursue the interest of shareholders (usually profit) to the best of their ability within the constraints of the law. That is why Friedman says that the "business of business is business". Thus far I am largely in agreement with Friedman's views. His position is in line with the Legal Fiction Theory and recognizes that the corporation is a legal creation for the benefit of society. There is nothing inconsistent about the corporation being an instrumental tool for the benefit of society and also maintaining that executives should not try to act socially responsibly but merely follow the shareholder primacy norm. As was suggested earlier, the reason is that the *corporate legal form* is a tool of the state that has a *role* to promote the welfare of its citizens, while any *actual corporation* is a vehicle with the *goal* to promote the interests of the incorporators. The granting of the corporate legal form is itself an instrumental use of the corporate form by the state to help promote economic growth and thus social welfare. The state may (and it does) legislate legal rights and duties for corporations in order to guide their behaviour in a socially desirable direction. As long as the corporation maximises profits within the constraints of the law it contributes to the welfare of society as a taxpayer, employer, and producer of goods and services.

Peter Drucker (1946: 17) put the point in a similar way. He said that the corporation is not free from "social obligations; on the contrary it should be so organized that it automatically fulfils its social obligations in the very act of seeking its own self-interest". In other words, by pursuing the interest of the shareholders within the constraints of the law the corporation automatically contributes to social welfare. There is no need to ask the executives to make use of corporate funds to promote social welfare as well. They have neither the political mandate nor the knowledge to contribute intentionally to social welfare. The role of the corporation is as a productive organization that can contribute to society by being a vehicle for economic growth. It is not created for (nor well suited for) satisfying a wide array of stakeholder interests or social problems.[23] It is not a political institution.

[23] I do not make a sharp distinction between stakeholder interests and social problems. Corporate stakeholder individuals are part of society more generally. For example, issues of fair wages, environmental pollution, and product safety are both stakeholder issues and social issues. As such stakeholder concerns may be regarded as social problems. However, from a corporation's perspective it is important to distinguish between problems caused by the corporations and social problem that exist independently of the corporation. It is more reasonable to demand that a corporation address stakeholder issues it causes and can control than it is to demand that it solve social problems more generally.

We already have political institutions of government to solve social problems. Let these institutions that have a political mandate and are better suited for solving social problems solve them. If we want the corporation to behave differently, then impose legislation. If we want the corporation to contribute more to social welfare, then one possible option may be to tax it more. But do not ask executives to solve social problems that they are neither authorized nor qualified to do.

Normative Stakeholder Theory would carry more normative weight if there was no one but the corporation to care for stakeholder interests. But all corporations operate within the confines of sovereign states. As such, arguments regarding corporate responsibilities always need to be put in relation to state responsibilities, which in all democracies involves greater or lesser measures to care for the welfare of citizens, manifest through legislation that is binding on corporations. It is no surprise then that Freeman argues for Stakeholder Theory on libertarian grounds, thus shifting responsibility from the state to the corporation (Freeman and Phillips 2002).

Freeman and Werhane (2003) label Friedman's position as a "minimalist conception of corporate responsibility". I would label his position differently. Although Friedman himself favours minimal government intervention in the market, there is nothing in the Shareholder Theory per se that promotes minimal government intervention. Strictly speaking the content of the law as it pertains to corporations may be minimal or extensive.[24] Therefore the Shareholder Theory is consistent with extensive corporate regulation and hence corporations may have extensive *legal* responsibilities.

- The Shareholder Theory: At its core the Shareholder Theory advocates the shareholder primacy norm. The theory implicitly assumes that the corporation is not a moral agent and that the corporation is primarily a legal fiction. Because the corporation itself does not have any moral or social obligations, any calls for corporations to act socially responsibly must be a call for *executives* to act socially responsibly. However, if executives spend corporate funds differently from the desires of shareholders then this amounts to the levying of a tax on shareholders. But only the state has a right to tax its citizens and moreover executives are not in a position to know how to best contribute to the social welfare. Therefore the fiduciary duty of executives is owed to shareholders and not some wider constituency. In the process of pursuing shareholder interests within the constraints of the law the corporation contributes to social welfare through economic growth, employment and the payment of taxes.

I shall now continue with a more thorough defence of the Shareholder Theory in relation to the philosophical underpinnings of the CSR movement.

[24]Friedman's libertarian views clearly indicate that he would favour minimal government intervention, but the view that corporations should primarily be regulated by the rule of law, rather than ethical self-restraint, remains a robust argument.

If one truly believes in the CSR prescription that corporations and thus their managers ought to pursue initiatives of social responsibility then arguably society ought to demand that managers should be trained in ethics and follow strict codes of ethics. After all they are expected to make decisions with vast amounts of resources for the benefit of society. This surely requires some training and guidance if they do not have a political mandate. For example medical doctors have professional codes, most of which are legally binding. If the same were the case for managers then we would in effect end up with a similar form of "legislate to regulate" position that I am advocating. The primary difference is that the legislation falls on managers as a profession rather than on the corporate legal entity.[25]

Some CSR advocates seem to think that corporations ought to contribute to solving social problems because they can. They regard corporations as a reservoir of resources that ought to be used to help solve the problems of society. If we disregard for a moment that corporations are not moral agents capable of having duties to society in this way, we must ask whether or not corporations in fact can contribute to solving social problems. I have already said that corporate executives are not in the best epistemic position to know how to intentionally contribute to social welfare. However, do they even have the financial resources to solve social problems?

If we for a moment assume that corporations are moral agents and that "ought" implies "can" then corporations only have a duty to be socially responsible if they are profitable. In other words, they only have a duty to solve social problems and to take care of non-shareholder interests if they have the financial resources to do so. It may however be argued that few corporations in a competitive environment will be in a position to be socially responsible (when this involves additional costs). At least in economic theory, companies engaged in "perfect competition" will only make "normal profits", which means profits at the level which is just sufficient for the entrepreneur to stay in the industry. We all know that in the concrete world there are no theoretically perfect markets and therefore the potential for "abnormal profits"[26] does exists, thus potentially supplying the corporation with discretionary funds.

Large multinational corporations in the oil, technology, or finance industries, often make eye-popping profits. But by far the most numerous corporations are SMEs that make nowhere close to those profits and can often struggle to survive. For example it is widely acknowledged that a majority of start-ups fail within 4 years.

---

[25]In the wake of the 2008 financial crisis several commentators have suggested that business schools do more to educate MBA students in ethics. Podolny (2009) argues in favour of an MBA code of conduct as one of a number of measures business schools could take to regain trust given criticism received in light of the financial crisis. He would have schools draw up codes of conduct and monitor compliance, revoking degrees of graduates who violate the code. It is however unclear how and on what basis a business school would sanction a student without relying on a court conviction, in which case revoking the degree is just an additional sanction beyond the court sentencing.

[26]Abnormal profits are profits beyond those that are necessary to keep the entrepreneur in the industry.

If CSR is a normative concept whereby stakeholder concerns should be addressed irrespective of their profitability, then clearly there are many companies that may not have the means to address these concerns. The premise that "ought" implies "can" has the implication that only those firms that make abnormal profits have an obligation be socially responsible. But if only corporations that are profitable have a duty to be socially responsible (and presumably the more profitable the more responsible) then this amounts to the moral equivalent of a progressive tax for corporations.[27]

Moreover, it can be argued that many if not most social problems are not solvable by any individual firm. For example saving the environment is not the social project of one firm. It requires that all corporations reduce their emission of pollutants. But no single corporation has the power or authority to tell other corporations what to do. The CSR prescription to be socially responsible is a moral prescription and it is voluntary. Not only that, but corporations are free to decide how to be socially responsible and may have very different views of what that implies which hinders a concerted market effort. Chamberlain points out that:

> "[E]very business... is, in effect, 'trapped' in the business system that it has helped to create. It is incapable, as an individual unit, of transcending that system... the dream of the socially responsible corporation that, replicated over and over again can transform society is illusory... Because their aggregate power is not united, not truly collective, not organised, they [corporations] have no way, even if they wished, of redirecting that power to meet the most pressing needs of society... Such redirection could only occur through the intermediate of government rewriting rules under which corporations operate" (source: Buchholz and Rosenthal 2002).

In other words the individual corporation is incapable of solving social problems that require a concerted effort because it is situated in a competitive environment. We value the efficient resource allocation of the market system and therefore we have anti-trust legislation against cartels and market collusions, which are meant to prevent collective action among market actors. However, we can have concerted action among market actors if the state legislates that all competing actors must fulfil their part of some common objective.

- CSR leads to the moral equivalent of a progressive tax, and competition in the market precludes concerted efforts among actors to solve social problems.

[27]Corporations need to be profitable. Even if altruistic incorporators were to start a CSR corporation they could not solve social problems without revenues covering all the costs. Thus even in the case of the socially responsible corporation profitability is still a central concern. (One might think that the corporation does not need profits in order to honour negative rights to abstain from harm. However, there are several forms of *indirect* harm that a corporation can cause as part of its normal business activity, often referred to as negative externalities, such as pollution. Abstaining from such externalities does not require profits per se, but rather present an added cost. This still requires the corporation to make up for that cost through added revenue, which amounts to the same as a need to be profitable.)

The moral prescription of CSR for corporations to voluntarily address non-shareholder interests is problematic and brings up a further question. Why should shareholders be "taxed" extra by placing demands of social responsibility on executives? Why not just increase the corporate tax rate or legislate desired corporate behaviour in order to solve a social problem? It might be argued by CSR advocates that corporations ought to solve some social problems rather than the state because the state is not performing the task that needs doing. In other words that the corporation ought to solve the problem because it is something that needs solving and it is a moral agent with a positive duty to help. This argument hinges entirely on the moral agency of the corporation because otherwise a positive duty to help cannot be substantiated. However, according to my position, which rejects corporate moral agency, the corporation has no positive moral duty to help and the solution to social problems does not lie in shifting responsibility from the state to the corporation. If the state is not solving a certain social problem this may be due to three different factors. Firstly, it might be that not enough people have voiced their concern about the problem through the political process for it to become an issue that needs solving. Secondly, it might be that there is a fault in the political process. Thirdly, it might be that the state is inefficient or incompetent at solving the problem.

Firstly, if it is not an issue that citizens feel concerned about enough then it is definitely not a problem that corporate managers should spend time and corporate resources on. Friedman (1970) expresses the point in a similar way: "If the executive imposes taxes and spends the proceeds in the aforementioned way, he has failed to persuade a majority of his fellow citizens to be of a like mind [with regard to social responsibilities] and is spending resources in an undemocratic/dictatorial fashion".

Secondly, if there is a problem with the political process then that is the problem. The solution lies in fixing the political process so that it voices the concerns of citizens. The solution is not instead to ask private corporations to perform tasks aimed at social welfare that they are not empowered to perform. Social problems demand social solutions. If the political process works and enough people feel strongly about an issue, then a social solution may be found through an initiative by the state. If this requires more resources, the state may then decide to finance the solution through increased corporate taxes or some other means.

Thirdly, if it is deemed that the state is inefficient or incompetent at solving the problem, then there is nothing hindering the state from contracting the task to the private sector. There is no need for the solutions to social problems to be executed by the public sector; there is only a need for a public initiative to identify the problem that needs solving so that resources are allocated to improve social welfare. A private enterprise contracted by the state to solve a social problem is not acting socially responsibly; it is acting as any other private enterprise in its own interest as it is specifically being paid to perform the task on behalf of the state.

- <u>A state tax is better than a moral tax</u>: The universal adoption of CSR would lead all corporations to act socially responsibly and try to contribute to the solutions of social problems. But this is simply another way of "taxing" the corporation with the sole difference that it is voluntary. But there is no inherent virtue in these contributions being voluntary because the aim is to solve social problems (many which require social solutions that are coordinated). Regulation overcomes problems of coordination that come with moral CSR prescriptions. If the state is not solving a social problem this is not an argument for corporations to solve it, but rather a reason to inquire why the state is not solving the problem.

CSR prescribes that corporations contribute to social welfare in part by helping to solve social problems. This involves a shift in responsibility for solving social problems from the state to corporate actors. If citizens decide that they want the state to stop solving (some) social problems, and instead prefer that they are solved by private corporations, then they are free to become shareholders in corporations that further their desired social ends. However this scenario presents two problems:

Firstly we may ask: Is the corporation the right type of vehicle for solving social problems? A corporation as part of its business produces product X which generates profits to solve social problem Y. It seems like a rather inefficient route to produce X to solve Y, when you could ask a public (or publicly contracted) organization to solve Y straight away. Moreover, if corporations use their business profits for solving social problem Y, then there may be little or no money left over for dividends. If that is the case, then corporate shares have little or no economic value, which begs the question why anyone would buy shares in such a corporation rather than just give it to a charity aiming to solve the same social problem? For such "socially responsible" corporations to exist we need to use another assumption about human motivation than rational self-interest; one that is more other-regarding; but such an assumption may unfortunately be unrealistic.[28]

Secondly, we might take CSR initiatives down a slippery slope. If corporations take over some (or all) of the role of solving social problems, then it is primarily those issues that individuals are willing to "invest" in or donate to that will be addressed. This in effect means that social problems are to be addressed by private initiatives, which means that those citizens that have few means are at the mercy of the charity of corporations or wealthy individuals. This involves a reversal of the welfare state that has evolved to institutionalize redistributive measures through taxation. This shift might work if citizens become as economically charitable as they currently must pay in taxes, but taxation is compulsory precisely because private

[28]It might be objected that this is clearly not true because there are corporations today that do engage in CSR. It is however my understanding that those corporations engage in strategic CSR, or are profitable in spite of CSR costs, which is in part evidenced by CSR being a prerogative primarily among big corporations that can afford it. I am here concerned with normative CSR, where stakeholder interests are taken into account irrespective of their effect on corporate goals, and for-profit corporations with such an outlook are nowhere to be found.

solutions to social problems are not forthcoming. A move towards private solutions for social problems disenfranchises those in society that are most in need. The state has a unique position to overview the ills of society that individual citizens do not have. The CSR movement seemingly wants both the state and business to solve social problems, but what is the point of shifting some public tasks to the private sector? If some corporations happen to have a unique competence to solve certain social problems, for which there is no profitable market, then the government should contract these corporations to solve the problem or give them other economic incentives to do so.

- The CSR movement inadvertently promotes a privatisation of social welfare: CSR prescribes that corporations ought to help solve social problems. This might be interpreted on a range from a mere dabbling in corporate philanthropy to corporations assuming the tasks of solving most of the social problems previously handled by the state. It seems that CSR advocates tend to prefer more corporate social responsibility to less and thus it does not seem unreasonable to assume that corporations ought to engage in solving many of society's problems. This view falters because it fails to realise that the costs associated with solving society's problems will often be paid out of the dividends of shareholders. If shareholders no longer obtain a competitive return on their investment the incentive for incorporators to start and maintain corporations disappears unless we unrealistically exchange our rational self-interest assumption with a more other-regarding assumption about human motivation. Even if we do so, we end up with an unflattering state of affairs where social welfare is handled by private corporations and thus social problems are addressed in relation to charitable desires rather than the preferences of citizens.

As was mentioned earlier, Stakeholder Theory as advocated by Freeman has libertarian normative foundations (Freeman and Phillips 2002). It is thought that stakeholders should negotiate their concerns directly with the corporation and not have the rest of society shoulder this responsibility through state regulation. The CSR movement as understood today, with its focus on voluntary activities, has primarily an American genesis. With America in general being much more sceptical of "big government" than many European countries, the CSR focus on voluntary activities is not surprising. But is a shift in social responsibility away from the state onto corporations desirable?

Shifting the responsibility of social welfare onto corporations would involve a complete restructuring of the functions of state and private enterprise. Similarly, implementing Stakeholder Theory would involve a monumental change to the status quo. If the purpose of the corporation is to serve as a vehicle for coordinating stakeholder interests without giving primacy to one stakeholder group over another then this would clearly spell the end for the corporation as a vehicle to further the interests of shareholders. But the consequences of such a change are far reaching indeed.

11.2.2.1 The Economic Efficiency of Shareholder Theory vs. Stakeholder Theory

Jensen (2002), Sundaram and Inkpen (2004a, b), Williamson (1984), and others have argued for the superior efficiency of shareholder primacy (generally construed as Shareholder Value Maximization (SVM)) over Stakeholder Theory. The most forceful efficiency arguments in favour of the shareholder primacy norm (SPN) are: (1) economic efficiency requires governance with a single objective function; and (2) control is best exercised by residual claimants.

1. The fact that corporations are exposed to competition frequently threatens their very survival and requires them to make strictly financial priorities. A financial measure for deciding better from worse performance is required in order to evaluate and attain efficient use of resources in the organization. Jensen (2002: 239–240) observes:

> Much of the discussion in policy circles concerning the proper corporate objective casts the issue in terms of the conflict among various constituencies or "stakeholders" of the corporation. The question then becomes whether shareholders should be held in higher regard than other constituencies... The real issue to be considered here is... what behaviour will get the most out of society's limited resources.

Economic efficiency requires that as much output as possible is produced with a given set of inputs. The output in a market economy is economic value, which is measured by consumers' willingness to pay for the goods and services that they receive. Our question then becomes what norm of corporate governance will produce the most value for the economy?

One might argue that the notion of economic efficiency defined above contains within itself the notion of a single value objective for the corporation. If the output to be measured is economic value then the sole efficiency that we are seeking to measure is productivity. Obviously, if one has more than one objective these can be pursued more or less efficiently judged on their own merits. The primary point I am making here is that, if an organization has multiple goals, such as enhancing employee wellbeing, caring for the environment, and producing efficiently, it is likely that it will produce less efficiently than if it only had the overriding goal of efficient production.

Stakeholder Theory implies that the board and management have a number of constituencies towards whom they are accountable. This does not require multiple objectives for management—the constituencies might all unite behind one objective (see, Freeman et al. 2007)—but it does seem likely given their often different needs. As Williamson (1984: 1215) suggests, the fear is that public representation on the board "would come at a high cost if the corporation were thereby politicized or deflected from its chief purpose of serving as an economizing instrument."

In the current climate the interest of shareholders is usually for the corporation to generate profits, but this is often not the primary interest of other stakeholders. Employees may want higher wages and greater job security. Customers may want better products at lower prices. Suppliers may want higher prices and longer lead times. Society wants efficient allocation of resources and a clean environment etc. Trying to negotiate how all these demands are to be taken into account without giving special preference to any one stakeholder group would be very difficult. It seems reasonable to assume that trying to balance a diverse spectrum of competing stakeholder demands is a difficult and inefficient mode of production.[29]

According to Jensen (2002: 237), Stakeholder Theory is "fundamentally flawed because it violates the proposition that any organization must have a single-valued objective as a precursor to purposeful or rational behaviour." The purpose of producing value for the economy would not be efficiently realized with multiple corporate objectives because "it is logically impossible to maximize in more than one dimension at the same time." (Jensen 2002: 238). Instead, focusing on profit as a measure of success gives "one objective function that will resolve the trade-off problem among multiple constituencies. It tells the firm to spend an additional dollar of resources to satisfy the desires of each constituency as long as that constituency values the result at more than a dollar." (Jensen 2002: 239).[30] This objective function directs the corporation to allocate resources efficiently to produce output that is valued more than its inputs.

Phillips et al. (2003: 485) concede that Stakeholder Theory cannot provide a *specific* objective function: "Stakeholder theory does fail to provide an algorithm for day-to-day managerial decision-making." They contend that this is due to the level of abstraction at which the discussion takes place and that Shareholder Theory is susceptible to the same criticism because "the managerial dictate to maximize shareholder wealth stands mute when queried, How?" (2003: 485). Although correct, this misses the point because the criticism concerns not the *specificity* of Stakeholder Theory but the fact that it promotes a multitude of objectives to be followed rather than a single objective.

Jensen (2002) and Phillips et al. (2003) appear to be talking past each other. Stakeholder Theory on its instrumental interpretation functions on a *managerial level* by advising managers to manage stakeholder interests in order to reach corporate goals. On the other hand, Jensen is setting out an efficiency argument for a single objective function on the *level of the goal* of the corporation. This is

[29]Note that Stakeholder Theory does not prescribe the solving of social problems per se, only the problems of stakeholders.

[30]It might be objected that a single value objective for the corporation expressed purely in financial terms will not enable the corporation to properly value or make use of society's resources that are not part of its production function (for example, negative externality effects on the environment). This is correct if we are to regard the corporation as an atomistic entity decoupled from a political context. However, in democratic welfare states it is essential that corporations are embedded in a political context. For example, one would imagine the existence of environmental regulation that either prohibits certain behaviour or taxes the behaviour to internalize the cost of pollution into the production function. It should also be noted that the argument here focuses on the *economic* efficiency of the corporation as a producer of goods and services, and it is with regard to this that a single objective is more productive than multiple objectives. Note that Jensen (2002) argues that society's resources are most efficiently utilized when corporations aim to maximize the *long-term* total firm value as distinct from shareholder value more specifically.

intended as a scorekeeping device to measure success and it might be that managing stakeholders instrumentally is a good means for achieving the corporation's single goal. This is not inconsistent with Freeman (2008: 18), who observes that, "If a business tries to maximize profits, in fact, profits don't get maximized, at least in the real world." But unlike Shareholder Theory, maximizing profits is not the main point of Stakeholder Theory. Donaldson and Preston (1995: 79–81) maintain that success for Stakeholder Theory lies "in satisfying multiple stakeholder interests—rather than in meeting conventional economic and financial criteria". Similarly, Collins (1997) maintains that irrespective of the efficiency of "participatory management" in corporations, the primary reason for adopting such a system of governance rests on its supposed ethical superiority.

That the single objective function of profit leads to economic efficiency does not per se single out shareholders as the sole group that has an interest in corporate profitability. It is possible for other corporate stakeholders, in particular employees, to have their remuneration tied to corporate profits. However, shareholders are special in that their *entire* remuneration is tied to the potential profits of the corporation.

2. To argue in favour of shareholder primacy does not mean ignoring other stakeholder interests: "long run value maximization cannot be realized by ignoring or mistreating any corporate stakeholder, be it customers, employees, suppliers, or community" (Jensen 2008: 23). Instrumental Stakeholder Theory recognizes that a corporation must satisfy its different stakeholders so as to gain their cooperation and achieve its goals.[31] Indeed, Hillman and Keim (2001) found that stakeholder management leads to improved shareholder value. However, engaging in stakeholder management is not the same as extending control rights to non-shareholding stakeholders.

Non-shareholding stakeholders, such as employees, customers, and suppliers, are contractual claimants on the firm's financial resources. Their remuneration is (generally) fixed and specified in legally enforceable contracts. It is only after these contracts have been honoured (and all other costs deducted from revenues) that shareholders may receive dividends if there is a residual (profit). It is thus primarily in the interest of shareholders as residual claimants that the organization is efficiently run in order to obtain the best chances of a residual.[32] Fixed claimants' pecuniary incentives for financial success disappear after break-even (when their

[31]One way of distinguishing between the instrumental and normative interpretations of Stakeholder Theory is to say that as a managerial (instrumental) theory stakeholders are those groups that can affect the corporation's ability to achieve its goals, while as a normative theory stakeholders are those groups that can affect *or are affected by* the corporation, thus including constituencies whose interests should matter in a non-financial sense to the corporation.

[32]Legally shareholders are not strictly speaking residual claimants because they have no legal right to *claim* a residual (Stout 2012). Dividends to shareholders are decided by the board, which has no obligation to issue dividends. However, shareholders primary possibility of obtaining dividends is if the corporation realizes a profit leading to a residual that can lead to dividends being issued.

claims are assured). As Sundaram and Inkpen (2004: 354) note: "Control rights should go to shareholders, because as residual claimants, they are the constituency that will value this right most." Employee salaries could be linked to the residual (e.g., a bonus) and thus they would value the residual more, but not in principle as much as shareholders, unless their entire salary is variable.

Fixed claimants have made agreements in the form of contracts that they expect to see honoured. Shareholders have no such explicit contracts as the residual amount cannot be specified *a priori* in a competitive system. One might say that they have an implicit contract with the legitimate expectation to receive a residual in proportion to the risk of their investment. Phillips et al. (2003: 489) suggest that under their conception of Stakeholder Theory, shareholders would get "a fair return on their investment" (they do not specify whether or not this would be proportional to risk). However, shareholder theorists argue that there needs to be incentives for the firm to focus on seeking a residual so as to realize the legitimate expectations of shareholders. This outcome of an indeterminate process cannot be completely specified in a contract, arguably providing justification for shareholders as the sole stakeholder group towards which management owes a fiduciary duty (Easterbrook and Fischel 1993); a duty difficult to enforce without the sole voting rights of shareholders.

Potential incorporators could find incorporation unattractive if it meant they lost considerable control upon incorporation and were not given priority as residual claimants. The very purpose of having the corporate legal form for productive cooperation could be undermined because a main benefit of this legal form is the pooling of investment capital; while limited liability and other characteristics are beneficial to shareholders, would they wish to invest in a vehicle that did not prioritize seeking a residual? There needs to be a proportionally expected upside to the risk taken. Unlike investing in bonds where a fixed return is (virtually) guaranteed, shareholders cannot legitimately expect a guaranteed return in a competitive environment. There are no legally guaranteed returns for shareholders, whereas all non-shareholding stakeholders expect to see their legitimate contractual expectations honoured, at least assuming the backing of the judicial system. It is arguably the case that shareholders, as the only constituency whose remuneration is entirely dependent on a residual, *should* be vested with real corporate control powers (see, Benz and Frey 2007), because they have the greatest incentive for efficient production.[33] To

[33]A potential argument against assigning control rights to shareholders of public corporations relates to the liquidity of such shares (Aglietta and Rebérioux 2005). Shareholders can enter and exit a position almost instantly which suggests that they should not have influence over corporate operations in order to avoid short-term strategies at the expense of the long-term. This argument is sound, but it is also largely a description of the status-quo. Shareholders do not have operational control. They only vote annually for the board of directors. This incentivises management to stay focused on creating a residual, while appropriate incentive schemes for management should ensure that the goal is to create a long-term residual. Arguably a consequence of this is that shareholders should have limited control rights over management remuneration in order to avoid short-term incentive packages.

maintain that Shareholder Theory is likely to lead to more efficient corporations is perhaps not surprising because efficiency is not the central concern of Stakeholder Theory.

The prescription to maximise profits does not make sense in relation to normative Stakeholder Theory, because the very purpose of the theory is to not give primacy to one criterion or stakeholder group. It does not even make sense to say that the corporation ought to maximise profits and then use all those profits to satisfy stakeholder interests. Should the corporation distribute its profits not only to shareholders, but to employees, suppliers, customers, and society at large?

Stakeholder Theory is simply not about redistributing profits from shareholders to other stakeholders. It is about not treating people merely as means to some end. As long as a corporation is focused on realizing one goal (e.g. profit) then the efforts of corporate members are directed towards realizing that goal. This goal is seen to take primacy over the ends of individual members and therefore they are used as means towards realising the corporate goal (if that goal is the sole focus of the organization).[34] Stakeholder Theory is about stakeholders participating in the decisions that concern them before tasks are to be done (ex-ante) and not about simply voicing their concerns when it comes to redistributing profits after they have been ordered to perform the necessary tasks (ex-post). For normative Stakeholder Theory the primary importance of the corporation lies not with efficiency nor productivity nor some other single criterion. What is most important is how things come to be decided. However, when no single stakeholder has primacy then there is no incentive for any group to start a corporation. If corporations are not started as private initiatives (assuming rational self-interest), then they would need to be started as public initiatives by the state. This would remove private shareholders from the set of stakeholders and replace them with public ownership. In effect we end up with an erosion of capitalism and slide into socialism.

The central problem with the CSR prescription that corporations ought to solve social problems is that it regards the corporation as an all-purpose tool; one that is capable of being not only an efficient producer of goods and service, but also one that has the ability to solve a wide range of society's problems. The CSR movement overlooks the fact that the corporation is good at being a productive organization precisely because it can focus its energy and resources on achieving *one* goal. The corporate legal form played an important role as a catalyst in the industrial revolution and is today all pervasive in society acting as the primary vehicle for production and economic growth. This may make it attractive to think that the corporation can be the solution to all kinds of problems especially given the vast resources of the biggest corporations. But to demand that the corporation solve social problems would be to change precisely what makes the corporation good at what it does. The corporation already contributes to social welfare as a producer,

[34]Recall Paas' (1996) argument that the categorical imperative does not preclude that stakeholders are used as means, it only precludes that they are used *merely* as means. Stakeholder participation in decision-making that affects them is not necessary for avoiding treatment as a mere means.

employer and tax payer. We should not ask it to also take care of social problems that it is neither competent nor empowered to do. Richard De George (1999: 208) writes: "Businesses are taxed and such taxes may be used for social purposes. The purpose of the corporation, however, is profitable production, distribution, not social welfare". Demanding that the corporation solve social problems would not only be bad economic policy, but also bad social policy.

- The Corporation is not an all-purpose Tool: The corporate legal form (regarded as a legal instrument of the state) contributes to social welfare by promoting economic growth which is materialised through the economic activity of actual corporations. This growth is realized through the self-interested and instrumental use of the corporate form by incorporators and not because they are driven by social welfare goals per se. To direct the corporation to follow social welfare goals may obstruct the substantial economic contributions to social welfare that the corporate form already contributes.

I have said that the main tenet of the business ethics stream of Corporate Social Responsibility is to say that corporations have responsibilities that stretch beyond merely satisfying shareholder interests. As long as this position prescribes a moral duty for a corporate moral agent then it will clash with the position that I am advocating. However, there is nothing that hinders these prescriptions be written into law. In other words, that the interests of different stakeholder groups are made to bear on corporations in the form of legislation. This means that stakeholder interests are incorporated into the corporation, not by asking the corporation or its managers to adhere to a moral duty, but by augmenting the restrictions under which corporations maximise their profits. Because legislation tends to be general and not specific to any single corporation, legislating stakeholder rights is not likely to be completely responsive to the specific stakeholder demands of specific corporations. Nevertheless, many of the interests of stakeholders can be accommodated in the current system by legislating them. For example, all western democracies today have extensive labour legislation that regulates everything from minimum pay to fair hiring practices to employment security. This is a good example of a stakeholder group whose interests have been taken into account through the public process of legislation rather than the private initiatives of individual managers.

11.2.2.2 Exogenous vs. Endogenous Corporate Safeguards[35]

All parties to the debate believe that safeguards are necessary in order to protect stakeholders, and citizens more generally, from the potential externalizing harms of business. However, disagreement abounds regarding whether such safeguards should be externally imposed (exogenous) or internally imposed (endogenous), as well as how extensive such safeguards should be.

---

[35]This section draws on Rönnegard and Smith (2013).

Exogenous Corporate Safeguards

The pursuit of shareholder interests, at the expense of other stakeholders, can be constrained by exogenous safeguards, primarily in the form of government regulation.[36] For example, employment law (e.g., to ensure equal opportunity), market regulation (e.g. to regulate product safety), competition law (e.g., to avoid excessive market power), environmental law (e.g., to regulate externalities), and tax legislation (e.g., to provide redistributive effects). Boatright (2002: 1849) notes that "the stockholder and stakeholder theories disagree not about whether third parties ought to be protected from unjust harm, but how best to provide this protection." Many concerns that stakeholder theorists wish to address are taken care of through laws protecting the interests of the different stakeholder groups. Referred to as *exogenous* safeguards by Freeman and Evan (1990: 346–347), they "effectively constrain the pursuit of stockholder interests at the expense of other claimants of the firm… they force management to balance the interests of stockholders and themselves on the one hand with the interests of customers, suppliers and other stakeholders on the other."

To the limited extent that Milton Friedman would impose safeguards on corporate behaviour, those safeguards would be exogenous rather than endogenous. Friedman asserted that the social responsibility of business is "to use its resources and engage in activities designed to increase its profits *so long as it stays within the rules of the game*" (1962: 133, emphasis added). In other words, corporate managers ought to work so as to realize the interests of the owners subject to exogenous constraints. Libertarian belief in absolute property rights inhibits endogenous constraints that would allow non-shareholder stakeholders to participate in corporate decision-making. However, as libertarians, they do also believe in strong negative rights of non-interference, which importantly precludes harming others. The limited role of the state is to put in place the legal and enforcement institutions that are needed to guarantee contracts and protect negative rights. The envisioned limited role of government implies that such a system of government would espouse limited exogenous constraints and regulation. For example, Friedman and Friedman (1979) believe there is a role for government to play in rectifying market-failures such as addressing negative corporate externalities ("neighbourhood effects") such as environmental pollution. Nevertheless, Friedman cautions against too readily turning to the government as a solution. "The imperfect market, may after all, do as well or better than the imperfect government" (1979: 218).

[36] Exogenous constraints on corporate behaviour can also stretch beyond legislation. For example, the state can grant other legal forms, such as the non-profit corporation, that act as vehicles through which citizens can organize to pursue special interests. One such special interest can be the monitoring of corporate behaviour, as is currently the case with many nongovernmental organizations (NGOs) (Campbell 2007). Nevertheless, NGOs cannot be allowed free rein in their activities merely because they do not operate from a profit motive. They can suffer from the same legitimacy problems as corporations, not being democratically legitimate representatives of the citizens (Scherer and Palazzo 2007).

Endogenous Corporate Safeguards

Instead of such exogenous constraints, Freeman and Evan (1990) propose a theory with *endogenous* safeguards that do not externalize the costs of activities among contracting parties on others. (A simple way to understand the demarcation between endogenous vs. exogenous constraints is that the former involves corporate self-constraint while the latter involves externally imposed constraints.) Endogenous safeguards are essentially corporate governance safeguards that give non-shareholder stakeholders means to have their concerns considered by management. For example, extending legally enforceable fiduciary duties to stakeholders, or as suggested by Freeman and Evan extending voting rights to stakeholders in order to have their interests properly represented by the board of directors.[37]

Freeman and Evan (1990) object to exogenous constraints primarily on two fronts: (1) that endogenous constraints are more effective in protecting stakeholder interests, and (2) that exogenous constraints externalize contracting costs onto society.

First, Freeman and Evan (1990) wish to grant stakeholder voting membership on the board because it is seen as more *effective* in protecting stakeholders' interests. In essence, they take the view that safeguards that are created endogenously to the corporation through bilateral contracting between the corporation and stakeholders, together with the more general safeguard of board stakeholder representation, will always be more effective than exogenous stakeholder safeguards imposed by government. This view is maintained because government cannot legislate in a manner that is tailored to the particular circumstances of stakeholders of individual corporations. However, it is not clear that endogenous safeguards are always more effective (or more efficient) for protecting stakeholder interests. Although Freeman and Evan are correct in their view that government cannot tailor its safeguards to every corporation, there will be many circumstances when exogenous safeguards through government regulation are both more effective and more efficient. For example bilateral-agreements may not give *effective* protection to one party if the other party is in a significantly stronger bargaining position, and this is not circumvented by equal voting membership on the board because any stakeholder group in a system of voting is subject to the risk of minority oppression. Exogenous safeguards can on the other hand give protection to stakeholder groups irrespective of the internal contractual dynamics of the corporation. Boatright (2002: 1842) believes that stakeholder theorists regard the shareholder-management relationship as an ideal for treating all stakeholders, but that "stakeholders usually derive little benefit from the set of rights negotiated by shareholders and generally prefer

---

[37]Given that the shareholder primacy norm is primarily perpetuated through shareholders sole voting rights for the board, extending such voting rights to non-shareholder stakeholders is the logical move to attenuate shareholder primacy for greater managerial concern of stakeholder interests. However, extending voting rights beyond shareholders (and employees) is mired with so many practical difficulties as to be essentially impossible. The difficulties primarily concern the identification of who the relevant stakeholders are and what weight to give their respective votes.

other safeguards for their interests. Instead of seeking a seat on the board of directors or the benefit of fiduciary duties, consumers, for example, settle for manufacturers' warranties, consumer and product safety laws, and a tort liability system." Furthermore, it can also be argued that exogenous stakeholder protections that are applicable to all corporations can be much more *efficient* for protecting the interests of stakeholders as it saves the contracting of each of these safeguards for every corporation for every stakeholder group (Child and Marcoux 1999).

Although formal constraints (endogenous or exogenous) are important, one should not characterize stakeholders as helpless minions at the mercy of all-powerful managers. Stakeholders are capable of engaging in strategies to further their own ends (Frooman 1999). Just as managers can engage in the management of stakeholders, stakeholders can engage in the management of managers. However, there will be differing power relationships and therefore different strategies across stakeholders if they are to get what they want (Mitchell et al. 1997).

Secondly, for libertarians positive rights only arise through individual consent and, moreover, state aid may violate some negative rights (such as the right not to have one's property infringed upon) through the need for taxation. This helps explain Freeman and Evan's second objection to exogenous safeguards that their costs "are spread over the entire society" (1990: 347). The cost of legislating and enforcing government regulation is spread across citizens, usually through taxation. This is objectionable to libertarians because it imposes costs on third parties to corporate contracting (without their consent). In other words those, and only those, who engage in contracting should bear the full costs that result from their agreements. However, it would be practicably unworkable and inefficient to internalize all the potential external costs of contracting as every potentially affected third party would need to engage in the contracting and be compensated bi-laterally (Child and Marcoux 1999).

Not only is it possible to take into account shareholder interests by placing exogenous legal restrictions on corporations, but it is also the best way to hold the corporation accountable. Given that the corporation is not a moral agent it does not assume any moral duties that guides its behaviour. Moreover, if we assume that incorporators are primarily guided by rational self-interest then they will not start or maintain corporations for the benefit of other stakeholders with endogenous safeguards (unless such safeguards are legislated too). This means that the only thing that restricts corporate behaviour are social restrictions. These restrictions take the form of either informal public opinion or formal legislation. However, from the individual corporation's point of view it makes little difference if the restrictions are formal or informal because they are nevertheless restrictions to furthering its goal. This view has been called "Corporate Social Responsiveness" and essentially says that the corporation should make its organization responsive to social pressures. The corporation thus responds to laws and social opinion, not because it has a moral obligation to do so, but because it is part of its economic environment and thus needs to respond to further its own goals. Arguably all corporate behaviour is like this. Therefore, while Corporate Social Responsibly advocates are encouraging the development of CSR (Corporate Social Responsibility) they are in fact only getting CSR (Corporate Social Responsiveness). It could be said that a moral CSR prescription functions like a public opinion restriction on the corporation to the extent that enough consumers care about the specific issue. But if enough consumers (who are also citizens of a state) care about an issue, then it is better that the prescription is enacted in law because then it is enforced with the sanctioning power of the state and is applicable equally to all corporations; not just the few that are exposed by the media or subjected to consumer boycotts.

- Stakeholder interests can and ought to be accommodated by legislation: If a certain issue is important to a stakeholder group then their interest can be accommodated through legislation and thus will be taken into account by managers because it is part of the corporation's economic environment. I have suggested that exogenous legal constraints are more efficient and possibly more effective at addressing stakeholder concerns. Furthermore, it is preferable that corporations respond to legislation rather than public opinion because then it applies to all corporations equally and is enforced with the sanctioning power of the state. Arguably all actions by corporations are responses to their environment and not performed out of a sense of responsibility because they are not moral agents. Therefore CSR advocates at best only obtain Corporate Social Responsiveness.

11.2.3 The Rationality of the Shareholder Primacy Norm

As has been mentioned previously, CSR advocates regard the legal force of the shareholder primacy norm as a substantial obstacle to promoting other stakeholder interests. However, I said that in practice the shareholder primacy norm does not hinder corporate satisfaction of stakeholder interests because the norm is muted by the business judgment rule and stakeholder constituency statutes.[38] Gordon Smith (1998: 323) writes: "Proponents of CSR have seized upon the shareholder primacy norm in the belief that it is an important determinant of corporate decision-making. The evidence, however, does not support that belief".

Given that there is little or no restriction in practice for corporations to engage in CSR and corporate philanthropy, it may be possible to explain continued adherence to the shareholder primacy norm in terms of the importance that is given to the owners of an enterprise in a private enterprise economy. As long as shareholders have a right to vote for the board of directors, then those working for the corporation will be geared towards pleasing shareholders if they wish to keep their jobs. The right to vote that comes with the share ownership self-enforces the shareholder primacy norm and not the legal enactment of the norm itself. However, there

[38]For further details of this argument please see the previous section titled "Shareholder Primacy Norm".

is a very interesting argument made by Thomas Smith (2000) that says that the shareholder primacy norm is not the most rational norm for shareholders to advocate. Very briefly his argument is as follows:

It is possible to distinguish between a director's fiduciary duty to shareholders on the one hand and a fiduciary duty to the corporation itself without falling into the trap of reifying the corporation. One can regard the corporation as an abstraction consisting of the sum of the values of all financial claims against the corporation. These claims are primarily shareholder claims and claims by bondholders and other credit providers. What Smith (2000: 216) argues is that "[i]f economic efficiency is the normative guidepost of substantive law, then the principal norm of corporate law cannot be the maximization of shareholder value". Instead the rational investor should choose a fiduciary duty that maximises the value of the corporation, i.e. the sum of the value of all financial claims against the corporation. The argument is based on the idea that rational investors would adhere to CAPM (Capital Asset Pricing Model) in their decision making. According to CAPM rational investors will diversify among all classes of capital assets including both corporate shares and bonds. All rational investors wishing to diversify away industry specific risk will hold the same "market portfolio", which consists of proportional slices of all capital assets in the market. Because investors hold both bonds and shares in every firm in the market "it would be irrational for investors to agree to a principle that required the value of shares to be maximised if it meant reducing the value of their bonds by more than the increase in the value of the stock" (Smith 2000: 217).

The idea here is the following: The value of shares is dependent on the net present value of the investments of the corporation. The value of bonds is dependent on the risk that the corporation will default on its payments. Because of limited liability, if the corporation is close to insolvency then it can make an investment that may benefit the shareholders if it is profitable, but need not harm shareholders if there is a loss greater than the value of equity because the loss must be carried by the bondholders.[39] Therefore there is a conflict of interest if bondholders and shareholders are different groups of people, but if they are the same as is prescribed by CAPM then it would be rational to maximise the value of all financial claims against the corporation and not just the value of the shares.

This is important if the corporation is to consistently fulfil its role an efficient allocator or resources. The limited liability of the corporation shields it from potential losses in such a way that an investment with a negative net present value (one that is expected to lose money, but may be profitable) can nevertheless be a good investment from the shareholders' point of view because potential losses are carried by bondholders. Therefore the shareholder primacy norm in this situation leads to an inefficient allocation of resources, because it mandates that the

[39]In other words, because shareholders' personal assets are shielded by the limited liability of the corporation they do not risk bearing the full burden of a loss bearing investment that leads to corporate bankruptcy. However, bondholders who have lent the corporation money may lose their financial claims on the corporation instead.

corporation engage in an investment that is expected to be loss bearing. However, the norm to maximise the value of all financial claims (both shares and bonds) against the corporation means that no negative net present value investments are possible. This is because all investors hold both shares and bonds and thus there is no sense in which shareholders can transfer their losses to bondholders. "If managers really are duty bound to maximize the value of shares, then they are duty bound to make inefficient choices" (Smith 2000: 224). Not only would rational investors not choose the shareholder primacy norm, but economic efficiency suggests that they ought to choose a norm that maximises the value of the corporation instead.[40]

- In order for the corporation to improve its role as an efficient allocator of resources the shareholder primacy norm ought to be replaced with a legal norm prescribing that the value of the corporation be maximised.

The shareholder primacy norm is not a hindrance to greater social responsibility in the sense that it legally restricts managers from taking into account stakeholder interests, but it does sometimes hinder the corporation from fulfilling its social role as an efficient allocator of resources. The efficient production and allocation of resources is the corporation's primary role in society, not social welfare. The state already exists as the established institution for representing the will of the people and solving social problems in accord with their preferences. CSR advocates often proceed in their discourse as if the state did not exist. But the state does exist and it has a primary role in solving social problems. This brings us to the next section which shall take a more in depth look at the division between private and public role responsibilities.

- Summarizing Remarks: I started this Sect. (11.2) by explicating the Stakeholder Theory and the Social Contract Theory and their importance for the CSR movement, which advocates that a wider constituency of stakeholder interests ought to be taken into account in managerial decision-making. Here I pointed out that the prescriptions of CSR, especially those founded on Social Contract Theory, rely on corporate moral agency. I then explicated the Shareholder Theory as put forward by Milton Friedman and contrasted how its adherence to the shareholder primacy norm stood in opposition to the central tenet of CSR. I then proceeded to argue against the prescriptions of CSR in favour of the Shareholder Theory. Some of the most important point were:
  - CSR leads to the moral equivalent of a progressive tax that is counter competitive thus undermining the market mechanism. Therefore a state tax

[40]The real market for capital assets is not as perfect as that hypothesized in CAPM. In real markets most investors do not hold a complete market portfolio and thus real investors may still choose the shareholder primacy norm to guide corporate directors. However, it still holds that following the shareholder primacy norm may lead to a socially inefficient allocation of resources when the corporation is near the point of insolvency. This inefficiency problem near insolvency is in practice addressed by courts piercing the corporate veil if limited liability has been abused, and several jurisdictions deem that fiduciary duties stretch to all financial claimants near insolvency.

is better than a moral tax because it is equal for all actors. Tax revenues can then be used by the state to help solve social problems.
- Competition in the market precludes concerted efforts among actors to solve social problems. State regulation can align the efforts of corporations while avoiding collusion among the actors.
- The CSR movement inadvertently promotes a privatisation of social welfare because it promotes private solutions to social problems.
- Stakeholder corporations are likely to be less economically efficient than shareholder corporations, because normatively balancing a diverse spectrum of stakeholder concerns is a difficult mode of production.
- The corporation is not an all-purpose tool. The corporation is a good producer of goods and allocator of resources because it only needs to focus on satisfying one criterion. If it is to try and satisfy the entire spectrum of stakeholder interests then that would undermine corporate contributions to social welfare in terms of production, employment and tax revenues.
- Stakeholder interests can and ought to be accommodated by legislation because then their interests are backed by the sanctioning power of the state and the same rules apply to all corporations equally. Legislation is also more efficient and arguably more effective at addressing stakeholder concerns.
- In order for the corporation to improve its role as an efficient allocator of resources the shareholder primacy norm ought to be replaced with a legal norm prescribing that the value of all financial claims against the corporation be maximised.

11.3 The Division Between Public and Private Corporate Responsibilities

It is not possible to answer what role the corporation ought to have in society without at the same time answering what role the state ought to have in society, unless the two roles overlap. Orts (2013) says that the institution of the "state" itself cannot be conceived metaphysically without a public/private distinction. "Without a designation of what is "public" and what is "private", everything potentially counts as "public" (i.e. totalitarian government) or nothing does (i.e. a radical anarchy)" (Orts 2013: 114).

The state can exist without the corporation but the corporation cannot exist without the state. Even libertarians agree to as much. Liberals think that the state should take care of many (or most) social problems, while libertarians at the other end of the political spectrum think that the state should do virtually nothing. These political positions also prescribe whether the corporate form ought to primarily be an instrument of the state or merely an instrument of the incorporating parties. Of course if the corporate form is an instrument of the state then the public role responsibilities of the corporation also ought to be set by the state through legislation.

Moreover, these political positions only advocate the degree of social intervention and responsibility of the state, but neither political view says that the corporation itself should *intentionally* take care of social problems. The prescription that corporations should take care of social problems only comes with the assumption that the corporation is also a moral agent. Nevertheless, if one does advocate corporate moral agency then the social responsibilities of the corporation will be contingent on what social responsibilities the state has not already assumed.

Seeing as I am not advocating a corporate moral agency position I shall not be focusing on the potential moral responsibilities of the corporation in relation to the state. I will instead be focusing on the legitimate interplay between the state and corporations on the assumption that the corporate legal form is an instrument of the state. There has been genuine concern over the years that corporations may wield such power that they in effect can manipulate the political system for their private agenda. For example in 1899 John Bates Clark wrote of "the power of corporations to make the political machine their instrument and the legislator their servant" (source: Samuels 1989). More recently Robert Monks has commented that "in our search for wealth and prosperity, we created the thing that is going to destroy us" (source: Bakan 2004). Corporations wield great economic power that can influence public policies and other state initiatives. Therefore I shall look more closely at the legitimacy of corporate involvement in public affairs.

I shall further explore the division between public responsibilities of the state on the one hand and private responsibilities of the corporation on the other hand. First, I shall evaluate how the public/private distinction bears on the responsibilities of the state and corporations. Secondly, I will discuss the normative justification for the market mechanism and how market regulation affects the duties of managers and executives who are moral agents. Here I will maintain that the justification of the market demands a zone of moral exception where actors may act purely out of self-interest while working within the boundaries of the law. Finally, I shall look at some of the normative and practical justifications for state intervention and regulation of market activities as they pertain to corporations.

11.3.1 The Public/Private Distinction

It is fairly common among political theorists to distinguish between a public sphere and a private sphere in society. Generally the purpose of this dichotomy is to distinguish the private sphere of life in society as an area that is out of reach from the powers of public intervention of the state. What is important here is to analyse which of these two spheres corporate activity falls into. To the extent that the corporation is part of the private sphere this places it out of reach from the regulatory arm of the state. It should be clear that the placement of the corporation in the private sphere is a normative decision supported by libertarian ideology. For example one may regard the conferring constitutional personhood to the corporation as an ideological shift in power from the state to the corporation; i.e. a shift away from the corporation regarded as a grant by the state towards a conception of the corporation regarded as a person with constitutional protections. Recall that the *Santa Clara* case, which ruled that the corporation was a person before the constitution, was decided on the basis of the Nexus-of-Contracts Theory, which itself has libertarian underpinnings. John Flynn (1989: 132) articulates clearly the ideological importance of recognising the corporation as a person with private protections:

> "Recognition of the corporation as a person for constitutional purposes is more significant, not because of some metaphysical debate over personhood, but because such recognition elevates this form of joint or collective action to a constitutional status with certain immunities from control by the community through government".

In a similar vein Orts (2013: 115) maintains that "the legal recognition and protection of some level of autonomy for self-organization through agency arrangements, organizational contracts, and the assembly of different constellations of property are needed for private business to arise and flourish". The position that I have been advocating is that we should regard the corporate legal form as an instrument of the state on the one hand, but regard actual corporations as instruments for the incorporators on the other hand. On this conception it seems appropriate to regard the corporate legal form as belonging to the public sphere while actual corporations as belonging to the private sphere.

I think we may regard the state with its political electoral process as containing a decision procedure for determining the ends towards which society aspires, while an actual corporation, with its procedures of corporate governance, contains a decision procedure about the means for achieving the ends articulated in the articles of incorporation. This yields a public/private distinction whereby the state is free to regulate the corporate legal form in line with society's goals, while actual corporations are free to decide which means will best realize their private goals within the confines of state regulation. This distinction may be more broadly characterized as a division between the political sphere and the economic sphere, where the political sphere regulates the playing field in which economic activity takes place for the benefit of society. This can be phrased as the corporate legal form having a *role* to serve the socioeconomic ends of the state, while actual corporations have as their *goal* to further the ends of their incorporators.

- Given that the corporate legal form is an instrument of the state and that actual corporations are the instruments of the incorporators, we then obtain a public/private distinction in which the state regulates the corporate legal form while actual corporations are free to decide on the best means to realize their private goals within the boundaries of the law.

Many of those who invoke the distinction between the political sphere and the economic sphere describe this as a relationship of conflict and tension. That is to say that the public agenda of the state to regulate corporations (and the market) conflicts with the interests of corporations to be as unregulated as possible. As a point of description this may very well be true. However, there are those (often of a libertarian leaning) who also prescribe this conflict of interests between the state and corporations as a checks and balances mechanism for keeping reins on the power of the state. Nevertheless, this representation of the conflict between the state and corporations cannot be fundamental to a free enterprise economic system. The interests of the state and that of corporations are often depicted as diametrically opposed because one is only considering the narrow issue of regulation. I think it is a healthy idea to keep checks on the state, but broadly speaking the interest of the state and that of corporations cannot be diametrically opposed because the very existence of actual corporations is contingent on the granting of the corporate legal form by the state. Recall the words of the dissenting Justices in *Bellotti*: "The state need not permit its own creation to consume it".

It is understandable that the interest of corporations is to be exposed to as little regulation as possible because this can affect profitability and thus there will be regulatory conflicts of interest between the state and corporations. Silk and Vogel write that: "The doctrine of 'corporate social responsibility' emerged in the United States, precisely because it is seen by many businessmen as a way of reducing the role of government in their affairs" (source: Smith 1990). However, the role that corporations perform as producers, employers, and taxpayers are all very much in the interest of the state. Conflicts of interest that arise between corporations and the state are often tangential to the general pursuit of business and do not detract considerably from their over-all contribution to society. At least this ought to be the case. A corporation that does not contribute positively to social welfare is parasitic on the rest of the socio-economic system and ought to have its charter of incorporation revoked.

- The interest of the state and corporations cannot be diametrically opposed: The interest of actual corporations may conflict with the states regulation interests, but the effects of corporate activity in the form of production, employment and tax revenue are all in the interest of the state. It is these positive public benefits that justify the states grant of the corporate legal form. If a corporation is not contributing positively to society it is entirely legitimate for the state to revoke its charter of incorporation.

There is a common misconception that a free enterprise economic system is somehow free from regulation. The "free" in "free enterprise" stands in contrast with command economies where all enterprises are publicly controlled. Therefore "free enterprise" has nothing to do per se with a lack of corporate or market regulation by the state. Peter Drucker (1946: 3) writes about free enterprise that: "It does not exclude government regulation or government limitation of business; but it sees the function of government in setting the frame within which business is to be conducted rather than in running the business enterprise". In other words the role of the state in a free enterprise economy is to set the boundaries that delimit a playing field of acceptable economic behaviour and not to control actual corporations. As Bowman (1996: 139) puts it: "Regulation should not be confused with state command or control of an enterprise".

Those who regard the corporation as having a role in the checks and balances of the state and who regard the ideal of free enterprise as consisting of as few regulations as possible tend to regard the economic sphere consisting of corporations as a counter weight to the state. During the mid-1970s the United States government took to using legislation in order to shape business conduct so that it would respond to a range of social problems. Business in turn responded by "attempting to influence the public and the legislature and regulatory process with regard to specific laws and regulations" (Buchholz and Rosenthal 2002). In other words, corporations decided to organize themselves in order to counter public policy and legislation that was not in their interest. There are now lobby organizations in Washington that represent oil interests, tobacco, guns, and pretty much every other product that might be subject to tougher legislation for the public good. It is part of the view I am advocating that corporations ought not to have the right to influence the political process unless specifically invited by the state to do so.[41] Corporations are not real entities with an existence independent from their state grant that legitimately places them in a position to act as a counter weight to the public initiatives of the state.

Actual corporations having been granted the corporate legal form ought not to be allowed to lobby against public policy and thus act as a counter weight to the state. This is because the corporate legal form is granted for the good of society and thus if corporations lobby against regulation that is enacted for the public's benefit then they are countering public measures for the good of society. It seems unreasonable that an instrument for the good of society should be allowed to counter legislation for the good of society. Not only is it unreasonable, it is also a bypassing of the democratic process.[42] When corporations manage to influence the legislature then the resulting legislation is not necessarily an expression of the public interest. Not only does lobbying constitute a bypass of the political process, the corporation does not even have a right to vote in the electoral process. Corporations may be afforded the status of personhood for certain purposes of the constitution but they are not American citizens. As much as corporations today have jumped on the bandwagon of declaring themselves "Good Corporate Citizens" they are not *actually* citizens and do *not* have the right to vote.

Nevertheless, it is surprising that corporations have been afforded the right to political speech under the First Amendment and may thus influence the political process. Bakan (2004: 103) writes: "Another significant change in corporate-government relations since the 1970s has been the expanded role and influence of corporate donations within the electoral system. In the mid-1970s the Supreme Court extended First Amendment constitutional protection to corporate financing of elections, a decision that has opened the door to corporation's near-complete

[41]In practice a ban on all lobbying might be a bit extreme. Governments are imperfect and as such may not know when to ask for relevant information when such information is available. Responsible lobbying might make important information available when it arises rather than merely when it is asked for. Therefore in practice a moderate stance would be to allow lobbying with reasonable restrictions in place.

[42]The ruling in *Citizens United* (2010) allows for corporations' influence the democratic electoral process by engaging in political speech. Such a ruling is inconsistent with the position I am advocating.

takeover of the electoral process". This has been further entrenched in *Citizens United* (2010) by allowing unlimited political expenditure for political speech in federal elections. It does indeed seem strange that corporate legal entities should be allowed to have such a pervasive influence on the electoral process when they are not even allowed to vote.[43] There are good reasons for not conferring the right to vote to corporations and equally there are good reasons to restrict corporations from influencing the electoral process. One obvious reason why corporations ought not to be allowed to vote is that they are human legal creations, and thus it would be possible to distort the electoral process simply by creating a multitude of "shelf-companies" each with a right to vote. However, the influence that actually occurs in the form of campaign financing and contributions is no less significant. Recall the words of Justice Brennan speaking on behalf of the majority in Federal Election Commission v. Massachusetts Citizens for Life:

> "The resources in the treasury of a business corporation . . . are not an indication of popular support for the corporation's political ideas. They reflect instead the economically motivated decisions of investors and customers. The availability of these resources may make a corporation a formidable political presence, even though the power of the corporation may be no reflection of the power of its ideas."

If we for a moment compare the "interests" of corporate persons and human persons, one thing that we can say in general is that corporate interests are considerably narrower in scope. The interests of corporations are primarily focused on the pursuit of the corporate goal as set out in its articles of incorporation. This means that if corporations are allowed to influence the electoral process then they will apply pressure to obtain such changes as are in their interest. This will generally be such things as less regulation and less taxation in their favour. Corporations are formed for the purpose of pursuing their stated goal and have no reason to take into consideration the public interest (except to the degree that regulation and public opinion influences their strategy). The dichotomy between corporate interests and the public interest is itself a problem if corporations have a pervasive influence over the electoral and legal process.

Corporate legal entities are not the type of entities that we ought to confer the right to vote and the right to political speech. This is in part because they are not citizens, and in part because their interests are entirely economically one-sided thus disregarding those important aspects of society that are not economically motivated. As Robert Hinkley (2002: 27) put it: "We must remember that corporations were invented to serve human kind, and not vice versa".

When corporations lobby government officials or make political contributions to the electoral process they are crossing over from the legitimate private sphere of activity into the public sphere where they do not belong. Arguably, this also applies to corporations engaged in CSR activities that use corporate funds to try and solve

[43] If all that is needed to influence the American electoral process is a corporation with vast amounts of financial resources, then this seems like a clear vulnerability that may be exploited by hostile foreign regimes.

social problems. Managers that use funds to solve social problems are "taxing" their shareholders, which only the state has a right to do, and the managers are attempting to solve a social problem, which they do not have the public mandate to do.

The private sphere of corporate activity is the realm of deciding the best *means* of achieving their goals within the rules of the game that are set by the state. Lobbying may be an effective strategy for the corporation to achieve its goals by influencing the state to change the rules of the game, but I am advocating that this kind of strategy ought not to be permitted because it is a bypass of the democratic process. Moreover, certain CSR activities might be in the interest of shareholders when combined with effective marketing and advertising, but these activities may still be objectionable if corporate resources are not spent well to actually solve social problems.[44] The role of corporations is not to try and influence the state to change the rules of the game, nor to assume the state's role responsibility of solving social problems. But now we may ask, how do public-private partnerships fit into this prescription?

Generally I believe that public-private *partnerships* are wrong. The main reason lies in that the concept of "partnership" implies a form of equality between the partners that is inappropriate in the relationship between the state and corporations. Bakan (2004: 108) expresses the point aptly:

> "Partners should be equals. One partner should not wield power over the other, should not regulate the other, should not exert sovereignty over the other. Partners should share the same mission and same goals. They should work to together to solve problems. Democracy on the other hand, is necessarily hierarchical. It requires that people, through the governments they elect, have sovereignty over corporations, not equality with them; that they have the authority to decide what corporations can, cannot, and must do".

Corporate interests will not tend to be the same as the public interest. That is to say, the type of social projects that the state is interested in pursuing will not be the type of projects that corporations will pursue on their own. There may be no profitable market for services that the state wishes to provide (public goods) and if there is then corporations will already be providing them. There might however be a profitable market for particular services (e.g. Healthcare & Education) that the market "undervalues" (merit goods) and thus the state may wish to provide or finance them for the public's welfare. Corporations may perform these services on

[44]Many CSR activities aimed at solving social problems are likely to be a net cost to corporations because they are expenditures unrelated to their core business. In some industries, however, where public opinion is very important or customers are especially conscious of corporate behaviour, it may be profitable to engage in CSR activities when combined with effective marketing and advertising. However, CSR activities may not solve the social problem at hand and may even worsen the situation, which has been called "Pernicious CSR" or "Delusional CSR" (Economist 2005). CSR activities that are profitable but worsen social problems are parasitic on society's welfare and are worse than mere window-dressing. A CSR activity that is profitable and helps solve a social problem seems to be unobjectionable because it is a win-win situation. Nevertheless, corporations are not in a good epistemic position to know ex-ante the wider positive or negative ramifications of their CSR activities.

behalf of the state and financed by the state, but this would not be characterised as a "partnership" where both parties concertedly engage with both financial resources and personnel on an equal footing.

Moreover, from time to time the state consults representatives of a certain industry with regard to their preferences and opinions on economic policy or regulation that will affect their industry. This is not and ought not to be a partnership relationship. It is an instance of the state needing factual information in order to form public policy in accord with its social objectives and not a matter of trying to specifically satisfy the regulatory interests of corporations. Corporations should not be in a position to decide the regulation that is to affect them. The role of the state is to further the public good. If the state satisfies the regulation interests of corporations it ought only to be done as part of a function to further the interests of the public. As we shall see a little bit later, furthering the public good may involve tradeoffs between greater regulation and accountability on the one hand, and greater investment and economic growth on the other hand.

- <u>Corporations ought not to be allowed to traverse the public/private divide:</u> The corporate legal form is an instrument of the state and as such the state need not and ought not allow actual corporations to act as a counter weight to its efforts to pursue the public good. When corporations lobby or make electoral donations they traverse the public/private divide because they stop merely concerning themselves with the best means to achieving their own goals and instead influence the publicly sanctioned regulations that define their playing field. However, corporations also traverse the public/private divide when managers use corporate funds to solve social problems, because they do not have the right to "tax" shareholders nor do they have the political mandate to solve social problems. Furthermore, public-private partnerships in the true sense of the term are wrong. The state should not relinquish its sovereignty over corporations in order to become an equal partner with them. This is because the corporate instrument is created for the public good and to transfer some control over public projects to a self-interested corporate entity will usually be counter to the public good.

So far I have maintained that the private sphere of the corporation is the realm of decision-making in pursuit of the best means to satisfy its own goals. But we may ask in this context if corporate managers are not bound by any moral norms within the defined playing field of regulation? Is the market a "zone of moral exception"? Next I shall discuss the normative justification for the market mechanism and how the market that is framed by the regulation of the state affects the duties of managers and executives who are moral agents.

11.3.2 *The Market as a Zone of Moral Exception*

Many would agree that morally good or acceptable behaviour requires that we as moral agents exercise a concern for others in our decision-making; that the realm of moral behaviour is encompassed by actions that are not purely self-interested in character and thus necessarily incorporates a regard for others. We may then ask: when managers work to satisfy corporate goals within the boundaries of the law does morality require of them that they also exercise a concern for others in their decision-making?

Let me first say a word about the value of the market mechanism itself. We make use of the market in our society because it is instrumental in transmitting price information to market actors which allows them to make efficient allocations of resources. There is no inherent value in the market, it is merely an instrument.[45] Moreover, the market cannot function as an efficient allocator of resources unless the actors in the market respond to the price information that they are given. Assuming that we wish to make use of the instrument of the market in our society for its resource allocation benefits, then this places a social expectation on market actors to act efficiently by responding to the price information they are given. Now, I shall maintain that because of the way we value the instrumental function of the market, this has the implication of making the market into a zone where the behaviour of market actors are part of a moral exception.

Market actors must respond to price information if they are to allocate their resources efficiently and so must most actors if the market is to function as an efficient allocator of resources on the whole. However, responding to price information is not commensurable with maintaining a moral concern for others. The market is characterised by competition rather than cooperation. For example, if a manager obtains market information that he is overpaying his staff then, other things remaining equal, he should give them a pay cut if he is to allocate corporate funds efficiently. This decision might be contrary to his personal concern for the employees, but the ideal of market efficiency and his fiduciary duty to the shareholders both suggest that he should issue the pay cuts. Another example might be how a manager considers the effects of his strategies on the competition. If moral concern for others was at stake, then the manager ought to choose strategies that helped his competitors or at least minimized the negative impact on the competition. The ideal of the market, however, says that the manager should not concern himself with negative impacts on the competition; in fact market efficiency follows a "survival of the fittest" ideology, which implies that the worse one's strategy affects the competition the better it is.

What I am saying is that we cannot both have our cake and eat it. It would be wonderful if we could allocate resources efficiently by being as charitable to as

[45]Other things remaining equal, if we could find a more efficient way of obtaining information about how much people value different resources there would be no argument against making such a shift away from the market mechanism. One might object that if we remove the market it will restrict people's freedom of choice. However, the market is merely a process whereby we reveal our preferences. If some other process revealed our preferences then the choices we would like to make would always be available. There may potentially be fewer options available, but a loss of options that we have no interest in choosing is not a restriction of freedom; rather it is an increase in efficiency of resource allocation.

many people as possible, but efficient allocation of resources and charity are two different and incommensurable activities. If we want to keep the market mechanism in our society, and we want it to perform the function that it is meant to perform, then we must expect and allow managers to make decisions that are based on self-interest (or rather corporate interest).

Make no mistake; this by no means absolves managers of moral responsibility. Every moral agent that intentionally acts in pursuit of a certain goal is morally responsible for his actions. However, those actions need not be morally reprehensible. Managers are morally responsible for the choices that they make, but we have created in our society a realm were self-interested behaviour is acceptable. For example, if the law states that a corporation may pollute amount X, and a manager makes sure that the corporation pollutes X (and no more), then the decision to pollute by the manager is not morally reprehensible. Although managers as moral agents are responsible for their self-interested behaviour they are not morally wrong in so doing as long as they play within the rules of the game.[46]

Heath et al. (2010) point out that business ethics as a field has proceeded largely as a domain of applied ethics, which focuses on the ethical decision-making of managers in particular situations. What might be regarded as a normatively proper decision, however, depends on the wider business and social context. This takes us into the domain of political philosophy. As such, the correct behaviour for corporations and their managers has less to do with the ethicality of conduct in a particular situation (e.g. whether it is good to pollute or not) and more to do with conduct within the publically recognized rules (e.g. how much it is permissible to pollute).[47]

Albert Carr (1968: 148) writes: "Violations of the ethical ideals of society are common in business, but they are not necessarily violations of business practices". This makes sense. For example, it may be considered morally reprehensible for an individual in his private capacity to display a lack of impartiality when recommending a product to a friend, while it is acceptable and expected for a business representative to be biased. Carr considers distortions of the truth (bluffing)

---

[46]In the theoretical ideal the legal framework (that defines the corporation's playing field) ought to be a reflection of the values of society and thus the actions conducted within that frame should be morally acceptable to that society. Of course such an ideal is unrealistic and many things that are legal may appear morally reprehensible to some. Corporate moral responsibility attributions (negative or positive) that may be made towards the corporation then lodge with those individuals within the corporation that are morally responsible.

[47]I am not conflating law and morality. I am saying that in this instance what is morally acceptable overlaps with the law because that which is deemed best for society is decided politically and enacted in law. Negative externalities such as pollution are an inevitable side effect of many business activities. If the production of all externalities were considered morally bad then we would in effect have to abstain from productive activities altogether in society. An acceptable social balance between negative externalities and the benefits of economic activity needs to be made. It seems reasonable that such a social balancing act be performed at the social level by democratically elected representatives that enact legislation, rather than by individual corporate managers who do not need to bear the costs of the externalities.

to be acceptable within the rules of the "business game". There is however a good argument to be made that truth distortions are counter to the market ideal of perfect information. Distortions of information adversely affect the ideal functioning of the market and ought not to be part of the rules of the "business game". Nevertheless, I think that there is an important distinction between biased information on the one hand and lying on the other hand. The former is inevitable for anyone who wishes to promote their own agenda, while the latter is deceitful manipulation of another person that amounts to fraud. Moreover, fraud is illegal and therefore does not fall within the rules of the game.

The point I am trying to make is that the market distinguishes itself as a realm in society where if you play within the rules of the game then *purely* self-interested behaviour is acceptable, whereas it would be considered reprehensible outside of that context.[48] The sport of professional boxing is an appropriate analogy. If you hit someone outside a boxing ring it is under most circumstances morally wrong and illegal, but if you do it inside the boxing ring it is acceptable and the applauded winner is the last man standing. In the same way the market and its accompanying legislation define a frame that demarcates a separation of where purely self-interested behaviour is acceptable and where it is not.

David Gauthier has famously put forward the argument that the *perfectly competitive* market (PCM) is a "morally free zone". The PCM assumes that all factors of production are privately owned and that all goods are private goods (i.e. each good enters the utility function of only one person). Furthermore, there are an infinite number of rational actors that have perfect information and the actors are mutually unconcerned with each other (i.e. their utility functions are independent from one another).[49] Moreover, the PCM presupposes an absence of force and fraud, and that there are no externalities. Given all these idealised conditions, Gauthier (1986: 93) argues that because the PCM guarantees individual gain through voluntary exchanges (a coincidence of equilibrium and optimality), therefore "morality has no application to market interaction under the conditions of perfect competition". He says that "[m]oral constraints arise only . . . when mutual benefit is not assured by the pursuit of individual gain" (Gauthier 1986: 93).

The idea is that moral constraints on the pursuit of individual self-interest have no role to play in furthering the welfare of individuals when that welfare is maximized by the self-interested pursuits of those individuals. However, the idealized PCM is set up not only to eliminate a *need* for moral concern for others (optimality and absence of externalities), but it also removes a concern for others from the

[48]*Purely* self-interested behaviour is morally acceptable under a system of perfect legislation. However, I shall maintain that *primarily* self-interested behaviour is acceptable in a democracy with an imperfect legal system. In both cases the market is a zone of moral exception.

[49]The PCM also assumes that the actors sell homogenous products that are perfect substitutes for one another. Together with the assumption that there are an infinite number of actors this implies that all actors are "price takers" and cannot influence the price of their goods through product differentiation or supply alterations.

preferences of the actors (independent utility functions). Within this hypothetical construction it is not very controversial to grant that the market is a "morally free zone".

Nevertheless, Gauthier (1986: 102) also says that "the morally free zone created by the market can arise only within a deeper moral framework". He says the market requires an absence of force and fraud to work properly, and I understand that such constraints are to count as the market's moral framework. Gauthier conceives of morality "as a system of rationally required constraints", and abstaining from force and fraud qualify as such constraints because they enable the mutual benefits of market interactions.[50]

Actual imperfect markets fail to live up to the idealized assumptions of the PCM and thus one cannot argue that actual markets are morally free zones based on this idealized conception. I do not argue that the market is a "morally free zone" but rather that it is a "zone of moral exception". Importantly, imperfect markets are characterized by imperfect information and negative externalities that open the door for market regulation to promote public welfare (for more on this please see Sect. 11.3.3). Society's normative preferences regarding market interactions are contained in the markets legal framework. Gauthier says that the market creates the morally free zone, while I say that it is the normative/legal framework that creates a zone of moral exception, which enables competitive markets. The constraints of the legal framework are not merely "rationally required", but also account for citizens mutual concern. The market is not morally free because it is normatively framed. The moral exception of the market is that actors need not practice self-constraint to the extent commonly expected by moral agents in society (guided in part by their concern for others), but can act out of self-interest within the teleologically imposed constraints of the law.

This places a big burden of responsibility on legislators to account for all the normative preferences of citizens for all the normative issues that might occur as part of business activity. It also places a large burden of responsibility on law enforcers to uphold the letter of the law in the face of actors pursuing their own self-interest. In the concrete world there are no perfect markets, no perfect legislators, and no perfect law enforcers. The world is not perfect. However, we need ideals towards which to strive in order to realize a good, yet imperfect society. If we value the market's efficient allocation of resources, then this ideal is not commensurable with cooperation among actors based on a mutual concern for each other because they must react to price information. Competition is the ideal. By recognizing this and that markets are imperfect we can further social welfare by asking market actors to pursue their self-interest with the constraints of (imperfect) legislation that aims to be perfect.

---

[50]It might be objected that such constraints imply that the market is not "morally free", but I interpret Gauthier as saying that the constraints are part of the framework of the market and thus do not act as constraints *within* the market.

An imperfect legal system will not contain all relevant normative constraints. This means that the normative framework of the market will have normative gaps.[51] This is problematic, but given that we are assuming imperfect markets we may also assume imperfect market actors; i.e. actors that unlike homo-economicus are not *purely* rationally self-interested. This allows for the possibility that market actors be guided by their own moral compass where the law contains gaps. Furthermore, it would be prohibitively expensive for law enforcers to try and detect every potential breach of law. Therefore, in reality a social and economic system is greatly aided by a general "ethical culture" to follow the rule of law and to abstain from harm that may be permissible through normative gaps in the law.

In a perfect legal system managers could not be morally blamed for business decisions that are within the constraints of the law. In an imperfect system, with normative gaps, managers could be morally blamed for decisions that are legal yet normatively wrong. In this particular context one could regard CSR prescriptions as suggestions to fill normative gaps in the law. This opens the door for advocating that managers follow some CSR prescriptions. The legitimacy of such prescriptions ought to stand in relation to the degree of imperfection of a legal system; i.e. how well/poorly it represents the normative preferences of citizens.[52] The ideal is that citizens of democratic sates ought to *primarily* make calls for legal enactments to hold the corporate legal instruments accountable to their preferences.

The market as a zone of moral exception is not contingent on a perfect legal system. The market is still a zone of moral exception with legal imperfections because it is morally acceptable to act *primarily* out of self-interest, in a manner that would not be acceptable outside of that context.

Would it ever be morally acceptable for managers to break the rules of a *perfect* legal framework that encompasses the market? The law generally distinguishes between legislation which regulates behaviour which is "mala prohibita" and behaviour which is "mala in se". Laws that prohibit behaviour which is *mala prohibita* are wrong to break merely because they are prohibited. An example is a law that forbids you from driving on the left side of the road. The British who all drive on the left side of the road are not all being immoral because they drive on the opposite side of the road to Americans.[53] *Mala prohibita* legislation are usually motivated on some instrumental justification for the social good and not because they prohibit behaviour that is morally wrong. However, laws that prohibit behaviour which is

[51] The method of the law is primarily negative (i.e. it issues prohibitions), so it is difficult from the outset to know in an imperfect system what is a normative gap and what is an intentional allowance.

[52] An instance of this view is to be found in Sweden that usually ranks top of world democracy rankings. Sweden has a well-functioning democracy and judiciary that has enacted extensive labour, environmental, and market legislation. As a consequence, CSR is primarily regarded as a foreign concern evidenced by the fact that the Swedish CSR Ambassador works for the Ministry of Foreign Affairs and primarily advises Swedish corporations on how to act outside of Sweden.

[53] Although if you knowingly drive on a different side of the road from the conventional side then this may be morally reprehensible as you are intentionally endangering the lives of others.

mala in se are justified on the grounds that the prohibited behaviour is morally wrong in itself. For example, murder or some other bodily harm.

Whether an offence will qualify as either *mala prohibita* or *mala in se* is bound to be a judgment call. For example, I am advocating that lobbying by corporations ought to be prohibited. Is the act of lobbying a *mala prohibita* or *mala in se* offence? That depends if one construes lobbying as 'industry information from a prohibited channel' or as a 'direct circumvention of the political process in order to serve a private agenda'. It is difficult to say, but I am inclined towards the latter.

Now, it may be argued that it is morally acceptable for managers to break *mala prohibita* legislation (for example antitrust legislation) in their role as managers. The justification lies in the system of deterrence for corporate breaches of the law. Deterrence of corporate behaviour is considered to be a function of the magnitude of the potential fine times the risk of being caught put in relation to the profitability of breaching the law. This is because managers are assumed to be rationally in pursuit of the corporation's financial interest and therefore will regard the potential financial penalties of breaching the law as a cost in their cost/benefit analysis for any investment opportunity. In this context it is the responsibility of the socially minded state to find an optimum level of deterrence; in other words the optimum breach of law is not necessarily zero. The reason is that extremely high fines that are thoroughly enforced might over-deter corporate investment because some investments that do breach the law may all things considered be of socio-economic benefit to society. For example, a breach of antitrust legislation by one corporation might be harmful to the competitiveness in an industry but it might create a great number of job opportunities and tax revenue, which on balance is seen as a social benefit. Furthermore, every investment opportunity also faces the risk of legal mistakes that translate into high expected costs if fines are high, which in turn also reduces the propensity to invest.

If the state itself engages in a cost/benefit analysis of the social good with regard to the level of acceptable legal breaches then such breaches are arguably acceptable. It is the responsibility of the state to deter breaches of *mala prohibita* legislation at an optimal level. Therefore it is part of the rules themselves that managers make cost/benefit analysis with regard to breaching the law. In other words, if the system of deterrence itself expects managers to breach *mala prohibita* legislation when it is profitable for them to do so, then it is not necessarily wrong for managers to do so in their positions as managers.[54]

This puts a heavy responsibility on the state to carefully calibrate the optimum fine for the optimal level of acceptable breaches of law. This precision of calibration may be unrealistic.[55] But neither is it possible to maintain that the corporation

---

[54]One suggestion might be to sanction managers for mala in se breaches of law while merely sanctioning the corporate legal entity when mala prohibita legislation is breached.

[55]Furthermore, there is a practical slippery slope counter argument. An acceptance for certain breaches of law serves to devalue respect for the law as a whole. In other words there is a risk that managers might come to regard all breaches of law as "acceptable".

has a moral obligation to follow the law irrespective of fines because it is not a moral agent. Corporations should be held liable for breaches of *mala prohibita* legislation while primarily individuals ought to be held liable for breaches of *mala in se* legislation. Let me explain.

Breaches of criminal law that are *mala in se* are not morally acceptable. I do not believe it ought to be part of the states socio-economic calculation that a certain level of such conduct is permissible. This is reflected in that the law generally prosecutes individual persons and not only the corporate entity for such legal transgressions, thus finding individual moral agents to *punish* for the *mala in se* breaches of law. *Mala in se* breaches of law pertain to the domain of criminal law and are punishable by jail sentences (rather than fines), which moves the focus away from an economic cost/benefit analysis and instead focuses more on punishing the wrongfulness of the act.

It might be argued that holding individual managers responsible for *mala prohibita* offences, rather than merely the corporate legal entity, might over-deter corporate investment that may be socially beneficial. However, such arguments ought not to be used when aiming to deter breaches of *mala in se* offences because matters of justice ought to take precedence over matters of social expediency. Furthermore, it seems normatively correct that the moral agents who are responsible ought to be held accountable for morally reprehensible breaches of law. For example, if a manager decides that breaching safety regulation on a new automobile design will cut costs sufficiently to cover all the expected legal penalties that are imposed due to an increased death toll, then this is not morally acceptable and the manager ought to be held morally as well as legally responsible. It is not part of the rules of the game that such breaches of legislation take place.

- The market is a zone of moral exception: Our society values the instrumental role that the market plays in allocating resources efficiently. For the market to perform its role it requires that market actors respond to price information, which is not always commensurable with a regard for others. Given that we nevertheless wish to make use of the market mechanism we must accept that market actors act on the basis of their own self-interest. For that reason we create a zone of moral exception in our society where it is acceptable to act purely out of self-interest while playing with the rules of the game.

Next, I shall move on to look at some of the normative and practical justifications for state intervention and regulation of market activities as they pertain to corporations.

11.3.3 The Justification for State Regulation

Regulation, like any other state intervention by a socially minded state, ought to be justified on the basis that it contributes positively to social welfare. Regulation contributes to social welfare primarily by forcing corporations to internalize the cost of their externalities, by filling the gaps of imperfect markets, and by protecting stakeholders from harm that corporate activity might cause.

Proponents of laissez faire economics advocate as little regulation as possible in order to allow the market to work uninhibited and allocate resources efficiently. Although the visible hand of the state might in many respects allocate resources less efficiently than the invisible hand of the market, there are still several areas where there are strong reasons for regulation. There are certain activities for which there is no market and thus the state can create one through regulation, and further there are certain markets that are sufficiently imperfect that regulation can help to fill the gaps. For example, there is no market for industrial pollution unless the state puts a limit on the amount of permissible pollution. Pollution is an externality of industrial activity as long as the environment is unregulated. Environmental legislation forces corporations to pay for the right to pollute, which internalizes the cost of pollution, thus making pollution a less attractive activity because it is no longer free. Regulation creates a market for pollution that leads to a decrease of emissions and provides revenues to help cover the costs of environmental cleanup activities. Assuming that society values the environment and does not want to bear the cost of pollution by corporations, then regulation provides a solution that contributes positively to social welfare.

Another example is product safety legislation, which protects consumers from potentially dangerous products, such as faulty electrical equipment or medication. Society benefits from regulating the market because it is imperfect due to incomplete information. It is not possible for consumers to look at a toaster or a pill and tell whether or not it is safe. For one, the relevant information is not immediately available and further, even if the information were available the average consumer lacks the knowledge to judge for himself whether the information means that the product is safe. The state thus intervenes to guarantee information in an imperfect market and to guarantee a certain standard of safety that the consumer himself cannot evaluate. One might argue that a company that harms its customers will not survive in a competitive environment and thus product quality is self-regulating. However, that argument only works ex-post after the damage is done and customers have stopped doing business with the company. Regulation serves as a preventive measure to avoid the harm in the first place and to raise safety standards above the level that companies with purely pecuniary motives might choose.

Many economists look at intervention and regulation of the market (especially government intervention) as creating a disturbance in the efficient allocation of resources. There are many instances of state intervention contributing to a less efficient allocation of resources. Nevertheless, because of market imperfections state regulation can also improve resource allocation efficiency. Ronald Coase (1988: 9) makes an interesting observation with regard to regulation and the working of markets. He says:

> "It is not without significance that exchanges like the stock exchange used by economists as an example of a perfect market and perfect competition are markets in which transactions are highly regulated (and this quite apart from any government regulation there may be). It suggests, I think correctly, that for anything approaching perfect competition to exist, an intricate system of rules and regulations would normally be needed".

Because the ideal of the perfectly competitive market does not exist, except on the drawing board of economists, there is potential room for regulation to augment the "natural market" so that it more closely approximates the ideal. For example, antitrust regulation exists to ensure that the market maintains a plurality of actors in order to keep a competitive environment for the efficient allocation of resources. Another example is the near perfect information that stockbrokers have about the shares they trade. They have this information, not because they are superhuman individuals, but because the gathering and dissemination of information is institutionalized and regulated. This then supplies an additional argument for legislating the social responsibilities of corporations rather than leaving social accountability to be pursued by the uncoordinated efforts of managers. Legislating the social responsibilities of corporations not only creates a level playing field for all involved, but it also creates the possibility of greater information and transparency regarding corporate activities. With institutionalized information gathering procedures and socially erected benchmarks, not only would consumers and regulators be better informed, but the homogeneity of the information would allow for a social comparison between corporations in a manner that today is virtually impossible.[56] Perhaps most importantly, if corporations are to have social responsibilities at all, then they ought to be legal responsibilities that are an expression of the concerns of society as a whole rather than a vocal few.

The goal of the socially minded state is not necessarily resource allocation efficiency per se, but improved social welfare. Thus regulation need not aim at creating a market solution to a social problem or to improve the workings of an imperfect market. Even if state regulation of medical drugs leads to a less efficient allocation of resources it may still be a positive contribution to social welfare because of the avoided health hazards etc. As Bowman (1996: 138) puts it: "Regulation provides a means whereby the public interest... can be invoked to subject corporate decision-makers to standards of social responsibility".

In this context of market freedom and state regulation it is often that Adam Smith is invoked to defend laissez faire free market polices. Smith believed, as do many economists today, that most state intervention in the market was negative. Instead he advocated that market actors be left to their own devices and let the invisible hand take care of the allocation of resources in society. Smith's statements, however,

[56]The Global Reporting Initiative (GRI) is starting to become an established standard reporting framework, although its voluntary nature means that far from everyone within an industry uses it, and furthermore measurements are often not homogenous enough to allow comparison.

need to be understood in the context of the environment in which he was living. Smith published "An Inquiry into the Nature and Causes of the Wealth of Nations" in 1776, which coincided with the very first years of the industrial revolution in Britain. He could not at the time have envisaged the dominance that corporations would come to have in the market. George Goyder (1987: 26) points out that at the time of Smith's publication the unit of enterprise was "a family or, if it were a company, a chartered company with clear social responsibilities". Smith thought that people's aspiration for being well thought of by their community and their family and friends was a sufficient incentive to maintain an underlying system of justice in social arrangements. He advocated a hands-off approach by government because the economic actors in his day were mainly individuals and families with their behaviour constrained by their "moral sentiments". Goyder (1987: 25) says that:

> "'[T]he invisible hand' of Adam Smith represents not so much the interplay of unrestrained impersonal economic forces, as the hand of Providence working through the family as a unit of social and local responsibility; a company of responsible individuals in a local society, in which the approbation of his fellow men restrained the entrepreneur by constantly reminding him of this duty as a parent and citizen".

The dawn of the industrial revolution with large scale organizations dominating the economy was not part of Smith's view. Large scale corporations removed individuals from day to day contact with customers and society. This removed them for the gaze of their communities and families thus shielding them behind the corporate veil. This not only removed individuals form the environment of social approbation of their communities, but also removed them from the social sanctions that Smith was relying upon to preserve a balance of justice. Nowadays citizens might direct their misgivings in the form of corporate responsibility attributions because the morally responsible individuals are hidden behind the corporate veil. However, the corporate entity is not a moral agent and it need not concern itself with the community's approval unless it affects its bottom line.

Social sanctions may work well on moral agents but not on corporate legal entities. Rather legal entities require legal rules coupled with legal sanctions. By defining the rules of the game through legislation and applying financial sanctions for breaches of law you hold the corporation accountable where it matters the most, namely its bottom line.

Given that the corporate legal form is a grant by the state for the public benefit this in itself implicitly puts restrictions on corporate conduct. On this assumption a corporation's raison d'être is based on its positive contributions to society, which places restrictions on the externalities that it can confer on society. Theoretically the corporation may not externalize more costs than the socio-economic benefits of its existence. On this premise, regulation is arguably an inextricable part of granting the corporate legal form because the state must restrict the actions of its legal creation so that it does not harm society, but rather works for its benefit.

Concern about how corporations were polluting the environment in the 1960s and 1970s was being voiced by activists such as Greenpeace and many others.

Corporations started reacting to these concerns in relation to the bad publicity that activists managed to generate for them. Slowly many of these concerns made their way into legislation. Today there is an extensive amount of environmental legislation in most developed democracies. Perhaps some of the concerns that today are being voiced by CSR activists will sometime in the future become legislation. The activists highlight their concerns to the general public, and if the public concurs they will in turn pressure their political representatives to make new legislation. However, I find it hard to believe that the public will pressure the government to ask corporations to solve social problems rather than just ask the government itself to solve the problem. Nevertheless, if for some reason they do, it is imperative that it manifests itself in the form of legislation as an expression of the will of the people rather than social pressure from a minority of vocal activists.

It might be objected that there is an important difference between (a) social problems caused by the corporation itself (externalities) and (b) social problems that exist independently of the corporation. The objection might be that the corporation has a responsibility to solve the problems it causes itself, but does not have such a responsibility with regard to independent social problems. If we are talking about moral responsibilities then the answer is that there is no difference between (a) and (b) because the corporation is not a moral agent and can neither have a moral duty to solve (a) nor (b). If (a) and (b) are conceived as legal responsibilities then the corporation may be legally responsible for either, neither or both (a) and (b) depending on what the legislation may be. However, legislation requiring that the corporation curb or eliminate its own externalities (a) seems much more reasonable than legislation requiring that it solve social problems more generally (b). This is because the corporation has the ability to abstain from its own social harm but is unlikely to be a good solver of unrelated social problems.

Today oil corporations are receiving a lot of heat related to potential plans for arctic drilling. In my view much of this blame is misplaced. Oil corporations drill for oil; that is what they do. Unless oil corporations are in some illegal way interfering in the public decision process over drilling rights they are not primarily to blame.[57] If the public does not want corporations to drill for oil in Alaska and their political representatives allow it anyway, then it is the democratically elected politicians that are primarily to blame for allowing it despite the public's interest.

- Regulation is justified on the basis of (1) internalizing the costs of corporate externalities, (2) to fill the gaps of market imperfections, and (3) to protect stakeholders from corporate harm. The goal of the socially minded state is social welfare and not necessarily the efficient allocation of resources per se. Thus it may be legitimate for the state to disturb the efficient allocation of resources if it leads to increased social welfare. The Smithian advocacy of laissez faire

[57]Clearly oil corporations are lobbying government to allow them to drill in Alaska as this is in their interest. In my view such lobbying is an illegitimate bypass of the political process and should be illegal. However, it is not illegal in the United States and thus it is not surprising that the oil corporations are putting pressure on politicians through lobbying activities.

economic policy is less applicable today than it was in his day because the dominant actors are now corporations, which are not moral agents, and need not be concerned with the approbation of local communities. Today we require legal rules with legal sanctions to hold the corporate legal actors accountable for their actions.

Making use of the market in our society for the efficient allocation of resources is like a double edged sword; it is a good instrument for resource allocation but you need to be careful that you do not hurt yourself when using it. Creating a zone of moral exception where competitive self-interested behaviour is acceptable is productive and efficient for society. However, the market also needs to be harnessed with regulation in order to protect society from potential harm. The market's realm of self-interested behaviour must be constrained. For example if you have a boxing match with no rules the winner may not be the last man standing but the last man still alive (as may be the result of any contest without any constraints). Adam Smith lived at a time when the economic actors were mainly individuals or families and thus the moral approbation of the community may have been a sufficient constraint on self-interest. Today when the market is dominated by actors that are legal agents through which individual moral agents operate out of sight from their communities then the social system of sanctions breaks down. Now we need legal sanctions tailored to the legal entities granted by the state. We may regard the market and its actors as the "economic engine" of the "social automobile" that needs to be steered through legislation by the state in the direction of the public good.

- Summarizing remarks: I have aimed to analyse the legitimate interplay between the state and corporations on the assumption that the corporate legal form is an instrument of the state and that actual corporations are the instruments of the incorporators. Given these assumptions we obtain a public/private distinction in which the role of the state is to regulate the corporate legal form, while the goal of actual corporations is to decide on the best means of realizing their private interests within the constraints of the law.

Furthermore, corporations ought not to be allowed to traverse the public/private divide through lobbying activities. Corporate lobbying efforts are an illegitimate bypass of the democratic process. The corporate legal form is an instrument of the state and it need not allow corporations to interfere in its pursuit of the public good.

We have created in our society a zone of moral exception where purely self-interested behaviour is acceptable because we value the efficient allocation of resources that such a zone provides. However, the market and its actors are constrained by legislation that defines the playing field within which actors pursue their interests. These regulations are justifiable on the basis that they internalize the costs of corporate externalities (by filling the gaps of market imperfections), and because they protect stakeholders from potential corporate harm.

11.4 Summary: The Role the Corporation Ought to Play in Society

I have aimed to explore three areas relating to the role that corporations ought to play in society. First I took issue with the libertarian position that advocates the Nexus-of-Contracts Theory both in its descriptive and prescriptive senses. This position stands in contrast with the view that I have been advocating which maintains that the corporate legal form is and ought to be an instrument of the state. Instead libertarians hold that corporations are the sole instruments of the incorporating parties who have inviolable property rights that prohibit state interference with the corporate legal form. I have argued that the Nexus-of-Contracts Theory, with its libertarian foundation, is descriptively false and prescriptively misguided. It is false because the corporate legal form could not have evolved as a private nexus-of-contracts because it is not possible to privately contract complete limited liability. Furthermore, the libertarian adherence to absolute property rights is normatively misguided because there is no robust non-instrumental argument for justice in initial acquisition of property, which makes an adherence to absolute property rights seem rather dogmatic. Once property rights are accepted as non-absolute this then opens the door for social welfare arguments to regulate corporations and augment the corporate legal form for the sake of the public good.

Secondly, having accepted that the corporate legal form is and ought to be an instrument of the state I took issue with the Corporate Social Responsibility (CSR) movement regarding whether or not the corporation ought to be used primarily as an instrument for the incorporators. The CSR movement advocates that a wider constituency of stakeholders than merely shareholders ought to be taken into account in managerial decision-making. I pointed out that in order to maintain this prescription CSR often needs to rely on an illegitimate assumption of corporate moral agency. Instead I argued in favour of an idealized version of Milton Friedman's Shareholder Theory while highlighting some of the main difficulties with the prescriptions of CSR. Among other things I said that the CSR movement inadvertently promotes a privatization of social welfare because it promotes private solutions to social problems. The force of the argument was that the corporation does not have a duty to engage in solving social problems and that the corporation ought not to engage in such problem solving. The corporation is not an all-purpose tool. Its role in society is to participate in the market by producing goods and services thus contributing to the efficient allocation of resources while also providing employment and tax revenue. The corporate form is not designed to solve social problems and moves that require corporations to do so may undermine their current contributions to society.

Finally, I have argued that there is a public/private demarcation between the role of the state and that of corporations. The role of the state is to regulate the corporate legal form while it is the role of actual corporations to decide on the best means to achieve their goals given the frame of regulation that defines their environment. This demarcation defines a normative line that corporations ought not to cross. Corporate intervention in the public sphere of activity is illegitimate because it is a bypass of the democratic process and corporate legal entities should to be allowed to act as a counter weight to the states pursuit of the public good.

Theodore Roosevelt once wisely commented about corporations: "They are indispensable instruments of our modern civilization; but I believe that they should be so supervised and so regulated that they shall act for the interest for the community as a whole" (source: Micklethwait and Wooldrige 2003).

The role that the corporation ought to play in society should be determined by the citizens of the state through the process of democratic representation. The corporate legal form is an instrument and as such it might be used for an array of different social ends. Today the corporate legal form is designed for corporations to be actors in the market's allocation of resources, although it is conceivable to change the corporate form to achieve some other end. However, it is not an all-purpose tool and cannot both be an efficient allocator of resources and a primary solver of social problems at the same time. This needs to be kept in mind so that society does not ask of corporations what they cannot simultaneously deliver. Because corporations are not moral agents, but merely legal persons, the citizens of democratic states should through representative government enact in law the duties they require their corporate legal instruments to fulfil in accordance with their preferences.

References

Aglietta, M., and A. Rebérioux. 2005. *Corporate governance adrift: A critique of shareholder value*. Cheltenham: Edward Elagar.

Bakan, J. 2004. *The corporation*. London: Constable.

Benz, M., and B.S. Frey. 2007. Corporate governance: What can we learn from public governance? *Academy of Management Review* 32: 92–104.

Blumberg, P. 1993. *The multinational challenge to corporate law: The search for a new corporate personality*. New York: Oxford University Press.

Boatright, J.R. 2002. Contractors as stakeholders: Reconciling stakeholder theory with the nexus-of-contracts firm. *Journal of Banking and Finance* 26: 1837–1852.

Bonnafous-Boucher, M. 2005. Some philosophical issues in corporate governance: The role of property in stakeholder theory. *Corporate Governance* 5(2): 34–47.

Bowman, S. 1996. *The modern corporation and American political thought: Law, power and ideology*. Pennsylvania: Pennsylvania State University Press.

Buchholz, R.A., and S.B. Rosenthal. 2002. Social responsibility and business ethics. In *A companion to business ethics*, ed. R.E. Frederick. Malden: Blackwell Publishers.

Campbell, J.L. 2007. Why would corporations behave in socially responsible ways? An institutional theory of corporate social responsibility. *Academy of Management Review* 32(3): 946–967.

Carr, A. 1968. Is business bluffing ethical? *Harvard Business Review* 46(1): 143–153.

Child, J.W., and A.M. Marcoux. 1999. Freeman and Evan: Stakeholder theory in the original position. *Business Ethics Quarterly* 9(2): 2007–2223.

Chilosi, A., and M. Damiani. 2007. Stakeholders vs. shareholders in corporate governance. *Journal of Corporate Governance* 6(4): 7–45.

Coase, H. 1988. *The firm the market and the law*. Chicago: University of Chicago Press.

Cohen, G.A. 1995. *Self-ownership, freedom & equality*. Cambridge: Cambridge University Press.

Collins, D. 1997. The ethical superiority and inevitability of participatory management as an organizational system. *Organization Science* 8(5): 489–507.

De George, R.T. 1999. *Business ethics*. Upper Saddle River: Prentice Hall.

Donaldson, T. 1989. *The ethics of international business*. Oxford: Oxford University Press.

Donaldson, T., and L.E. Preston. 1995. The stakeholder theory of the corporation: Concepts, evidence, and implications. *Academy of Management Review* 20(1): 65–91.

Drucker, P.F. 1946. *Concept of the corporation*. New York: John Day.

Easterbrook, F., and D. Fischel. 1985. Limited liability and the corporation. *University of Chicago Law Review* 52: 89–117.

Easterbrook, F., and D. Fischel. 1993. Contract and fiduciary duty. *Journal of Law & Economics* 36: 425–451.

Economist. 2005. The union of concerned executives. *Economist*, January 20.

Evan, W.M., and R.E. Freeman. 2003. A stakeholder theory of the modern corporation: Kantian capitalism. In *Ethical theory and business*, ed. T.L. Beauchamp and N.E. Bowie. London: Prentice Hall.

Flynn, J.J. 1989. The jurisprudence of corporate personhood: The misuse of a legal concept. In *Corporations and society: Power and responsibility*, ed. W.J. Samuels and A.S. Miller. London: Greenwood.

Freeman, R.E. 1984. *Strategic management: A stakeholder approach*. Boston: Pitman Publishing.

Freeman, R.E. 2008. Ending the so-called "Friedman-Freeman" debate. In Dialogue: Towards superior stakeholder theory. *Business Ethics Quarterly* 18(2): 153–190.

Freeman, R.E., and W.M. Evan. 1990. Corporate governance: A stakeholder approach. *Journal of Behavioral Economics* 19(4): 337–359.

Freeman, R.E., and R.A. Phillips. 2002. Stakeholder theory: A libertarian defense. *Business Ethics Quarterly* 12(3): 331–349.

Freeman, R.E., and P.H. Werhane. 2003. Corporate responsibility. In *A companion to applied ethics*, ed. R.G. Frey and C.H. Wellman. Oxford: Blackwell Publishers.

Freeman, R.E., J.S. Harrison, and A.C. Wicks. 2007. *Managing for stakeholders: Survival, reputation and success*. New Haven: Yale University Press.

Friedman, M. 1962. *Capitalism and freedom*. Chicago: University of Chicago Press.

Friedman, M. 1970. The social responsibility of business is to increase its profits. *The New York Times Magazine*, September 13.

Friedman, R.D., and M. Friedman. 1979. *Free to choose: A personal statement*. New York: Harcourt, Inc.

Frooman, J. 1999. Stakeholder influence strategies. *Academy of Management Review* 24: 191–205.

Galai, D., and Z. Wiener. 2008. Stakeholders and the composition of the voting rights of the board of directors. *Journal of Corporate Finance* 14(2): 107–117.

Gauthier, D. 1986. *Morals by agreement*. Oxford: Oxford University Press.

Goedecke, W. 1976. Corporations and the philosophy of law. *The Journal of Value Inquiry* 10: 81–90.

Goyder, G. 1987. *The just enterprise*. London: Deutsch.

Heath, J., J. Moriarty, and W. Norman. 2010. Business ethics and (or as) political philosophy. *Business Ethics Quarterly* 20(3): 427–452.

Hillman, A.J., and G.D. Keim. 2001. Shareholder value, stakeholder management, and social issues: What's the bottom line? *Strategic Management Journal* 22: 125–139.

Hinkley, R. 2002. How corporate law inhibits social responsibility. *Business Ethics: Corporate Social Responsibility Report*, January/February.

Jensen, M.C. 2002. Value maximization, stakeholder theory, and the corporate objective function. *Business Ethics Quarterly* 12(2): 235–256.

Jensen, M.C. 2008. From conflict to cooperation for promotion of the common good. In Dialogue: Towards superior stakeholder theory. *Business Ethics Quarterly* 18(2): 153–190.

Kymlicka, W. 1990. *Contemporary political philosophy*. Oxford: Oxford University Press.

Mitchell, R.K., B.R. Agle, and D.J. Wood. 1997. Toward a theory of stakeholder identification and salience: Defining the principle of who and what really counts. *Academy of Management Review* 22(4): 853–886.
Micklethwait, J., and A. Wooldrige. 2003. *The company*. New York: Modern Library.
Nagel, T. 1995. *Other minds: Critical essays, 1969–1994*. New York: Oxford University Press.
Nozick, R. 1974. *Anarchy, state, and utopia*. Oxford: Blackwell Publishers.
Orts, E.W. 2013. *Business persons: A legal theory of the firm*. Oxford: Oxford University Press.
Paas, D. 1996. Stakeholders and participation in corporate governance: A critique of some of the arguments. *Business and Professional Ethics Journal* 15(4): 3–17.
Phillips, R., E.R. Freeman, and A.C. Wicks. 2003. What stakeholder theory is not. *Business Ethics Quarterly* 13(4): 479–502.
Pickering, M.A. 1968. Company as a separate legal entity. *Modern Law Review* 31: 481.
Podolny, J.M. 2009. The buck stops (and starts) at business school. *Harvard Business Review* June: 62–67.
Rawls, J. 1999. *A theory of justice*. Cambridge, MA: Belknap Press of Harvard University Press.
Rönnegard, D., and N.C. Smith. 2013. Shareholders vs. stakeholders: How liberal and libertarian political philosophy frames the basic debate in business ethics. *Business and Professional Ethics Journal* 32(3): 183–220.
Samuels, W.J. 1989. The idea of the corporation as a person: On the normative significance of a judicial language. In *Corporations and society: Power and responsibility*, ed. W.J. Samuels and A.S. Miller. London: Greenwood.
Scanlon, T. 1976. Nozick on rights, liberty, and property. *Philosophy and Public Affairs* 6(1): 3–25.
Scherer, A.G., and G. Palazzo. 2007. Towards a political conception of corporate social responsibility: Business and society seen from a Habermasian perspective. *Academy of Management Review* 32(4): 1096–1120.
Schrenk, L.P. 2006. Equity versus stakeholder and corporate governance: Developing a market for morality. *The Business Renaissance Quarterly* 1(3): 81–90.
Smith, N.C. 1990. *Morality and the market: Consumer pressure for corporate accountability*. London: Routledge.
Smith, D.G. 1998. The shareholder primacy norm. *The Journal of Corporate Law* 23: 277.
Smith, T.A. 2000. The efficient norm of corporate law: A neo-traditional interpretation of fiduciary duty. *Michigan Law Review* 98: 214.
Stout, L. 2012. *The shareholder value myth: How putting shareholders first harms investors, corporations and the public*. San Francisco: Berrett-Koehler Publishers, Inc.
Sundaram, A.K., and A.C. Inkpen. 2004. Stakeholder theory and "The corporate objective revisited": A reply. *Organization Science* 15(3): 370–371.
Testy, K. 2002. Linking progressive corporate law with progressive social movements. *Tulane Law Review* 76: 1227–1252.
Williamson, O. 1984. Corporate governance. *Yale Law Journal* 93: 1197–1230.
Wolff, J. 1991. *Robert Nozick, property, justice and the minimal state*. Oxford: Polity Press.
Wolff, J. 1996. *An introduction to political philosophy*. Oxford: Oxford University Press.

Conclusion

This book has argued four major points:

- The corporation *is* <u>not</u> a moral agent.
- The corporate legal form *is* descriptively an instrument of the state.
- The corporate legal form prescriptively *ought* to be an instrument of the state.
- Actual corporations prescriptively *ought* to be primarily the instruments of their incorporators.

This conclusion will briefly summarize the main arguments for these points but also highlight how these points are interconnected.

First, I argued that the corporation is not a moral agent by setting up three necessary conditions for moral agency which are: an ability to intend an action, an ability to perform an action, and an ability to autonomously choose an intentional action. These three abilities are the metaphysical foundation that any corporation would at least have to meet in order to qualify as a moral agent. As I progressed with the explication of the theories of Peter French and other advocates of corporate moral agency I found that disagreement did not lie in the choice of conditions for moral agency, but primarily in the interpretation of the moral agency abilities. The morally relevant sense of these abilities was then further specified. I said that awareness of one's intentions and one's choices are necessary for lodging moral responsibility with an agent for its actions, which suggests that the intention and autonomy abilities are metaphysically mental states. The ability to perform an action was also specified further. I maintained that a moral agent must be able to perform an action on its own or through the help of non-free agents who do not act independently when representing their principal. This is because moral responsibility is not transferable from an agent to a principal if the agent is acting independently.

I primarily considered the theories of French, De George, Donaldson, Werhane, and Pettit, who all advocate some form of corporate moral agency that may be logically distinct from the corporate members. I found that these theories

D. Rönnegard, *The Fallacy of Corporate Moral Agency*,
Issues in Business Ethics 44, DOI 10.1007/978-94-017-9756-6

could not satisfy the three necessary and morally relevant criteria in part because they instrumentally attribute moral agency abilities to the corporation rather than showing that the corporation can possess these abilities itself as distinct from its corporate members. This instrumental attribution of moral agency abilities to corporations parallels our linguistic use of corporate names as the subjects of moral responsibility attributions. However, we cannot simply move from a semantic attribution of moral blame to corporations and then claim that corporations are moral agents in a metaphysical sense.

Nevertheless, making sense of our linguistic use of corporate names for attributing moral blame is far from irrelevant. I went on to discuss what it is we are referring to when we use corporate names as the subjects of moral responsibility attributions, which is the flip side of inquiring whether or not a corporation is a moral agent. Having already maintained that a corporation is not a moral agent logically distinct from its members, I suggested that the corporate names refer to the corporate structure, which in turn specifies the positions that corporate members fill. Because it might only be a subset of the corporate membership that are morally responsible for a certain event we only use the corporate name to broadly encompass those in whom responsibility resides, but we do not distribute responsibility until it is transparent exactly who those individuals are.

I then proceeded to explore if we could construct a more robust theory of corporate moral responsibility with the aid of either Bratman or Tuomela's theory of collective intentionality. The idea was that it might be possible to construct a better theory of corporate moral agency that meets our necessary moral agency conditions if the theory is based on the intentionality of the corporate members who are themselves moral agents.

Part I was summed up with a taxonomy of two illegitimate and two legitimate corporate moral responsibility attributions where my expansion Tuomela and Bratman's theories took part. I said that a Moral Responsibility Attribution to a Collective Whole (my expansion of Tuomela's position) is illegitimate primarily because the attribution of responsibility encompassed some members who are not responsible. I also said that a Moral Responsibility Attribution to a Corporate Structure (in accord with Peter French and others) is illegitimate because the responsibility attribution does not lodge with a moral agent. In other words the corporate structure as distinct from its members simply does not satisfy our three necessary conditions for moral agency. Next, a Moral Responsibility Attribution to a Unanimously Intending Collective (my expansion of Bratman's position) was said to be legitimate because every single member is morally responsible for the event being attributed. I finally maintained that an Elliptical Moral Responsibility Attribution to a Collective Whole is also legitimate because the attribution of the responsibility aims to lodge with those members who are morally responsible for the event, but one abstains from distributing responsibility until the corporate veil is pierced and the identity of those individuals is revealed. The central conclusion to be drawn from Part I is that moral responsibility may only be legitimately attributed to corporations when that responsibility is meant to lodge with corporate members and that corporations are never moral agents in and of themselves.

Having established that the corporation is not moral agent Part II proceeded to inquire about the role of the corporation in society, both descriptively and prescriptively. I started by establishing descriptively what the corporation *is* by tracing the evolution of the corporate legal form in English and American law. This involved explicating the historical development of the main corporate legal attributes which are: the shareholder primacy norm, the separation of the corporation from its incorporators, that corporate shares count as a separate form of property, and finally that shareholders are afforded limited liability. By following the development of these legal attributes I suggested that the corporation is primarily a legal agent and that the corporate legal form is an instrument of the state to promote the public good.

This historic evolution of the corporate legal form was in part viewed through the perspectives of the three competing legal theories over the nature of the corporation: the Legal Fiction Theory, the Nexus-of-Contracts Theory, and the Real Entity Theory. The Legal Fiction Theory maintains that the corporation is an artificial creation of law that is granted to an association of individuals, but is legally a distinct entity from the incorporating members. I argued that the Legal Fiction Theory is descriptively more accurate because it is the only one out of the three that is consistent with all the legal characteristics of the corporation and it is the only one that is consistent with the actual historical granting of the corporate form by the state. The historical impact of the corporate form as part of the industrial revolution was then traced. In this context we could clearly see the *role* of the corporate legal form as an instrument of the state to further socio-economic ends, but also the significance of the corporate form as an instrument for furthering the *goals* of individuals when incorporated in actual corporations.

I then moved on to consider the two prescriptive questions of whether the *corporate legal form* ought to be an instrument of the state and whether *actual corporations* ought to primarily be the instruments of the incorporating parties. It was argued that the corporate legal form ought to be an instrument of the state, in part, by showing that the libertarian nexus-of-contracts argument to the contrary is not tenable. Libertarians maintain that state augmentation of the corporate form is a violation of the incorporators' absolute property rights as shareholders. However, on examination of the justification for absolute property rights we find no robust argument for justice in initial acquisition of property and no good reason for why property rights should be absolute and outweigh all other considerations of justice in our society. Instead the best justification for private property rights rests on instrumental grounds for the economic benefits that such rights enable by making a free market economy possible. By conceiving of property rights instrumentally they may be construed in whatever way that promotes the public good. Accepting that property rights are not absolute and that the government has a role to play in promoting the public good (in accordance with the preferences of citizens) this then opens the door for the state to use the corporate legal form as an instrument for promoting such goods.

The prescription that actual corporations ought to be primarily the instruments of their incorporators was then set against the prescriptions espoused by the Corporate Social Responsibility movement (CSR). The CSR movement primarily advocates that a wider constituency of stakeholders than merely shareholders ought to be taken into account in managerial decision making, which might range from a mere dabbling in philanthropy to more engaging projects of solving social problems or even restructuring the corporation to take equal consideration of stakeholder interests. However, I maintained that such normative prescriptions often rely on the illegitimate assumption that corporations are moral agents. Instead I advocated a version of Friedman's Shareholder Theory (which prescribes the primacy of satisfying the interests of shareholders), and I explained some of the adverse effects of an increasing adherence to the CSR agenda. I maintained that the prescriptions of CSR inappropriately promote private solutions to social problems, which usually demand social solutions.

As a legal instrument the corporation can be put to use for many different purposes, but the force of my argument is that the corporation is not a good all-purpose tool. It is as an efficient producer and allocator of resources and to ask it to also perform social tasks that it cannot simultaneously deliver may interfere with its considerable contribution to society as a producer, employer, and tax payer.

The train of thought that has run through this book has started with the issue over corporate moral agency. The corporation is not a real entity that *participates* in business that is guided by moral obligations; it is merely a vehicle through which business is done. To believe otherwise puts undeserved faith in corporations holding themselves accountable in the absence of legal constraints. As legal fictions created by the state the law should be the primary tool for corporate accountability. In a democracy we know that the ends of the state are a reflection of the normative preferences of citizens and that the state manifests those preferences regarding public policy through legislation. Therefore if citizens have preferences regarding how corporate legal entities ought to behave it seems reasonable that they should make calls for legal enactments in accord with their preferences. Actual corporations are then free to focus their attention on pursuing the goals for which they were created while acting within the constraints of the law.

This model of accountability assumes a well-functioning democracy that represents the will of the people and a well-functioning judiciary that faithfully represents those preferences in the law. However, the dominant actors in our global economy are *multinational* corporations that are active not only in democracies with just legal systems, but also in developing countries with varying degrees of democracy and functioning judiciaries. Should corporations merely satisfy shareholder interests within the constraints of the law in these developing democracies?

My scope here is abridged to focus on the moral and political *ideal* of corporate accountability and does not tackle corporate accountability under undemocratic regimes. That much said, one can firmly acknowledge that a continued misperception of corporations as moral agents that are led by moral duties and held accountable to their own conscience does nothing but hinder corporate accountability at home and in the world. This book is a work in ideal theory, and while no countries in the world are ideal, it provides a direction towards which we can strive. Only when we know where we want to go can we take steps to get there. A well-functioning democracy with legislation that addresses stakeholder concerns is the way forward.

Bibliography

Aglietta, M., and A. Rebérioux. 2005. *Corporate governance adrift: A critique of shareholder value*. Cheltenham: Edward Elgar.
American Law Institute. 1994. *Principles of corporate governance: Analysis and recommendations*. St. Paul: American Law Institute Publishers.
Anand, U., B.E. Ashforth, and M. Joshi. 2004. Business as usual: The acceptance and perpetuation of corruption in organizations. *Academy of Management Executive* 19: 9–23.
Anderson, E. 2000. Beyond homo economics: New developments in theories of social norms. *Philosophy and Public Affairs* 29(2): 170–200.
Arnold, D. 2006. Corporate moral agency. In *Shared intentions and collective responsibility*, ed. P.A. French and H.K. Wettstein. Cambridge, MA: Blackwell Publishers.
Bakan, J. 2004. *The corporation*. London: Constable.
Benz, M., and B.S. Frey. 2007. Corporate governance: What can we learn from public governance? *Academy of Management Review* 32: 92–104.
Berle, A.A. 1931. Corporate powers as powers of trust. *Harvard Law Review* 44: 1049–1074.
Berle, A.A. 1932. For whom are corporate managers trustees: A note. *Harvard Law Review* 45(7): 1365–1372.
Berle, A.A., and G. Means. 1932. *The modern corporation and private property*. New York: Macmillan.
Blumberg, P. 1993. *The multinational challenge to corporate law: The search for a new corporate personality*. New York: Oxford University Press.
Boatright, J.R. 1994. Fiduciary duties and the shareholder-management relation: Or, what's so special about shareholders? *Business Ethics Quarterly* 4(4): 393–407.
Boatright, J.R. 2002. Contractors as stakeholders: Reconciling stakeholder theory with the nexus-of-contracts firm. *Journal of Banking and Finance* 26: 1837–1852.
Bonnafous-Boucher, M. 2005. Some philosophical issues in corporate governance: The role of property in stakeholder theory. *Corporate Governance* 5(2): 34–47.
Bowman, S. 1996. *The modern corporation and American political thought: Law, power and ideology*. Pennsylvania: Pennsylvania State University Press.
Bratman, M.E. 1979. Practical reasoning and weakness of the will. *Noûs* 13: 131–151.
Bratman, M.E. 1987. *Intention, plans, and practical reason*. Cambridge, MA: Harvard University Press.
Bratman, M.E. 1993. Shared intention. *Ethics* 104: 97–113.
Buchholz, R.A., and S.B. Rosenthal. 2002. Social responsibility and business ethics. In *A companion to business ethics*, ed. R.E. Frederick. Malden: Blackwell Publishers.
Buss, S. 2008. Personal Autonomy. In *The Stanford Encyclopedia of Philosophy*, ed. Edward N. Zalta. URL: http://plato.stanford.edu/archives/fall2008/entries/personal-autonomy/.

D. Rönnegard, *The Fallacy of Corporate Moral Agency*,
Issues in Business Ethics 44, DOI 10.1007/978-94-017-9756-6

Campbell, J.L. 2007. Why would corporations behave in socially responsible ways? An institutional theory of corporate social responsibility. *Academy of Management Review* 32(3): 946–967.

Cane, P. 2002. *Responsibility in law and morality*. Oxford: Hart.

Carr, A. 1968. Is business bluffing ethical? *Harvard Business Review* 46(1): 143–153.

Child, J.W., and A.M. Marcoux. 1999. Freeman and Evan: Stakeholder theory in the original position. *Business Ethics Quarterly* 9(2): 2007–223.

Chilosi, A., and M. Damiani. 2007. Stakeholders vs. shareholders in corporate governance. *Journal of Corporate Governance* 6(4): 7–45.

Cialdini, R.B., and M.R. Trost. 1998. Social influence: Social norms, conformity and compliance. In *The Handbook of Social Psychology*, vol. 2, ed. D.T. Gilbert, S.T. Fiske, and G. Lindzey, 151–92. New York: McGraw-Hill.

Clarke, R. 1992. Free will and the conditions of moral responsibility. *Philosophical Studies* 66: 53–72.

Coase, H. 1988. *The firm the market and the law*. Chicago: University of Chicago Press.

Cohen, G.A. 1995. *Self-ownership, freedom & equality*. Cambridge: Cambridge University Press.

Collier, Jane. 1998. Theorising the ethical organization. *Business Ethics Quarterly* 8: 621–654.

Collins, D. 1997. The ethical superiority and inevitability of participatory management as an organizational system. *Organization Science* 8(5): 489–507.

Cooper, D.E. 1968. Collective responsibility. *Philosophy* 43: 258–268.

Danley, J.R. 1994. *The role of the modern corporation in a free society*. Notre Dame: University of Notre Dame Press.

Danley, J.R. 2002. Corporate moral agency. In *A companion to business ethics*, ed. R.E. Frederick. Cambridge, MA: Blackwell Publishers.

De George, R.T. 1981. Can corporations have moral responsibilities? *University of Dayton Review* 5: 3–15.

De George, R.T. 1992. Agency theory and ethics of agency. In *Ethics and agency theory*, ed. N.E. Bowie and R.E. Freeman. Oxford: Oxford University Press.

De George, R.T. 1998. Can corporations have moral responsibility. In *Ethical theory and business*, ed. T.L. Beauchamp and N.E. Bowie. London: Prentice Hall International.

De George, R.T. 1999. *Business ethics*. Upper Saddle River: Prentice Hall.

Dees, J.G. 1992. Principals, agents, and ethics. In *Ethics and agency theory*, ed. N.E. Bowie and R.E. Freeman. Oxford: Oxford University Press.

Dennett, D. 1987. Fast thinking. *The Intentional Stance*, 324–337. Cambridge, MA: MIT Press.

Diskant, E. 2008. Comparative corporate criminal liability: Exploring the uniquely American doctrine through comparative criminal procedure. *Yale Law Journal* 118: 126–176.

Dobson, J. 1999. Is shareholder wealth maximization immoral? *Financial Analysts Journal* 55(5): 69–75.

Dodd, M.E. 1932. For whom are corporate managers trustees? *Harvard Law Review* 45: 1145–1163.

Donaldson, T. 1982. *Corporations and morality*. Englewood Cliffs: Prentice Hall.

Donaldson, T. 1989. *The ethics of international business*. Oxford: Oxford University Press.

Donaldson, T., and L.E. Preston. 1995. The stakeholder theory of the corporation: Concepts, evidence, and implications. *Academy of Management Review* 20(1): 65–91.

Downie, R.S. 1969. Collective responsibility. *Philosophy* 44: 66–69.

Drucker, P.F. 1946. *Concept of the corporation*. New York: John Day.

Dubbink, W., and J. Smith. 2011. A political account of corporate moral responsibility. *Ethical Theory and Moral Practice* 14: 223–246.

Easterbrook, F., and D. Fischel. 1985. Limited liability and the corporation. *University of Chicago Law Review*. 52: 89–117.

Easterbrook, F., and D. Fischel. 1993. Contract and fiduciary duty. *Journal of Law & Economics* 36: 425–451.

Economist, 2005. The union of concerned executives. *Economist*, January 20.

Eshleman, A. 2009. Moral responsibility. In *The Stanford Encyclopedia of Philosophy,* ed. Edward N. Zalta. URL: http://plato.stanford.edu/archives/win2009/entries/moral-responsibility/.
Evan, W.M., and R.E. Freeman. 2003. A stakeholder theory of the modern corporation: Kantian capitalism. In *Ethical theory and business*, ed. T.L. Beauchamp and N.E. Bowie. London: Prentice Hall.
Feinberg, J. 1968. Collective responsibility. *Journal of Philosophy* 65: 674–688.
Fisse, B., and J. Braithwaite. 1993. *Corporations, crime and accountability*. Cambridge: Cambridge University Press.
Flores, A., and D.G. Johnson. 1983. Collective responsibility and professional roles. *Ethics* 93: 537–535.
Flynn, J.J. 1989. The jurisprudence of corporate personhood: The misuse of a legal concept. In *Corporations and society: Power and responsibility*, ed. W.J. Samuels and A.S. Miller. London: Greenwood.
Frankfurt, H.G. 1969. Alternate possibilities and moral responsibility. *Journal of Philosophy* 66: 828–839.
Frankfurt, H.G. 1971. Freedom of the will and the concept of a person. *Journal of Philosophy* 68: 5–20.
Freeman, R.E. 1984. *Strategic management: A stakeholder Approach*. Boston: Pitman Publishing.
Freeman, R.E. 2008. Ending the so-called "Friedman-Freeman" debate. In Dialogue: Towards superior stakeholder theory. *Business Ethics Quarterly* 18(2): 153–190.
Freeman, R.E., and W.M. Evan. 1990. Corporate governance: A stakeholder approach. *Journal of Behavioral Economics* 19(4): 337–359.
Freeman, R.E., and R.A. Phillips. 2002. Stakeholder theory: A libertarian defense. *Business Ethics Quarterly* 12(3): 331–349.
Freeman, R.E., and P.H. Werhane. 2003. Corporate responsibility. In *A companion to applied ethics*, ed. R.G. Frey and C.H. Wellman. Oxford: Blackwell Publishers.
Freeman, R.E., J.S. Harrison, and A.C. Wicks. 2007. *Managing for stakeholders: Survival, reputation and success*. New Haven: Yale University Press.
French, P.A. 1984. *Collective and corporate responsibility*. New York: Columbia University Press.
French, P.A. 1991a. The corporation as a moral person. In *The spectrum of responsibility*, ed. P.A. French. New York: St. Martin's Press.
French, P.A. 1991b. *Corporate ethics*. Jovanovich: Harcourt: Brace.
French, P.A. 1992. *Responsibility matters*. Kansas: University Press of Kansas.
French, P.A. 1994. Responsibility and the moral role of corporate entities. In *Business as a humanity*, ed. T. Donaldson and R.E. Freeman. Oxford: Oxford University Press.
French, P.A. 1995. *Corporate ethics*. Jovanovich: Harcourt: Brace.
Friedman, M. 1962. *Capitalism and Freedom*. Chicago: University of Chicago Press.
Friedman, M. 1970. The social responsibility of business is to increase its profits. *The New York Times Magazine*, September 13.
Friedman, R.D., and M. Friedman. 1979. *Free to choose: A personal statement*. New York: Harcourt, Inc.
Frooman, J. 1999. Stakeholder influence strategies. *Academy of Management Review* 24: 191–205.
Galai, D., and Z. Wiener. 2008. Stakeholders and the composition of the voting rights of the board of directors. *Journal of Corporate Finance* 14(2): 107–117.
Garrett, J.E. 1989. Unredistributable corporate moral responsibility. *Journal of Business Ethics* 8: 535–545.
Gauthier, D. 1986. *Morals by agreement*. Oxford: Oxford University Press.
Gentile, Mary. C. 2004. *Corporate governance and accountability: What do we know and what do we teach future business leaders?* The Aspen Institute Business & Society Program: http://www.google.se/url?sa=t&rct=j&q=&esrc=s&source=web&cd=1&ved=0CCAQFjAA&url=http%3A%2F%2Fwww.aspeninstitute.org%2Fsites%2Fdefault%2Ffiles%2Fcontent%2Fdocs%2Fbsp%2FEABIS.GENTILE.2004-1.DOC&ei=ojADVZeJNpH-sATU64LoAQ&usg=AFQjCNGa2TqCU-fUtWTE16ekhx1zpWv8zw

Ghoshal, S. 2005. Bad management theories are destroying good management practices. *Academy of Management Learning & Education* 4: 75–91.
Gilbert, M. 2000. *Sociality and responsibility*. London: Rowman & Littlefield Publishers.
Goedecke, W. 1976. Corporations and the philosophy of law. *The Journal of Value Inquiry* 10: 81–90.
Goodpaster, K.E. 1983. The concept of corporate responsibility. *Journal of Business Ethics* 2: 1–22.
Goyder, G. 1987. *The just enterprise*. London: Deutsch.
Griffiths, O., and E.M. Taylors. 1949. *The principles of company law*. London: Textbooks.
Hasnas, J. 2012. Reflections on corporate moral responsibility and the problem solving technique of Alexander the Great. *Journal of Business Ethics* 107: 183–195.
Heath, J., J. Moriarty, and W. Norman. 2010. Business ethics and (or as) political philosophy. *Business Ethics Quarterly* 20(3): 427–452.
Held, V. 1991. Can a random collection of individuals be morally responsible? In *The spectrum of responsibility*, ed. P.A. French. New York: St. Martin's Press.
Hess, K.M. 2013. "If you tickle us . . . ": How corporations can be moral agents without being persons. *Journal of Value Inquiry* 47: 319–335.
Hillman, A.J., and G.D. Keim. 2001. Shareholder value, stakeholder management, and social issues: What's the bottom line? *Strategic Management Journal* 22: 125–139.
Hinkley, R. 2002. How corporate law inhibits social responsibility. *Business Ethics: Corporate Social Responsibility Report*, January/February.
Horwitz, M.J. 1989. Santa Clara revisited: The development of corporate theory. In *Corporations and society: Power and responsibility*, ed. W.J. Samuels and A.S. Miller. London: Greenwood.
Hospers, J. 1978. Free enterprise as the embodiment of justice. In *Ethics, free enterprise, & public policy*, ed. R.T. De George and J.A. Pichler. New York: O.U.P.
Ireland, P. 1996. Capitalism without the capitalist: The Joint Stock Company share and the emergence of the modern doctrine of separate corporate personality. *Journal of Legal History* 17: 41–73.
Jensen, M.C. 2002. Value maximization, stakeholder theory, and the corporate objective function. *Business Ethics Quarterly* 12(2): 235–256.
Jensen, M., and W.H. Meckling. 1976. Theory of the firm: Agency costs, managerial behavior and ownership structure. *Journal of Financial Economics* 3: 305–360.
Kohlberg, L. 1981. *The philosophy of moral development: Moral stages and the idea of justice*. San Francisco: Harper & Row.
Kraakman, R.R., P. Davies, H. Hansmann, G. Hertig, K.J. Hopt, H. Kanda, and E.B. Rock. 2004. *The anatomy of corporate law: A comparative and functional approach*. New York: Oxford University Press.
Kymlicka, W. 1990. *Contemporary political philosophy*. Oxford: Oxford University Press.
Ladd, J. 1970. Morality and the ideal of rationality in formal organizations. *The Monist*54: 488–516.
Ladd, J. 1991. Corporativism. In *The spectrum of responsibility*, ed. P.A. French. New York: St. Martin's Press.
Lewis, H.D. 1984. Collective responsibility. *Philosophy* 24: 3–18.
Mander, J. 1992. The myth of the corporate conscience. *Business and Society Review* 81: 56–63.
Manning, R.C. 1984. Corporate responsibility and corporate personhood. *Journal of Business Ethics* 3: 77–84.
Marmor, A. 2004. The rule of law and its limits. *Law and Philosophy* 23: 1–43.
May, L. 1990. *The morality of groups: Collective responsibility, group-based harm, and corporate rights*. Notre Dame: University of Notre Dame Press.
May, L. 1991. Vicarious agency and corporate responsibility. In *The spectrum of responsibility*, ed. P.A. French. New York: St. Martin's Press.
May, L. 1992. *Sharing responsibility*. Chicago: Chicago University Press.
McMahon, C. 1995. The moral status of organisations. *Business Ethics Quarterly* 5(3): 541–554.
Micklethwait, J., and A. Wooldrige. 2003. *The company*. New York: Modern Library.

Mill, J.S. 1991. Reply to Mr. Mansel. In *Collected works of John Stuart Mill*, ed. J. O'Grady. London: Routledge.
Mitchell, L.E. 1995. Cooperation and constraint in the modern corporation: An inquiry into the causes of corporate immorality. *Texas Law Review* 73: 477–538.
Mitchell, R.K., B.R. Agle, and D.J. Wood. 1997. Toward a theory of stakeholder identification and salience: Defining the principle of who and what really counts. *Academy of Management Review* 22(4): 853–886.
Moore, G. 1999. Corporate moral agency: Review and implications. *Journal of Business Ethics* 21: 329–334.
Nagel, T. 1995. *Other minds: Critical essays, 1969–1994*. New York: Oxford University Press.
Nozick, R. 1974. *Anarchy, state, and utopia*. Oxford: Blackwell Publishers.
Orts, E.W. 2013. *Business Persons: A Legal Theory of the Firm*. Oxford: Oxford University Press.
Ouyang, G., and R.A. Shiner. 1995. Organisations and agency. *Legal Theory* 1: 283–310.
Ozar, D.T. 1985. Do corporations have moral rights? *Journal of Business Ethics* 4: 277–281.
Paas, D. 1996. Stakeholders and participation in corporate governance: A critique of some of the arguments. *Business and Professional Ethics Journal* 15(4): 3–17.
Pennington, R.R. 1987. *Directors' personal liability*. London: Collins Professional and Technical.
Pettit, P. 2002. Groups with minds of their own. In *Socializing metaphysics*, ed. F. Schmitt. Lanham: Rowman & Littlefield.
Pettit, P. 2007. Responsibility incorporated. *Ethics* 117: 171–201.
Phillips, M.J. 1992. Corporate moral personhood and three conceptions of the corporation. *Business Ethics Quarterly* 2: 435–459.
Phillips, M.J. 1994. Reappraising the real entity theory of the corporation. *Florida State University Law Review* 21: 1061–1123.
Phillips, R., E.R. Freeman, and A.C. Wicks. 2003. What stakeholder theory is not. *Business Ethics Quarterly* 13(4): 479–502.
Pickering, M.A. 1968. Company as a separate legal entity. *Modern Law Review* 31: 481.
Podolny, J.M. 2009. The buck stops (and starts) at business school. *Harvard Business Review* June: 62–67.
Rawls, J. 1996. *Political Liberalism*. New York: Columbia University Press.
Rawls, J. 1999. *A Theory of Justice*. Cambridge, MA: Belknap Press of Harvard University Press.
Rawls, J. 2001. *Justice as Fairness: A Restatement*. Cambridge, MA: Belknap Press of Harvard University Press.
Ronnegard, D. 2008. Collective responsibility; Collective punishment. In *Encyclopedia of Business Ethics and Society*, ed. Robert W. Kolb. Thousand Oaks: SAGE publications.
Rönnegard, D. 2013. How autonomy alone debunks corporate moral agency. *Business and Professional Ethics Journal* 32(1–2): 77–106.
Rönnegard, D., and N.C. Smith. 2013. Shareholders vs. stakeholders: How liberal and libertarian political philosophy frames the basic debate in business ethics. *Business and Professional Ethics Journal* 32(3–4): 183–220.
Samuels, W.J. 1989. The idea of the corporation as a person: On the normative significance of a judicial language. In *Corporations and society: Power and responsibility*, ed. W.J. Samuels and A.S. Miller. London: Greenwood.
Scanlon, T. 1976. Nozick on rights, liberty, and property. *Philosophy and Public Affairs* 6(1): 3–25.
Scherer, A.G., and G. Palazzo. 2007. Towards a political conception of corporate social responsibility: Business and society seen from a Habermasian perspective. *Academy of Management Review* 32(4): 1096–1120.
Schneider, B. 1975. Organizational climate: An essay. *Personnel Psychology*. 28(4): 447–479.
Schrenk, L.P. 2006. Equity versus stakeholder and corporate governance: Developing a market for morality. *The Business Renaissance Quarterly* 1(3): 81–90.
Seabright, M.A., and L.B. Kurke. 1997. Organizational ontology and the moral status of the corporation. *Business Ethics Quarterly* 7(4): 91–108.
Searle, J. 1980. Minds, brains and programs. *Behavioral and Brain Sciences* 3: 417–57.
Searle, J. 1995. *The construction of social reality*. London: Allen Lane.

Skadden. 2011. Air Products & Chemicals, Inc. v. Airgas, Inc. *Skadden Newsletter*, February 16. Available at: http://www.skadden.com/newsletters/Air_Products_Chemicals_Inc_v_Airgas_Inc.pdf. Accessed: 14 May 2013.

Smith, N.C. 1990. *Morality and the market: Consumer pressure for corporate accountability*. London: Routledge.

Smith, D.G. 1998. The shareholder primacy norm. *The Journal of Corporate Law* 23: 277.

Smith, T.A. 2000. The efficient norm of corporate law: A neo-traditional interpretation of fiduciary duty. *Michigan Law Review* 98: 214.

Soares, C. 2003. Corporate versus individual moral responsibility. *Journal of Business Ethics* 46: 143–150.

Stout, L. 2012. *The shareholder value myth: How putting shareholders first harms investors, corporations and the public*. San Francisco: Berrett-Koehler Publishers, Inc.

Sundaram, A.K., and A.C. Inkpen. 2004a. The corporate objective revisited. *Organization Science* 15(3): 350–363.

Sundaram, A.K., and A.C. Inkpen. 2004b. Stakeholder theory and "The corporate objective revisited": A reply. *Organization Science* 15(3): 370–371.

Taylor, R.S. 2005. Kantian personal autonomy. *Political Theory* 33: 602–628.

Testy, K. 2002. Linking progressive corporate law with progressive social movements. *Tulane Law Review* 76: 1227–1252.

Thompson, D.F. 1987. *Political ethics and public office*. Cambridge, MA: Harvard University Press.

Treviño, L.K., and G.R. Weaver. 2003. *Managing ethics in business organizations*. Stanford: Stanford Business Books.

Tuomela, R. 1993. Corporate intention and corporate action. *Analyse und Kritik* 15: 11–21.

Tuomela, R. 2000. Collective and joint intention. *Mind and Society* 1: 39–69.

Tuomela, R. 2002. *The philosophy of social practices*. Cambridge: Cambridge University Press.

Tuomela, R. 2003. *The We-mode and the I-mode*. From his webpage: http://www.valt.helsinki.fi/staff/tuomela/papers/Midwest_Studies_paper_Tuomela.htm.

Tuomela, R. 2007. *The Philosophy of Sociality: The Shared Point of View*. New York: Oxford University Press.

Velasquez, Manuel G. 1983. Why corporations are not morally responsible for anything they do. *Business and Professional Ethics Journal* 2: 1–18.

Velasquez, Manuel G. 2003. Debunking corporate moral responsibility. *Business Ethics Quarterly* 13: 531–562.

Waldron, J. 2005. Moral autonomy and personal autonomy. In *Autonomy and the Challenges to Liberalism*, ed. J. Christman and J. Anderson. Cambridge, MA: Cambridge University Press.

Watson, G. 1975. Free agency. *Journal of Philosophy* 72: 205–220.

Werhane, P.H. 1985. *Persons, rights, & corporations*. Englewood Cliffs: Prentice Hall.

Werhane, P.H. 1989. Corporate and individual moral responsibility: A reply to Jan Garrett. *Journal of Business Ethics* 8: 821–822.

West, D.M. 2011. *The purpose of corporations in business and law school curricula*. Governance Studies at Brookings: http://www.brookings.edu/~/media/research/files/papers/2011/7/19-corporation-west/0719_corporation_west.pdf.

Williamson, O. 1984. Corporate governance. *Yale Law Journal* 93: 1197–1230.

Wilmot, S. 2001. Corporate moral responsibility: What can we infer from our understanding of organizations. *Journal of Business Ethics* 30: 161–169.

Wolff, M. 1938. On the nature of legal persons. *Law Quarterly Review*. 54: 494–505.

Wolff, J. 1991. *Robert Nozick, property, justice and the minimal state*. Oxford: Polity Press.

Wolff, J. 1996. *An introduction to political philosophy*. Oxford: Oxford University Press.

Zimmerman, M.J. 1991. Sharing responsibility. In *The spectrum of responsibility*, ed. P.A. French. New York: St. Martin's Press.